JN045704

シュミット堀佐知……［編］
SCHMIDT-HORI, Sachi

シュミット堀佐知／佐々木孝浩／日比嘉高／江口啓子／マーク・ブックマン／
セツ・シゲマツ／末松美咲／クリストファー・ローウィ／ディラン・ミギー

なんで日本研究するの？

Why Study Japan?

文学通信

第 **1** 部
言葉の壁・方法論の谷・技術という橋

第 2 部
エンパワーメントとしての知の創造

第**3**部
周縁的なものに光をあてる

Part 1

The Linguistic Barrier, the Methodological Gulf, and the Technologies to Bridge the Gaps

Part 2

The Creation of Knowledge as Empowerment

Part 3

Illuminating the Peripheries

06 **Let's Demystify "Classical Literature"**

Connecting Classical Japanese Literature to the World: Tales Retold and Reinvented

Misaki Suematsu (Nagoya Gakuin University)
Translated by Brian Bergstrom

07 **Inter-scriptal Storytelling**

Japanese Literature at the Intersection of Text and Narrative Content

Christopher Lowy (Carnegie Mellon University)

はじめに

シュミット堀佐知

1.「日本研究」って何？

『なんで日本研究するの？』という本書のタイトルを出版社に提案した時、「日本研究」という言葉は、（日本の）読者にとってあまり馴染みのない言葉かもしれない、というコメントを編集の方からいただいた。なるほど、と思い、幼なじみのＦに、「日本研究」という言葉を聞いたことがあるか、その言葉をどう思うか、と尋ねてみたところ、日本生まれ日本育ちで、研究者ではないＦの答えは、「聞いたことがない」「あまりにも大雑把な括り方だから変に聞こえる」というものだった。その理由を説明してもらうと、いくつかの興味深い事実が明らかになった。

まず、Ｆにとって「研究」という言葉は「不可解で特殊なものの真相を科学的に明らかにすること」を意味し、古代文明の遺跡発掘調査や、電子顕微鏡による細胞や微生物の観察にこそ相応しい語なのだそうだ。ゆえに、「日本研究」という言葉を聞いてすぐに「日本のなにを採取して、どうやって分析するんだろう。地層の研究のことかな」という疑問が頭に浮かんだらしい。次に「ジャパン・スタディーズ」という言葉をどう思うかと訊くと、今度は「え、それならピンとくる。学問っぽい」という反応が返ってきた。「ジャパン・スタディーズ」という英語は、Ｆにとって、「不可解で特殊なもの（＝日本）の真相を明らかにする」という「研究」のイメージにぴったり当てはまったようである。もちろん、この場合の研究者は「西洋人」でな

くてはならない。

　「日本研究」という語があまり日本で定着していないのは、日本の教育・研究機関に所属する人文学・社会科学分野の専門家のうち、日本の文化・政治・歴史・文学・美術などを研究する人の割合が多いので、「日本研究」という枠が、Fの言う「大雑把な括り方」になってしまい、機能的ではないという単純な事情による。言い換えれば、日本国外で「日本研究」という枠が通用する理由は、日本を専門とする研究者が少ないからである。とはいえ、世界中のほとんどの国は、「中近東」「カリブ諸島」「北アフリカ」「東欧」などのように、近隣の国々と一緒に地域レベルで研究対象とされることが多いのも事実だ。それを考えると、世界各地に日本研究を専門的に学ぶことのできる教育機関があり、日本研究に特化した学会や学術誌が存在するのは、非常に単純で俗っぽい言い方をすれば、「すごい」ことなのかもしれない。

　もちろん、地域研究が誕生した背景にあるのは、西洋列強による近代植民地政策・世界大戦・東西冷戦・国際安全保障の歴史であり、この学術分野の枠組みに対する批判が絶えないというのも事実である。しかしながら、地域研究の歴史的・政治的・経済的背景への批判に対する答えは、地域研究を見捨てることではあり得ない。そもそも、アカデミアという世界は、印欧語を母語とし、中流階級以上の教養を持ち、キリスト教の教義にもとづく倫理観を標榜する、異性愛者で健常者のヨーロッパ系成人男性の主観を「人類普遍の客観性」とみなすことを前提として成り立っている。それゆえ、仮に学界の周縁的一部分を占めるに過ぎない地域研究を撤廃したとしても、知の創造に関わる矛盾や不平等が解決するわけではない。それよりも、地域研究に携わっている人々が、この分野の不完全さや限界を充分に自覚し、その上で、矛盾や不平等を改善するための対話や協働に力を入れていくことの方が建設的である。もちろん、世界中の日本研究者たちにも、専門・使用言語・方法論などの違いにとらわれず、オープンに対話を行う姿勢が求められているのだ。

2．なんで『なんで日本研究するの？』なの？

　このバイリンガル・エッセイ集は、2021年に立ち上げた「スプリングボード・ジャパン」という日本研究プロジェクトの一環である。2021年と言えば、COVID-19が世界中で猛威を振るっていた時期であり、このプロ

ジェクトを立ち上げたきっかけも、コロナ禍と無関係ではない。

　私が住んでいるアメリカでは、COVID-19 パンデミックという世界史に残る惨事は、新型コロナウィルスの蔓延だけではなく、民主政治の終焉をもたらしかけた、社会的大惨事でもあった。その理由は、2017 年のトランプ政権発足以来、表面化してきた保守 / 革新、マイノリティ / 白人、労働者 / エリート、都市 / 地方間の対立が、コロナ禍によって一層激化され（これはトランプ政権の思惑でもあった）、さまざまな社会情勢不安をもたらしたからである。その間、マスク着用・ワクチン接種・学級閉鎖などの判断が、医学的根拠ではなく、共和党支持か民主党支持かという、個人もしくは自治体の政治的アイデンティティによって、決定された。このような社会全体を覆う不信感と危機感は、最終的には、2021 年アメリカ合衆国議会議事堂襲撃という、クーデター未遂事件にまで至ってしまった。

　市民の武装権を憲法で保障しているアメリカでは、社会がこのような一触即発の状態になると、拳銃やマシンガンが飛ぶように売れる。2021 年 5 月 29 日付の『ニューヨーク・タイムズ』紙の記事によれば、銃器の売り上げは、パンデミックによる行動規制の開始以来伸び続け、この記事の掲載時には、アメリカ史上最高の水準に達したのだという。人種・階級間の緊張感が高まり、誰がいつどこで発砲するか分からない状況下で、警官の職権乱用・過剰防衛・過失のために無抵抗の黒人市民が亡くなる事件が頻発した。そのような事件に抗議する Black Lives Matter (BLM) 運動が全米を席巻するとともに、武装した反・BLM 派による煽動行為も激化した。実に、2020 年初頭から 2021 年の終わりまでの約 2 年間は、多くのアメリカ市民が、パンデミックの脅威だけなく、人災の可能性にも日々怯えなくてはならない、暗くて悲しい時期であった。

　誤解を恐れずに言えば、アメリカに住むアジア人として、リアルな衝撃と恐怖を感じたのは、新型コロナウィルスが中国の武漢で発生したことによって多発した、アジア系市民に対する嫌がらせや無差別暴行・致死事件であった（そのもっとも悲惨な例は、8 人の犠牲者を出した、2021 年 4 月のアトランタ連続銃撃事件である）。警官による黒人市民の暴行致死が、正当防衛という大義名分と警察当局の黙認のもとで起きる、組織的な人種・階級差別行為であるのに対し、アジア人へのヘイトクライムは、一般市民が白昼堂々と、時には衆人環視の中で行ったことは注目に値する。これは黒人市民よりもアジア系市民

の方が同情されるべきだという議論ではないのだが、「危険そうな人物を服従させる」という名目が一切通用しない状況で、散歩をしていたり、バスを待っていたりしているだけの女性や高齢者を、アジア系だからというだけで攻撃できる心理は、アジア系市民がこの国では「永遠のよそ者」であるという、周知の事実を端的に表している。

　私は1997年にアメリカに移住し、2000年に帰化した「アメリカ人」で、2024年には、私のアメリカ国民歴は日本国民歴に追いついてしまう。しかし、この国では、私の「アメリカ人らしさ」などというものは、3時間前にジョン・F・ケネディ空港に降り立った金髪碧眼のデンマーク人観光客の足元にも及ばないであろう。ハワイやカリフォルニアに住むアジア系アメリカ人3世4世たちも、別の州を訪れると、英語の話せない観光客と間違われる、という話も聞く。アジア系の人々に対する不信感が、もっともあからさまな形で表面化したロックダウン中のアメリカで、私は、アメリカのアカデミアに籍を置く日本出身の日本研究者として、自分の生業の意義をもう一度深く考えなければならない、と強く感じたのである。

　そんな中、西海岸や日本の研究者仲間と、ズームなどで近況を知らせ合う機会が増えた。パンデミック以前は、互いに忙しすぎて、用件のみの連絡ばかりだったのだが、ロックダウンを機に、オンライン上の交流が普通になったのは、不幸中の幸いだったと言える。その一連の会話の中から生まれたのが、「スプリングボード・ジャパン」いうプロジェクトだ。「スプリングボード」というのは、器械体操の跳躍台のことで、日米アカデミアの間にそびえる言葉・文化・政治などの壁を跳び越えるための踏み台であれ、という意味を込めた名前だ。発足以来、日本研究や教育に関わる人々、そして日本語や日本文化を学んでいる学生などのために、過去に出版された学術研究の翻訳や、研究者同士の対談などを日本語と英語でウェブ公開（https://sites.dartmouth.edu/springboard-japan-demo/）したり、シンポジウムを開催したりしてきた。大学の仕事と自分の研究の合間に細々続けている無償の副業なので、蝸牛の歩みではあるものの、本書もこのプロジェクトの成果である。

3．本書の内容と構成

　本書は、私を含む9人の日本研究者たちが、直接的もしくは間接的に「なんで日本研究するの？」という問いへの答えをエッセイの形で綴り、その日

本語版と英語版を 1 冊にまとめる、というコンセプトで始まった企画である。頭の中で構想を練っていた段階では、「いろいろな分野の研究者が、自分自身の知的探求史を振り返るきっかけになりうるような本」を、漠然とイメージしていた。しかしながら、できあがったのは、学術研究という狭い世界に携わる人々だけでなく、どんな職業や年齢や国籍の人が読んでも、思わず引き込まれてしまう、刺激的な本であった。教養書ではないが、教養も学べ、語学教材ではないが、語学の教材にもなり、しかも、読む人の人生を豊かにしてくれる、さまざまなアイディアまでギュッと詰まっている──『なんで日本研究するの？ Why Study Japan?』は、そんな珠玉のエッセイ集なのである。

　本書は前半が日本語（オリジナル 5 篇と英語エッセイの日本語版 4 篇）、後半が英語（オリジナル 4 篇と日本語エッセイの英語版 5 篇）のバイリンガル・エッセイ集で、前半・後半ともに 9 篇のエッセイを 4 部構成で収録した。**第 1 部は「言葉の壁・方法論の谷・技術という橋」**というテーマで、佐々木孝浩氏の「私はなぜ海外に日本の書物文化を発信するのか」、日比嘉高氏の「なんで、どうやって私は『英語でも』研究をするようになったのか」、そして江口啓子氏の「私は『変』じゃない──私が日本研究する理由」の 3 篇から成る。

　この 3 本のエッセイは、人文学研究における英語の有用性と、人文学研究者が英語という「言語の壁」を乗り越えるためのヒントが、執筆者それぞれの観点から描かれていて非常に興味深い。また、佐々木氏の専門である書誌学や、日比氏と江口氏の専門である文学研究において、研究の使用言語が異なれば、たとえ扱う書物やテクストが同じであっても、「方法論の谷」と私がここで呼んでいるものが自ずと生じてくる。そのような「言語の壁」と「方法論の谷」を越えるための重要な架け橋となるのが、テクストや画像・映像のデジタル化や AI による翻訳である（「技術という橋」）。テクノロジーは、既存の問題の解決に貢献してくれる有難い文明の利器であるものの、新たな問題を生じさせる可能性をもはらんでいるのは言うまでもない。さまざまな技術は、人間同士の対話や協働に取って代わるものではなく、研究者たちは、ほどよい距離を保ちつつ、テクノロジーを有効活用すべきだというメッセージも、これらのエッセイから伝わってくる。

　しかしながら、一読いただければ分かるように、第 1 部の内容は、決し

て巷に溢れる「ハウツー情報」などではないことを強調しておきたい。この3篇は、書き手の人柄がにじみ出る筆致と、心の琴線に触れるエピソードが堪能できる随筆（つまり文芸作品）でもあるのだ。個人的には、第1部の醍醐味は、現在それぞれの分野で活躍するお三方が、小説家になることを夢見ていた少年時代、LAでロンドン留学中の夏目金之助と自分を重ね合わせた若手研究者時代、「世間的な標準」から決別することを決めた大学生時代を振り返り、そこからの出発と軌跡を、生き生きとした言葉で綴っていることだと思う。

　「**エンパワーメントとしての知の創造**」と銘打った**第2部**は、日本研究者であるだけでなく、それぞれの分野で運動家としても活躍してきたマーク・ブックマン氏とセツ・シゲマツ氏のエッセイ――「アメリカ人障害者として日本で暮らすこと」と「白人性と日本研究」――から成る。第1部を読み終えて第2部にやってきた読者は、主題の違いもさることながら、日本語原文のエッセイと、英語を日本語に翻訳したエッセイのニュアンスの違いにも気づくと思う。概して、アカデミックな英語に求められる書き方というものは、明確さと、読者を納得させる力強さであると思う。ブックマン氏とシゲマツ氏の運動家・研究者としての雄弁さは、日ごろ一般教養として扱われがちな人文学の実践的側面を物語っている。それは、知の創造が、社会的弱者にとってのエンパワーメントになり得るという事実であり、この2篇のエッセイは、研究や教育を机上の空論で終わらせてはいけない、というメッセージを思い出させてくれるものだ。

　第3部（「**周辺的なものに光をあてる**」）には、末松美咲氏の「世界とつながる日本古典文学」とクリス・ローウィ氏の「テクストと物語をつなぐ日本文学」を収録した。

　末松氏のエッセイを読むと、日本古典文学、とくに中世後期から近世にかけて挿絵付きで人気を博した作品世界が、時代だけでなく、言語や国境をも越えて翻案・継承され、身近なモチーフとして現代でも愛され続けていることがよく分かる。このような、情報としての価値はもちろん、末松氏のエッセイが、日本人の歴史や伝統に対する無関心という問題を取り上げている点にも注目していただきたい。私の勤めているダートマス大学には、英語学習者のためのプログラムはなく、日本からの留学生は、すでに英語で大学の授業を受けられる帰国子女かインターナショナルスクール出身者ばかりだ。彼

らは、子供の時から日本の歴史や文学作品に触れる機会が少なかっただけでなく、そもそも日本文化への関心自体も薄いらしく、自分のルーツに無知であることに、それほど抵抗を感じていないように見える。「日本人だから」「常識だから」のような馬鹿げた理由で日本に関する知識を彼／彼女らのような学生に押し付けるのはナンセンスであるが、国語・日本史・国文学・日本文学などの教育者は（自分も含め）、末松氏がすでに実践しているように、前近代日本の文化が決して現代社会と切り離されてはいないということを学生に気づかせつつ、彼らの興味と関心を引き出すことのできる教授法を模索していかなくてはならないのだと思う。

　ローウィ氏も、そのエッセイの中で、一見周縁的だが実は非常に本質的なテーマを扱っている。これは、日本語の文章が、他の言語には見られない柔軟性（文字の種類、ルビ、文の方向など）を特徴とするにも関わらず、この視覚性が日本語で書かれた文学作品にもたらす重層的効果について、これまでほとんど研究されてこなかったという問題である。実際、英語圏の大学で日本文学を教える場合、教員は当然英訳テクストを使う必要があるのだが、それだけでなく、英語を母語とする日本文学研究者の場合、リサーチには時間の節約のために英訳をメインに使い、原文は必要に応じて部分的に参照するだけ、という人はザラである。そのため、日本語の文学テクストに見られる、英語に翻訳不可能な視覚的修辞は、英語圏の日本文学研究者にとって、一種のパンドラの箱である感は否めない。しかしながら、ローウィ氏によって、すでに賽は投げられた。彼のような多才な若手研究者が、英語圏での日本文学研究方法論を革新していく時代が到来したのである。

　本書を締めくくる**第4部「日本とアメリカのあわいで」**は、拙稿「なんでアメリカで日本古典文学研究するの？」とディラン・ミギー氏の「根無し草たちの日本研究」である。拙稿とミギー氏のエッセイにも書かれているように、私たち2人は、それぞれのパートナーが生まれ育った国で外国人として暮らしており、日常的に外国語を駆使し、日本文学を研究し、日米2つの文化を受け継ぐ子どもを育てている。日本とアメリカのあわいに佇み、2つの文化と言語の間で揺れ動く自己は、この2篇のエッセイによく表れているのではないかと思う。

　ミギー氏の原稿を最初に読んだ時、直接言語化されていないけれども、彼の伝えようとしていることが、僭越ながら、手に取るように分かったような

気がした。そして、このエッセイを翻訳するにあたり、「根無し草」という比喩を使わせてもらった。これは、私自身がアメリカで日常的に感じている違和感と、日本とアメリカ双方の束縛から自由でいられる身軽さを表現する言葉だ。本書に所収されているエッセイの中で、もっとも文学テクストに近いのはミギー氏の文章であり、意訳ではあるが、このイメージをこの織物の縦糸として使いたいと思ったのである。この提案にミギー氏が快く賛成してくれたことを非常に嬉しく思う。

第**1**部

言葉の壁・方法論の谷・技術という橋

日本研究の本場は日本だけじゃない

私はなぜ海外に
日本の書物文化を
発信するのか

佐々木孝浩（慶応義塾大学・斯道文庫）

1. 何故英語が必要なの？

　高校時代は授業中も小説を読んでいた。小説家になりたいと思い、東京の私立大学の文学部に進学した。上手く滑り込めた慶應義塾大学の文学部は、2年時から専攻に分かれることになっていた。国文学か日本史学かで悩んだけれども、歴史分野は政治思想が重んじられるようだったので、気楽だろうと国文学専攻に進んだ。

　小説は好きだけれど、研究の対象にするのは違うような気がして、中世文学のゼミに進んだ。卒業論文は、10世紀初めに天皇の命令で編纂された『古今和歌集』の、15世紀に書かれた注釈書を対象に選んだ。卒論より問題だったのは、卒業後の進路のことだった。大学入学後は、高校生のころのように無心に小説を書くことができなくなって、作家になりたいという夢は萎んでいた。かといって進みたい業界や職種も見つからなかった。自分は教師に向かないと思って、教員免許に必要な科目は履修していなかった。進路を決められないことに、どんどん追い詰められている気持だった。

　ある飲み会の席で、ゼミの先生から進路はどうするのかと質問された。何も決まっていなかったので、出まかせ半分で、「落語家にでもなろうかと思います」と答えた。時折寄席には行っていたものの、入門したい落語家がいるわけでもなかった。とっさとはいえ、どうしてそんな返事をしたのか、自分でも不思議である。

普通の教師なら、もっとまじめに考えろとたしなめたのかもしれないが、返ってきた言葉は、「今は大学出の落語家は珍しくない。だがな、大学院を修了した落語家はまだいないぞ」であった。大学院への進学など、それまで考えたこともなかったので、その手があったかと、かすかに光明が見えた気がした。修士に進めば、とりあえず2年間は進路決定を先延ばしできることに気づいたのである。

　しかし、ここで立ちはだかったのが、中学校以来苦手意識が付きまとう英語が試験科目にあることだった。英語で落第して大学院の進学を諦めた先輩がいたので、その二の舞になりそうで怖かった。欧米の影響の色濃い日本近代文学を研究するのなら理解できるが、自分が専門にしようとする13〜16世紀の日本古典文学に、英語は無関係だと固く信じ、学ぶことを放棄していたのである。

　辞書持ち込みで、長文を日本語に翻訳するだけの問題だったので、なんとか潜り抜けて、大学院に進学できた。履修する授業を考えていた時に、先輩から「斯道文庫の授業には当然出るよな」と訊かれた。現在私はその斯道文庫の専任教員をしているが、大学院入学までは、慶應義塾大学に斯道文庫という変わった名前の研究所があることを、まったく知らなかった。

　やがて、斯道文庫が漢字を使う国々の古い書物を研究する研究所だと知った。江戸時代以前の書物である和本には、学部時代に触れたことはあったけれども、演習で調査を担当した16世紀初めの写本は、見ているだけで幸せな気持になれた。自分が日本の古い書物が好きであることに気付いたのである。しかしそれを研究対象にしようとは思わなかった。お金も時間もかかる分野であることが、容易に想像できたからである。

　修士の2年間でも進路を決めることができず、流されるままに博士課程への進学を考えた。しかし、博士課程の入試には、なんと2か国語が課せられていたのである。苦手な英語に加えて、1年しか学んだことのないフランス語までが加わるのだ。私には不条理なことにしか思えなかった。外国語のためではないと思いたいのだが、1度落第し、翌年再受験し、なんとか進学することができた。さすがにこの頃には、古典文学研究者として、大学教員になれればよいな、と考えるようになっていた。

2. 世界の日本研究との出会い

　博士課程の2年目も終りに近づいた頃、斯道文庫の恩師から、国文学研究資料館の助手に応募する気はあるか、と訊かれた。就職に関して具体的に考えたことはなかったので、深く考えもせずにその話に飛びついた。

　国文学研究資料館は、日本文学に関係する諸学会の要請で1977年に創設された、日本文学の情報を集積して、研究者に提供するとともに、先進的な共同研究を推進する、国立の研究機関である。現在は東京西郊の立川にあるが、当時は品川区戸越という下町情緒あふれる場所にあった。

　履歴書と業績一覧を提出して面接を受けると、幸運にも採用が決まった。当時の助手は、助教授には昇任できず、いずれは出なければならない決まりであったが、任期は無かった。とりあえず給料をもらって生活できる、研究者の端くれになれたのである。今もそうだが、当時も博士課程を単位取得退学しても、就職できない人は少なくなくなったから、自分が非常に幸運であることは、さすがに自覚していた。

　助手としての任務は、国文学関係の論文目録を作成することであった。現在は「国文学論文目録データベース」が公開されているが、当時は1年に1巻の冊子が刊行されていた。全国から送られてきた研究雑誌に掲載されている論文の情報を、1本ごとに1枚のデータシートに記入し、時代と分野などで区分して蓄積し、区分内での順序を定めてから、出版社に入稿するのが、所属する部署の仕事であった。助手の役割は、データの内容チェックとキーワードの付与、データの排列を決めることであった。

　当時は、『源氏物語』の論文だけでも年間に500本以上あったので、すべての論文の内容をある程度理解して並べていくのは非常に大変な任務であった。自分の専門外の分野の論文にも触れざるをえなかったので、大いに勉強になったのは確かである。

　国文学研究資料館には、6年間在籍した。そろそろ出なければ、と考えていたころ、恩師から、斯道文庫の定年退職者の後任にならないか、との声が掛かった。書物の研究者になることに迷いはしたが、古い書物は好きであるし、どこかの大学に転出できる保証もないので、誘いを受けることにした。ただし、身分は助手のままであった。

　斯道文庫の話があった頃、若手研究者の海外留学を推奨する動きがあり、1年間欧米の大学に行かないか、とのお誘いもいただいた。魅力は感じた

が、自分の英語力のなさと、斯道文庫への転出の話もあったのでお断りした。今からすると、斯道文庫の助手就任は1年待ってもらって、無理にでも留学すべきであったと思うけれども、当時はそんなアイデアを思いつくこともなかったのである。

結局、斯道文庫に戻る形になったけれども、国文学研究資料館に在籍したことの意味は大きかった。同館は、国内に散在する古典籍の調査と、マイクロフィルムによる収集を大規模に行うとともに、海外に存在する日本の古典籍の調査も積極的に行っていた。また、海外からの日本研究者も、客員教員として受け入れていた。それらに直接関係する部署に所属していた訳ではなかったが、それでも海外の日本研究や日本古典籍に関する多様な情報を得ることができた。自分の所属は、様々なデータベースの構築を始めとして、デジタル技術を国文学研究で活用する方法を研究する部門であったので、デジタル上での漢字利用の実態の調査を目的として、ヨーロッパとアメリカに1度ずつ出張することができた。私の欧米における日本研究との本格的な出会いとなる経験であった。

初めてのヨーロッパは、デンマークのコペンハーゲンで開催される、ヨーロッパ日本学会大会に出席するための出張だった。同大会は市庁舎で市長主催のレセプションパーティーが開催されるほどの、規模の大きな催しであった。チボリ公園横の大きなレストランを貸し切りにしたフェアウェルパーティーに至るまで、日本の学会との違いに、ただただ驚き続けた数日間であった。繁華な市街の中にある、中世以来の伝統的な大学に、世界中から多くの日本研究者が集まり、分野ごとに分かれて、講演や研究発表が数日間行われた。様々な人種・国籍の人々が、公用語である英語と日本語を交えながら、日本の古典文学や芸能・美術などについて熱く討議しているありさまは、会場の建物の雰囲気とあまりにもミスマッチな感じがして、頭がくらくらした。どうして外国の人が日本のことでこんなに熱心になれるのだろう、と不思議でならなかった。

学会発表はやはり英語が中心で、日本語で行うのは日本人のみだった。もちろん、日本人の中にも英語で発表する人がいて、素直にまぶしく見えた。英語の発表の内容はほとんど理解できず、時折混じる固有名詞などで、勝手な憶測を巡らせるばかりであった。学生時代に英語をしっかり学ばなかった付けが回ってきたのを、この時はっきりと実感したのである。

初めての渡米は、斯道文庫に移籍する直前のことであった。ニューヨークからワシントン DC、オハイオ州のコロンバス、サンディエゴにロサンゼルスと、空路でアメリカ大陸を横断した。オハイオ州に本部のある Online Computer Library Center（OCLC）を始め、各地の図書館や博物館などにおける、デジタルカタログ上での漢字の使用状況などを視察して回ったのだが、日本の古典籍や美術品の収蔵・管理などの状況を見学することもできた。

メトロポリタン美術館やスミソニアン博物館群のサックラー・ミュージアムでは、展示されている日本美術品の質と量に圧倒されたが、それぞれ大規模な修復のための施設を館内に有しており、日本で技術を学んだ修復の専門家が所属していることにも驚かされた。議会図書館は別格として、コロンビア大学と UCLA の和本コレクションも、想像をはるかに超える充実ぶりであった。

　この出張で私は味を占めてしまった。アメリカで優れた日本のコレクションを所蔵する機関には、必ず日本人か日本語が堪能な担当者がいて、たどり着きさえすれば英語ができなくても困らないという事実に、である。その後も私はこの事実に甘え続け、今に至っている。何度か日本語のできる人がいない瞬間があって、苦労したこともあるけれども、何とかなってしまったのである。

　斯道文庫に就職してからは、国内の和本調査を主要な任務として、あちこちに出かけて行き、様々な和本に触れた。自分の専門分野に限定せず、多様な分野の書物を調査したことは、結果として、和本の総合的な特徴を考える上で、とても役に立った。国文学研究資料館でも斯道文庫でも、視野を広げざるをえない業務に就いたことは、非常に幸いであった。

　また、国文学研究資料館で築いた人脈により、韓国の国立中央図書館に所蔵されている、朝鮮総督府図書館旧蔵日本古典籍の調査メンバーにも加わることができ、合計すると 20 回以上ソウルに出張した。このコレクションも分野が広いものであったので、多くを学ぶことができた。それだけでなく、朝鮮半島の活字印刷本を中心とする書物とその文化を学ぶ機会ともなり、日本の書物を相対化して観ることができるようにもなった。

　やはり国文学研究資料館との縁により、コレージュ・ド・フランスの日本学高等研究所のシンポジウムに参加し、和本について発表する機会を得るこ

ともできた。そして、それがきっかけとなり、フランスの日本研究者たちとの国際共同研究にも参加した。親しくなったあるフランス人研究者の、和本に関する知識があまりにも豊かなことに驚かされた。

フランスのメンバーの研究テーマには、日本の大学や学会ではあまり見かけないタイプのものがあり、大学の専攻の枠組みに縛られた日本国内の研究よりも、視野が広く、日本文化の本質を突いたものであることにも気づいた。日本研究は日本が本場だとふんぞり返っていられない状況に突入していることを実感したのである。この思いは、この後頻繁に北米を訪れるようになって、どんどん大きくなっていった。

3. 世界に向けて和本文化を発信

海外出張に慣れてくると、不思議とその機会が連続するようになった。海外での調査を行うには、日本学術振興会の科学研究費補助金（通称：科研費）を代表として、様々な団体の研究補助を得るのが一般的な方法である。単独で申請することもあれば、複数のメンバーで複数年にわたるプロジェクトとして申請することもある。その在外日本古典籍の調査研究プロジェクトのメンバーに加わることを、求められることが多くなったのである。

慶應義塾大学文学部には、室町後期から江戸前期にかけて製作された絵入り写本である、奈良絵本の専門家として著名な石川透教授が在籍している。奈良絵本は見た目に美しく楽しいものでもあるので、来日した外国人が購入して持ち帰ったために、世界中に非常に多く伝存しているのである。石川氏はそれらの調査を積極的に行ってきた、海外出張のスペシャリストであり、調査プロジェクトの立案・実行の能力にも長じた人物である。

私は石川氏のプロジェクトに度々参加させていただいたし、他大学の研究者が立案した計画にも何度も加わることができた。こうして研究代表に随行する形で海外出張を重ね、欧米における日本の古典籍の所在情報や管理状況の知見を増やし、日本研究に関係する多くの方と面識を得ることができた。これは何物にも代え難い私の貴重な財産である。

私にとって大きな転機となったのは、やはり石川氏を代表とする、2009年から5年計画で実施された、文部科学省私立大学戦略的研究基盤形成支援事業「15～17世紀における絵入り本の世界的比較研究の基盤形成」（通称「絵入り本プロジェクト」）のメンバーに加わったことであった。慶應義塾大

学の西洋・中国・日本の書物の専門家のみでなく、日本のキリシタン史やイスラム史の専門家も加わっており、研究会を通して自ずと視野が広がった。フランスのノルマンディー地方で西洋の中世写本を見学したり、ポルトガルで日本のキリシタン版の調査を行ったりしたことなどは、比較的視点を得るための貴重な経験になった。

またこのプロジェクトは、個人でテーマを決めて活動することもできた。自分で立てた計画に従って、占い本の国際比較シンポジウムを開催し、初めて1人でフランスやアメリカに出張した。何程のことでもないように見えても、英語が不自由な人間にとっては、なかなか勇気のいることなのである。1週間のみのことながら、パリのギメ美術館図書館に1人で通った時は、留学している気分になったものである。

忘れられないのは、アメリカのプリンストン大学への訪問である。同大の知人を頼って、図書館と博物館所蔵の和本の調査をさせていただいた。その折に、数年前から考えていたことを、実行に移すことにした。海外のシンポジウムやワークショップなどに参加して、和本に関する研究発表を行ったことは何度もあったものの、和本に関する基礎的な知識をお話ししたことがないことを、私は少し残念に感じていた。所蔵されている本を、その大学やその国の研究者が、研究や教育などに活用することが望ましいのは言うまでもない。折角日本から出かけていくのだから、研究や教育に必要となる和本の情報や知識を現地の方々と共有することができれば、と前々から考えていたのである。

英語で説明できればよいのだろうけれど、それはできないので、その知人にお願いして、日本研究をしている大学院生に集まってもらい、日本から持参した和本類を手にとってもらいながら、3時間ばかり日本語でお話しをした。現物に触れるのが理解を促進する一番の方法であるのは言うまでもないし、和本に興味をもってもらうのにも、それに優る方法はないのである。

その時に参加してくれた院生さんが、今や、全米屈指の日本美術コレクションを有する美術館のキュレーターや、州立大学の日本研究の教員に就任しているのは、何の因果関係もないことながら、個人的には大変感慨深いものがある。そしてもう1つ忘れられないことは、調査でお世話になった図書館の日本書担当の専門司書の方が、この講習会に参加して下さったことである。

北米やヨーロッパでは、日本関係資料の公開と利用の促進などを目的として、図書館司書や大学教員などから成る組織が結成されている。North American Coordinating Council on Japanese Library Resources（北米日本研究図書館資料調整協議会、略称NCC）と、European Association of Japanese Resource Specialists（日本資料専門家欧州協会、略称EAJRS）と呼ばれるグループで、メンバーによる情報の共有や、所属を越えた協力を通して、欧米における日本研究を強力にバックアップしてくれているのである。またNCCには上部組織として、Council on East Asian Libraries（東亜図書館協会、略称CEAL）も存在する。

　プリンストン大学の日本書担当司書の方は、NCC および CEAL の主要メンバーのお１人で、私の話に興味を持って下さり、CEAL の年次大会に併せて開催する、和本のワークショップの講師をする気はないか、と声を掛けて下さった。私にとっては、考えていたことをより強力に推進できる機会なので、二つ返事でお引き受けした。

　翌年３月、シカゴで開催された Association for Asian Studies（アジア研究学会、略称 AAS）の年次大会に合わせて、CEAL や NCC の会合も催された際に、シカゴ美術館の日本美術部門の部屋をお借りして、「CEAL Workshop on Japanese Rare Books in Chicago」を行った。部屋の大きさから定員は 20 名となったが、応募者は 40 名を越え、和本の知識を必要としている方が多いことを実感した。カナダやイギリスから参加された方もおられ、日本書担当司書だけでなく、日本研究者も少なくなかった。やはり日本から持参した和本と、シカゴ美術館に所蔵される和本を囲んでお話しさせていただいたが、参加者の熱意をひしひしと感じることができ、私にとっては至福の１日であった。

　プリンストンでの思い付きの試みが、シカゴでより具体的な形となったことは、まさに夢を見ているような気分だった。そのことに満足を感じていたのだが、このワークショップは、終着点ではなく、実は本格的な出発点であった。その後、参加者の方にお誘いいただき、ブリティッシュ・コロンビア大学やハワイ大学マノア校、南カルフォルニア大学などで、ワークショップや講演会の講師を務めることになったのである。

4. MOOC という追い風

　次の大きな転機は、シカゴのワークショップ後まもなくやってきた。所属する慶應義塾大学が、Massive Open Online Course（大規模公開オンライン講座、略称MOOC）のプラットフォームの1つであり、ロンドンに本部を置くFutureLearn に加盟することになったのである。

　日本からの初加盟ということで、最初のコースは日本関係の内容がよかろうということになり、学内から文学・歴史・美術などの諸分野の日本研究者が集められ、説明会が開催された。私もその中の一人であった。MOOC の歴史や状況などについての説明が行われ、最初の講座を誰が担当するかという話になった際に、私は率先して立候補した。ワークショップなどの経験を通して、和本について知りたいと思っている人が、世界に一定数存在することや、そうでない人にも興味を持ってもらえる対象であることに、確信を持っていたからである。

　自薦は承認され、和本に関する講座のリード・エデュケーターをすることになった。ワークショップの内容を転用できるので、コースの内容も半分以上完成しているようなものであった。ただ、現物に触れてもらうことは不可能なので、ビデオや画像を通して、できる限り多種類の和本を鑑賞できるように工夫した。テキストは日本語で書き、ビデオの中でも日本語で説明したが、世界に公開するものなので英語字幕をつける必要があった。幸い、アメリカの大学院で日本古典文学を学んだイタリア出身の知人が、翻訳を担当してくれることとなった。

　こうして、2016 年 7 月に「Japanese Culture Through Rare Books」が公開された。紹介のためのトレーラーのビデオでは、命じられて私が英語でコース紹介をした。英語を苦手にしている自分が、世界に向けて英語で受講を呼び掛けていることが、とても信じられない気がした。しかもそのビデオは YouTube にもアップされたのである。自分が知らない場所にいるような、不思議な気分になったことをよく覚えている。

　開講中一番問題だったのは、受講者からのコメントや質問に対する回答であった。一方通行の講義とならないように、また受講者同士でも意見交換ができるように、コメントを書き込めるシステムになっているのだが、当然のことながら、基本的に英語で書くことになっている。初回の公開では、判明するだけで 140 ヵ国の 9000 人近い登録者があり、コメントの数は 8000 を

超えた。

　それらは英語で書かれているだけでなく、詳しい説明を求める質問であったりするので、とても私の英語力で手に負えるものではなかった。そのためコース制作にも関与していた、英語に堪能な大学院生に協力してもらい、重要と考えられる質問をピックアップして日本語に訳してもらった。その質問に私が日本語で答え、それをその院生が英訳して、正式に回答をする、という作業を行ったのである。

　そのプロセスは大変なものであったが、様々な立場の方々からの具体的な質問は、非常に勉強になった。オンラインコースの公開は、エデュケーターの学びの場でもあるのだと実感した。翻訳サイトは当初から利用していたが、分かりやすい翻訳にはなっていない感じがしていた。しかし、公開の回数を重ねるうちに、翻訳の精度も上がっていき、現在では、ほぼ翻訳サイトの利用だけで、回答ができるようになっている。私は、多くの人々だけでなく、デジタル技術の発展にも助けられてきたのである。

　最初の講座は幸いに好評で、欧米の知人から、授業で利用したという報告を受けることもあった。オンラインコースを公開してからも、イェール大学やコロンビア大学、フリーア・サックラー・ミュージアム、イギリスのケンブリッジ大学や、フランスのギメ美術館図書館やストラスブール大学などで、ワークショップを開催していただいたが、その際にMOOCのクラスを受講したと伝えて下さる方が次第に増えていった。オンラインと対面開催が上手く連携し、一つの理想的な形式が完成したような気持ちになった。

　そのような時に、世界中を巻き込んだ新型コロナの騒動が始まった。FutureLearnの授業は、通常は3か月間の公開と休止を繰り返すことになっているのであるが、新型コロナの期間は休止をしなかった。また、パンデミック以前に計画されたイベントは、すべて延期となってしまったが、自宅に籠ることを余儀なくされた方々によるオンラインコースの受講は増えた。そして、そのような受講者から有意義な時間の使い方ができた、との感謝のコメントをもらうようになった。公開回数は曖昧になってしまっているものの、現在までに約140ヵ国の2万5千人ほどの方が登録して下さっており、コメント数も約2万に上っている。その後、延期されていたシンポジウムやワークショップは、オンラインで開催された。和本に直接触れていただけないのが残念ではあるけれども、対面のイベントではありえない、広範囲な

地域からの多数の参加があったことは、不幸中の幸いであると感じている。

5. これからのこと

　初回のコースが好評であったので、関連講座の制作を薦められた。やはりリード・エデュケーターとして、和本に使用された和紙に焦点を当てたコースを企画し、「The Art of Washi Paper in Japanese Rare Books」を 2018 年 7月に公開した。また、大英図書館との共同で制作したヨーロッパと日本の書物を比較するコースは、新型コロナのために完成が遅れたものの、2022 年 6月に開講できた。

　現在、書物の国際比較研究が世界的に盛んであり、それに関するオンライン・カンファレンスやシンポジウムなども次々に開催されている。声を掛けていただくこともあるのだが、それらのイベントは英語を使用するものがほとんどである。幸い、多くの方の協力を得て、なんとか和本のことを紹介させていただいてきたとは言え、活発な議論に参加するのが難しいことは、言うまでもない。

　研究すればするほど、英語という、私にとっての大きな壁が立ちはだかってくるのである。そこから逃げて、日本国内だけで活動するのは簡単であるけれども、和本文化を世界に発信するのは天命であると自分に言い含めて、できる限りのことをしていきたいと考えている。それが、これまでに私を助けて下さった多くの方々への恩返しになるはずであるし、これまで主体性なく何となく生きて来た私に、和本がそれを命じているように思われてならないからである。

　和本は海外の日本研究を、より活性化させるための重要な存在であり、海外での日本研究の発展は、日本国内の研究を守り育てることにもつながるはずである。願わくは、私が、英語のできない日本人の日本研究者の、最後の世代でありますように。

　第１部　言葉の壁・方法論の谷・技術という橋

なんで、どうやって私は「英語でも」研究をするようになったのか

日比嘉高（名古屋大学）

1.「なんで」英語でも研究しはじめたのか

　気がつけば、英語を使って書いた論文が長短あわせて3本になっていて、今年2023年にはあと2本が出版を待っている。日本で日本近代文学を研究していた自分が、こんな仕事の仕方をするようになったとは、と私は驚く。

　自慢話を始めようというのではない。相も変わらず、私の英語はお粗末なものだ。英語のニュースを読んだり見たりしても、わからない単語がボロボロ出て来るし、研究発表や講演を聴いても、話が入り組んでくると頭に入らなくなる。学会の質疑応答はいやな汗ばかり出てきて、できれば逃げ出したい。だから、これから書いてみようとしているのは「私は英語でも論文を書いてるんだぞ」という自慢などではなく、むしろ逆に、「こんな体たらくですが、なんとかなるもんです、だからあなたも一歩踏み出してはどうか」といういわゆる「先ず隗より始めよ」式の話である。

　話の中心は「どうやって」に関わるものになるのだが、まずは「なんで」の方の話をしておこう。なぜ、私は「英語でも」研究をするようになったのか。いくつかの理由があるが、いずれも特別なものではない。研究は差異を競う。差異を生み出す1つの方法は、既存のパラダイムの外に出ることである。日本語以外で行われる研究の世界を知ることは、外を知り、差異を提示するための知的な源となる。とりわけ英語の学術世界は活気があり、理論的な更新の速度も速い。これが1つ目の理由である。また、研究者とし

ての行動範囲の魅力もある。日本語のみで研究をしていると、おおむね日本国内で活動し、たまに海外に出る程度になる。一方、英語を使うようになると、海外で発表する機会は格段に広がる。それも、その気にさえなれば、北米だけではなくヨーロッパでもオセアニアでも、アジア諸地域でも機会は見いだせるようになる。知らない町を訪れ、普段接しない人たちと数日を過ごしながら研究交流をする魅力は、とても大きい。最後に、もちろん日本の大学を取り巻く状況も無視はできない。多くの大学で、英語の教育は重視されているし、留学生の受け入れにも積極的である。大学によっては、教員に対し、授業を英語で行うよう求める場合もある。私はそうした英語偏重の流れには反対だが、だからといって英語を用いて研究することまでも否定しようとは思わない。

　さて、この先がこのエッセイの本題である。どのようにして、私は「英語でも」研究をするようになったのか。個人的な回顧が多くなりそうだが、私のわずかな経験が、これから英語や、その他日本語以外の言語を使って研究してみたいと思っている人や、あるいはもしかしたら日本語を外国語として習得して日本研究をしているものの、イマイチ日本語の運用に自信がない人へのヒント、あるいは誘いになれば幸いである。

2.「どうやって」英語で研究をするようになったのか

　私が、英語で行われている日本文学研究について最初に意識したのは、大学院生の時である。私は日本の私小説の研究をするつもりでいたが、所属していた講座は文学理論や比較文学などを主たる研究範囲とする研究室だったので、教員はむしろ外国文学や比較文学の専門家が多かった。そのうちの１人の先生が、あるとき私に言ったのである。「ひびくん、英語の日本文学研究の論文には、レベルが高いのもあるよ、これからはそういうのも読まないとだめだよ」。

　私が大学院に入ったのは 1995 年で、そのころは文芸批評理論やポストモダニズムの思想がとても流行していた。私も、雑誌の『批評空間』や『現代思想』をよく手にしていたし、文芸批評理論や現代哲学の単行図書も、どのような新刊が出るのか注意して見ていた。インターネットで新刊情報が流れてくるような時代ではなかったから、学内の書籍購買（丸善が入っていた）を頻繁に見に行った。棚に並ぶ文芸批評理論や現代哲学の論文、単行図書は、

フランス語や英語からの翻訳が多かった。みすず書房や法政大学出版局の白く光るブック・カバーが知的な香りを放っていた。翻訳された理論書こそがより先端的だと、当時の私には思えた。だから、先生から、外国語の文献も読みなさいと言われたとき、私は素直にそうするべきだと受け入れた。もっとも、それをどれだけ実行できたかといえば、口ごもらざるを得ない。わずかばかり、自分の博士論文に関わる文献を、読んだだけであった。

　大きな決心をしたのは、博士号を取得し、筑波大学の助手になってからだった。米国の日本研究の雰囲気やレベルがどのようなものなのか、知っておいた方がいいという気持ちが強くなっていた。それに、博士論文を書き終え、次に取り組むべき新しい研究テーマを探していた。そのころ、まだ文部科学省の「在外研究員」という制度があった。申請した教員は審査に通れば、旅費と滞在費が支給されて、1年を上限に、国外の研究機関に籍を置いて研究を行うことができる仕組みだった。決まるまで、いろいろ曲折もあったのだが、それは省略する。ともかく私は、周囲にさまざまな迷惑をかけつつ、米国に行くことを決め、幸いにも申請を通過することができたのだ。

　受け入れてくれた大学は、カリフォルニア大学ロサンゼルス校（UCLA）の日本研究センターだった。当時私には、1人として、アメリカ人の日本文学研究者の知人はいなかった。しかし受け入れ研究者の承諾なくして、在外研究に申し込むことはできない。私は細い細い線をたどらざるを得なかった。学会で、米国で教員をしている知人の話をしていたKさんに、その知人Uさんに取り次いでもらえるようお願いした。Uさんは親切にも、何も知らない私の相談に乗ってくれ、そのテーマであるならば、UCLAがいいだろう、ついてはマイケル・ボーダッシュさんに取り次いであげようと言って下さった。

　そのテーマ、というのは日系アメリカ文学の中の日本語文学についての研究だった。包み隠さず言えば、そのときの私に深い考えがあって、このテーマを選んだわけではなかった。新しい研究テーマは、ポストコロニアル系の問題関心に接するようなものにしたいこと、米国で在外研究を行うことに正当性を与えるような領域にしたいこと、という2つの動機の交点になるものを選んだだけであった。このテーマの面白さを見いだしたのは、決めてから後のことである。

　ボーダッシュさんの受け入れ許可をもらい、在外研究が正式に決定したあ

と、9. 11が起きた。その日私は、いつものとおり食事の後、NHKの定時ニュースを見ていた。ニュースの時間になり、画面が切り替わると、何の説明もないまま、黒煙を上げる超高層ビルの映像が映し出された。私は深夜まで、釘付けになってテレビを見続けた。

　それからしばらく、何人もの人に、「本当に行くのか」と尋ねられた。ニューヨークの次は、ロサンゼルスが危ない、という説を読んだりもした。私には、どれくらいそこが危険なのか、よくわからなかった。しかし、このチャンスを逃したら、次はいつになるかわからないことだけは確実だった。私は、行くことに決めた。出発は翌年5月だった。

　出発に向けて、英語の勉強はした。評判のいい会話教本の類いを買って勉強した。これは、そこそこよかった。先生の家へ行って教えてもらう形式の、英語の家庭教師もお願いした。こちらは、正直言って、役に立ったかどうかはわからない。

3. ロサンゼルス、2002年

　5月のロサンゼルス。最初に印象に残ったのは、星条旗と、ロサンゼルス・レイカーズの旗だった。米国のプロバスケットボールリーグに、大した関心もなかった私は、街中の車がレイカーズの黄色い旗を取り付けて走り回っているのを見て、なにごとかと驚いた。レイカーズはこのとき、3年連続のNBAプレーオフ進出を賭けて戦っており、3連覇の期待がかかっていた。レイカーズの黄色い旗とならんで、星条旗がどの車にも、どの窓にも、どのビルにもあるようにみえた。戦争を戦っている国にいるのだ、と私は実感した。

　結論を先に言ってしまうと、1年足らずのロサンゼルス滞在で、私の英語の力は大して伸びなかった。当たり前である。私は、ほとんどの時間を自分のアパートと大学図書館との往復で過ごした。大学図書館では、20世紀初頭のサンフランシスコで刊行された日本語新聞のマイクロフィルムを、ひたすら読んでいた。友人らしい友人はまったくできなかった。当時日本近代文学を教えていた教員は、マイケル・ボーダッシュさんとセイジ・リピットさんだったが、タイミングの悪いことに、2人ともそろってサバティカルと何かで、その年は授業を教えていなかった。

　私は大学院時代に結婚しており、ロサンゼルスには妻の天野知幸（日本近

代文学を専攻する同業者だ）も一緒に来た。彼女は彼女で、日本でのチャンスをなげうって米国に来ていた。ロサンゼルスでは、彼女の方が自由に、そして積極的に活動していたが、それでも2人で過ごす時間が圧倒的に多かった。それは2人の支えになったが、家に閉じこもる要因の1つとなったことも確かだろう。

　私は、冗談でも何でもなく、ロンドンで群狼に混じったムク犬として過ごした夏目金之助のことを思い、自分もノイローゼになる日は遠くないだろう、と思っていた。キャンパスの学生たちは楽しそうで、晴天続きのロサンゼルスは光にあふれていたが、私は彼らの群れの中にはいなかった。CNNのキャスターが言っていることは、よくわからなかった。FOXテレビは、やや聞きやすかったが、女性キャスターが派手だった。一番わかるのは子供向けの番組で、中でも『テレタビー』を愛していた。テレタビーたちは、英語を話さなかった。

　英語を読み聞く力についてはゆっくりしか伸びず、書く力にいたってはまったく進歩しなかったが、しかし振り返れば、米国の長期滞在は、私にとって多くの意味があった。まず、言語以外の習慣、意識、ルールや米国社会の実情の一部を、身をもって知り得たことの意味は大きかった。図書館の使い方、買い物の仕方、公共交通機関の使い方。初対面の人に、にこやかに挨拶をすること。レストランやタクシーでチップを払うこと。言葉の不自由な東洋人は、排斥はされないまでも、冷遇はされること。英語といっても、さまざまな社会的民族的なまりが飛び交っていること。危険な場所、危険な時間帯の街の危険さは、日本とは比較にならないこと、などなど。米国で講演会やセミナー、学会に参加できたことも、次につながった。会場の様子、会の進行、質疑の仕方、歓談の仕方などのフォーマットを知ったことは、帰国後も、米国だけでなく他の国の学会や研究会に出る際に、とても役立った。

　自分が外国人になるという経験も大きかった。日本にいた私は、無自覚なマジョリティだった。言葉がわからないこと、習慣がわからないこと、制度がわからないこと、頼れる人が身近にいないことが、どれだけつらく、不安であるか、不利であるかを、身をもって知った。そのことは帰国してからの自分の振る舞いや考え方に、長く影響を残していると思う。

　米国の大学では、もう1度だけ短い滞在をした。2009年に、ワシントン

大学のテッド・マックさんが、滞在研究員として招聘してくれたのだった。私は名古屋大学に移動したばかりで職場の状況が許さなかったため、一ヶ月足らずの滞在になったが、それでもありがたい経験だった。シアトルでは、テッドさんと一緒に日系移民関係の調査もすることができた。日本語を多く使ったが、このときには英語を使うことも慣れてきていたので、シアトルでの私の調査活動の範囲は広がった。

4. 英語で学会発表をする

　一番最初に英語で学会発表をしたときのことは、よく覚えている。2004年の香港だった。筑波大の元同僚のY先生が、国際比較文学会にパネルを出そうと誘ってくれたのである。ものすごく、緊張した。英語の読み上げ原稿は作成したものの、質疑応答はできる気がしなかった。初めて訪れる香港は楽しく、猛烈に暑い8月の街歩きも楽しんだが、私は不安の塊だった。会場は、驚くべきことに、一番大きなレクチャーホールがあたっていた。ホテルの部屋で翌日の準備をしながら、その講堂が聴衆で一杯になり、その中で質疑応答が進行し、何も答えられず立ち往生する自分、という妄想に取り憑かれた。もっとも当日、蓋を開けてみれば聴衆は自分たちと他数人でしかなかった。閑散とした空間にマイクロフォンの声が響き、掃除担当者でいいから部屋に入ってくれば少しは賑やかになるかもしれない、とさえ思えた。

　研究で用いる英語という、言語面での力について言えば、私の場合、米国滞在の10ヶ月よりも、その後、さまざまな学会で行った学会発表とそれに向けての準備のほうが、より上達につながったと思っている。目標が目の前にあり、必要とされる能力や情報が明確であり、ゴールの日時も決まっている。なにより、恐ろしいから必死に準備する。

　英語で発表する学会を経験するためには、パネル発表に加えてもらうのが一番の近道だろう。個人発表を申し込んでもよいが、準備から当日に至るまでのすべてを自分で行わなければならないから、ハードルが高い。パネル発表ならば、オーガナイザーが準備も含めた全体を取り仕切ってくれるし、パネルの仲間がなにくれと手伝ってくれ、相談に乗ってくれる。当日の質疑も、助けてくれる。関心や研究テーマの近い外国語話者の研究者と出会ったならば、いつかパネルを組もうと声をかけておくといいと思う。

　いくらかの経験を積むと、英語による質疑応答だとしても、基本的なベー

スとなるのは、自分が日本語で日頃行ってる研究の蓄積だということがはっきりしてくる。相手の言うことがある程度理解でき、こちらの言いたいことについての語彙が浮かびさえすれば、それを四苦八苦してつないでなんとか答えらしいものにできる。決してスマートではないし、相手にも聞き取りの負荷をかける。

　言葉の流暢さや発音の「正しさ」は、私はもうあきらめつつある。それよりもむしろ、きちんとかみ合った議論をし、有用な知見をその場に運ぶことの方が重要だ。逆の場合を考えてみればいい。日本語はものすごく達者だが、言っている中身はつまらないという研究者と、日本語はこちらのサポートが必要だが、中身はものすごくおもしろいという外国人研究者がいたとする。自分がどちらと仕事をしたいか。私なら、迷わず後者を選ぶし、自分もそうありたいと願っている。

5. 英語で書くこと、あるいは機械翻訳について

　英語を用いる私の仕事に、大きな変化を与えつつあるのが、ここ数年の機械翻訳の進歩である。書く際も読む際も、かなりの精度で翻訳をしてくれる。読むことについては、専門書に関しては自分で読んだ方が正確だとは感じる。ただし、スピードは比べものにならないから、大意がつかめればいい場合や、時間がないときには機械翻訳も使う。

　書く際には、私の場合、より劇的だ。「Google 翻訳」を使っていた 2010 年代半ばには、自分で英文を書き、部分的に「Google 翻訳」を参考にする程度だった。それが 2019 年に「みらい翻訳」が登場してから、一気に変わった。「みらい翻訳」が吐き出す英文の自然さをみて、私は自分の英作文の力では、到底これを越えるものは書けないと観念した。その後、学術的用途においてはさらに上を行く「DeepL 翻訳」が登場した。私は、私に求められる能力が、ゼロから英文を作る力ではなく、機械翻訳が出力する英文を自分の意図通りになっているかどうかチェックする力へと変化していることを知った。だからいまや私は、私の英語運用能力を、「自分＋機械翻訳」で合算して考えることに決めている。

　とはいえ、人力と機械翻訳の力を合わせても、十分ではない。学会発表や英文原稿を書く場合、私は機械翻訳を使った上で、英文校正の業者に依頼をする。まず日本語で完全原稿を作り、機械翻訳にそれをかけていき、出力さ

れた英文を直していく。完成したら、英文原稿を業者に送り、数日後にはそれが返ってくる。それをさらに直す。学会での短い口頭発表なら、これでなんとか許されるレベルにはなっているはずである。なお、機械翻訳にかけやすい日本語というものがあるから、それに留意すると効率が上がる。主語を明確にし、文章の構造をシンプルにすることだ。

ただこれでも、十分かといえば、残念ながら、そうとは言えないようだ。論文や研究発表のスタイルそのものが違うということもあるが、なにより本当に高いレベルで研究を行うには、高度な言語運用能力が必要とされてもいるからだ。もしかしたら、それが人文系分野の特色かもしれない。文章であれば文体が、弁舌であればその雄弁さが、研究者としての力の保証になるし、魅力にもなる。日本語であっても英語であっても、真に高度な議論は、圧倒的な専門的知識量を前提に、繰り出される言葉の細かなニュアンスまで制御しながら行われる。とりわけ、テキストの詳細な読解を行ったり、繊細な議論が求められるような話題に立ち入ったりする場合において、そうである。

そして口頭と文章とを比べれば、後者への要求水準が高い。とりわけ出版社から刊行されるような文章の質を求められるとき、要求のレベルが格段に上がる。先日、私が提出した英文の原稿は、校正業者によるネイティブ・チェックを経ていたにもかかわらず、編集担当の研究者によって徹底的に直された。選ばれる語彙や言い回しが、違うのである。おそらく私の文章は、高校生レベルの語彙、言葉遣いだっただろう。だが、求められているのは、人文系の研究者レベルの語彙、言い回しである。私も機械翻訳も校正業者も、そんなハイレベルな能力は持ち合わせていない。こうなるともう、完全にお手上げである。

が、私はもう開き直っていて、お手上げで仕方ないと今は考えている。今生において、私の英語がそこまで到達する日は来ない。生まれ変わって再チャレンジすることのできない私にできるのは、まず最初に準備する、日本語の原稿の質を上げることである。その先は、できるところまでやればよろしい。英語の文章として拙いならば、拙いと思っただれかが、助けてくれる。それで、十分である。

6. 日本文学研究のシンギュラリティ？

　機械翻訳の質がさらに上がっていったら、研究の未来はどうなるだろうか。このエッセイを閉じるにあたって、デジタル環境がもたらす変化をめぐって、もう少し踏み込んで考えてみよう。

　少し前に、「シンギュラリティ」というアイデアが流行した。レイ・カーツワイルが示した未来予測で、人工知能が人間の能力を超えるときを指しているようだ。私がここで想像してみたいのは、もう少し小規模で、しかし、もしかしたらもう目の前に迫っているかもしれない問題である。仮にそれを《日本文学研究のシンギュラリティ》と呼んでおこう。

　日本文学研究者がＡＩに駆逐される日──は当分の間来ないであろうから、ここで言う《シンギュラリティ》とは、研究のパラダイムが、テクノロジーの発展によって革命的かつ不可逆的に変わる瞬間、という程度の意味である。たとえば、こんな未来はどうだろう。

（1）機械翻訳がほぼ実用的になり、各言語で書かれた日本研究論文をかなり自然な自国語に訳して読める。また自国語で書いた論文をかなり自然な他言語に翻訳できる。
（2）各国・各言語の論文データベースが相互接続され、串刺しで横断検索できる。
（3）日本語で書かれた過去そして現在の文学作品や関連する書物・雑誌の内容が、全文テキスト検索できる。

　10年、20年後にはありえそうではないだろうか。《日本文学研究のシンギュラリティ》が到来したとき、私たちの研究、そして教育は、どのように変わるだろう。研究の視野は、相当変わるに違いない。読まなければならない論文の量が相当増えるので、ものすごくめんどうだが、しかし各地域の最も新しく、そして個別の関心に根ざした論考が、ほぼ刊行と同時に読めるようになる。母語以外で行う研究発表の敷居も、多少は下がるだろう。同時通訳者のいる研究発表会場を想像するといい。同時通訳者がスマートフォンに置き換わることになる。発表者や質問者は、母語でそれを行うことができる。言葉の不自由を理由に質疑応答にびびることも、減るだろう。

　大きなメリットとなるのは、研究の報告が、母語によってなされつづける

ということだ。現在、日本文学研究は、世界のさまざまな国や地域の内部で
コミュニティが作られ、互いにアド・ホックな連携を保ちつつも、おおむ
ね、それぞれの中で自己完結的に進められている。たとえて言えば、それは
互いに、ちょっとした往来のある島宇宙群のようなものだ。だが、全員が英
語、あるいは全員が日本語で研究を行うような時代になったとき、日本研究
の世界が内包している島宇宙の多様性の多くは消えていく。機械翻訳は、島
宇宙を平坦に均さないままに、生き延びさせる鍵になる。

　だがもちろん、よいことばかりではない。いかに同時通訳が優秀であって
も、直接対話を交わすことがもたらす親密さは、通訳という媒介者の存在に
よって低減されてしまう。パンデミックの間に、私たちは人と人の距離がも
たらす親密さ／疎遠さについて、多くのことを考えた。人と人とのつながり
は、空間と時間を供にして対話をしたり、食事をしたりすることからもたら
される。そうしたつながりを強化し維持するためには、機械や通訳者に頼り
切るのではなく、やはり自分自身で他言語や他文化を学ぶ姿勢を、もった方
がよい。

　研究の島宇宙についても、その存続はよいことばかりではあるまい。日
本、北米、ヨーロッパ、中国、韓国、台湾、ASEAN、南米、それぞれの日
本文学研究に、それぞれの事情やお国柄がある。どのような研究が面白く、
先端的だと感じるかという基準も異なる。日本文学研究の立ち位置も、それ
ぞれの国や地域で違うだろう。日本文学研究が「国文学」としてある場合も
あれば、地域研究、たとえば東アジア研究の一部としてある場合もあろう
し、単に数多くある外国文学の１つとして見なされている場合もあるだろ
う。植民地支配や留学によって結びついた、自国の近代文学史の一部として
考える必要がある地域もあれば、日系移民コミュニティが存在することで、
日本文学がエスニックグループのルーツの一部としてある場合もあろう。日
本文学研究の位置によって、日本文学研究に求められる役割が変わり、研究
者が差し出す研究成果の宛先も変わる。

　《日本文学研究のシンギュラリティ》が到来したとき、国境による分断
が、研究の分断のままであり続けることはなくなるだろう。島宇宙同士が接
し、融合が始まれば、差異を消そうという力が働き始める。どの方向に向
かって消すかを議論し出したとき、影響力の強さをめぐる葛藤や駆け引きが
起こるかもしれない。現実の問題として、人口や言語、距離、地政学などに

よって、同じ日本文学研究であっても、影響力の強い／弱いが存在するであろうから。

《シンギュラリティ》の3項目は、目の前に迫っている。日本の国立国会図書館では、現在の雑誌 1,320,000 点、973,000 点について本文の全文検索が可能となっている（「国立国会図書館デジタルコレクション」を使う）。国会図書館の蔵書のかなりの部分がデジタルテキスト化され、全文検索が可能になる時代は、もう始まっている。私たちの——とりわけ近現代文学の——研究は、変わらざるをえない。関連資料を多数所蔵する大図書館へのアクセス性が研究の優位性へと結びつく場面は、減っていくだろう。一方、居ながらにして大量に見つかる資料をどう評価し、どう位置づけ、どう使うかがという問いが突きつけられる。そして大量に収集した資料をいかにして分析するか（当然、コンピュータを用いた機械読解もここに含まれる）が改めて問われることになろう。どんな研究が可能になるのか、心から楽しみだ。

とはいえ、そうした時代は、情報科学という領域が用いる「言語」との間の翻訳が、問題となるような時代の始まりかもしれない。私が 10 年後に書くべきエッセイは、「なんで、どうやって、『コンピュータを使って』研究をするようになったか」になっている、だろうか。

　第１部　言葉の壁・方法論の谷・技術という橋

「いま」「ここ」の当たり前を問いなおす

私は「変」じゃない

私が日本研究する理由

江口啓子（豊田工業高等専門学校）

　昔から、良くも悪しくも「普通」から外れる子どもであったことは自覚している。たびたび親（主に母親）の手を煩わせて育った。中学時代あたりから、友人たちに「変わっている」と言われることを苦痛に感じるようになった。周囲（多数派）の予測（あるいは期待）から外れる行為、言動をするたびに「変わっている」と言われた。今振り返ると、思春期の私は無自覚に自分は多数派に属していると思っていたし、多数派であることで安心感を得ようとしていたのである。世間で「当たり前」とされることに疑念を持ったり、「当たり前」とされることとは異なる言動をしたりする自分を正当化したいという強い欲望が、昔も今も自分の日本研究をする動機となっている気がする。

1.「BLっていつからあるんだろう？」

　高校時代の私の目標は「普通」になることであった。自分の好きなものを手放す必要はないが、少なくとも世間一般でよいとされるものは嗜み、世間一般から浮かない振る舞いをする、というのが高校時代の自分に課したものである。果たして目標は達成されたか。当時はある程度果たされたと思っていたが、これも振り返ってみると大して達成されていなかったように思う。しかし、努力はした。そして高校を卒業するときに痛切に思った。なんと愚かしい努力をして、3年を無駄に費やしたのかと。以降、私は周囲から

どう思われようと好きにすることに決めた。しかし、だからといって自分が「変」であるというレッテルを貼られることを受け入れた訳ではなく、そのような評価は甚だ遺憾であった。

そこで、大学に入った私は、自分が「変」ではない証拠を探すことで世間（実体のない、私の中の想像のもの）に対抗することにした。もちろんこれは自己満足であり、ただ自分が安心するための行為である。しかし、その安心がなければ生きて行くのは少々辛いと私は感じていたのである。では、大学に入った私は何をしたか。とった方法は2つあった。1つは海外からの留学生と交流すること。今という時間を共有する人間同士であっても、国が違えば「当たり前」とされることは違う。そこで、海外に自分の考える「当たり前」を有する存在を見つけることで、私は日本においては「変」かもしれないが、世界的には「変」ではないということを証明しようとした。そして、自分が「変」ではないということを確認するためのもう1つの方法が、昔の日本を研究することであった。私はもともと歴史と文学に興味があり、それを勉強したくて文学部に入学した。歴史や古典を学ぶと、過去の日本は空間的には地続きでありながら、現代とはずいぶんと異なる「当たり前」が存在していたことがわかる。私は過去を遡ることで、自分の仲間を探そうとした。そうすることで、私は今の日本では「変」かもしれないが、歴史的には「変」ではないということを証明しようとしたのである。

結論から言うと、この2つの作戦は大成功であった。留学生たちとの交流を通じて、例えば、日本ではやたらと推奨される「5分前行動」が喜ばれない文化もあることを知った。友人の家を訪問するのに、約束の時間ちょうどに行くことがマナーとされる国もあれば、むしろ遅れていくことがマナーの国もある。人間関係の築き方、親愛の情の示し方など、例は枚挙に暇がないが、「今」「ここ」で「当たり前」とされることが絶対的なものではないという、ある意味、当たり前の事実を確認することができて、私は大変安心した。

さて、大学1年生の時に、その後長くお世話になることになる恩師との出会いがあった。1年次に大学における学問の作法を学ぶための授業として「基礎セミナー」なるゼミ形態の授業があったのだが、その時私が選んだ授業の担当教員が、のちの私の指導教員となる先生だった。シラバスに「本について学ぶ」としか書かれていなかったその授業は、そもそも「本」の定義

　第1部　言葉の壁・方法論の谷・技術という橋

から始まる、1年生にとっては恐ろしくマニアックな授業であった。その授業のグループ学習の発表課題で「最初の本を探す」というものがあった。「最初の本」とは？象形文字やくさび形文字で書かれた本を紹介すればよいのか？私たちのグループは、そういう発想は他のグループとかぶるであろうという判断から、「○○についての最初の本」を探すことにした。

　時に20世紀の末、1999年のことであった。アイディアを出し合っているうちに、当時ＢＬ（ボーイズラブ）と呼ばれ出していた、男性同士の恋愛を描いた物語ジャンルの話になった。かつては何となくひそやかに愛好されていたそのジャンルが、最近（1999年当時）は書店でも堂々と売られ始めた、などという話から、「そういえば、ＢＬっていつからあるんだろう？」という疑問にたどり着いた。奇しくも同じグループに韓国からの留学生がいて、韓国ではこの年、初めてゲイ向けの雑誌が刊行された、という情報も提供してくれた（注：これは1998年に創刊したゲイ・レズビアンの専門雑誌『BUDDY』のことだと判明した［柳、三本松2015］）。そこで、私たちのグループは「日本で最初のＢＬの本」について発表することにしたのである。

　さて、読者のみなさんは、最初のＢＬはいつ頃書かれたと想像するだろうか（注：ここでいうＢＬとは、あくまで「男性同士の恋愛物語」を指す）。まだインターネットよりも書籍を主たる情報源としていた時代であり、私たちはその答えを探すべく図書館へと向かった。そして図書館で見つけたのが『耽美小説・ゲイ文学ブックガイド』（柿沼瑛子・栗原知代編著、白夜書房、1993）なる本である。ちなみに「ＢＬ」というジャンル名は1994年頃から使われ初め、1996年以降に定着した呼称で、それ以前は「耽美小説」とも呼ばれていた（堀、守編著2020）。「日本で最初のＢＬ」を探していた我々にはうってつけの本であり、その本のおかげで、私は『秋夜長物語（あきのよのながものがたり）』の存在を知ることとなる。

　『秋夜長物語』とは14世紀に作られた物語で、比叡山の僧桂海と三井寺（園城寺）の児梅若との悲恋を描く。児（ちご）とは、寺院で僧の側近くに仕えた少年のことで、僧たちの性愛の対象になることもあった。主に中世に作られた、僧と児の恋愛を主題として描く作品を「児物語」と呼ぶ。もちろん、児物語を現在のＢＬと同列に扱うことはできないのだが、19世紀初頭に一般化した呼称とはいえ、児物語というジャンル名が作られるほど、男性同士の恋愛を描く作品が多数、過去の日本に存在していたことは、大学1年生の

私には衝撃的であった。私たちは「最初のＢＬ」として『秋夜長物語』について発表することにしたが、このテーマで果たして教授は受け入れてくれるのか、という一抹の不安も抱えていた。

　ところが、予想は鮮やかに裏切られ、受け入れてもらえた。さらに衝撃的であったのは、発表を終えた時の教授の言葉であった。なんと、２年生以上が選択できるゼミで現在『秋夜長物語』を輪読しているというのだ。私が何に驚いたかというと、自分が趣味で愛好するＢＬが、大学でのアカデミックな研究のテーマになりうる、ということであった。当時の私は、娯楽を目的とするメディアは研究の対象にはならないと信じていた。それが「当たり前」だと思っていた。世間の「当たり前」に苦しんでいた自分もまた、根拠のない「当たり前」を無自覚に受容していたということである。しかし、この「当たり前」の認識が破壊されたことによって、私は研究の道を志すようになったのである。

2. 愛すべき室町時代のはみ出し者

　主人公の貴族男性が女装の少年を寵愛したことから悲劇に見舞われる『風に紅葉』という作品で卒業論文を書き、無事に大学院に進学した私に、新たな運命的な出会いが訪れる。恩師に紹介されて知った、男装の少女を主人公にした『新蔵人』という物語絵巻だ。卒論で扱った『風に紅葉』は文章のみの物語であったが、この『新蔵人』絵巻は文章だけではなく挿絵を伴う作品で、さらに挿絵の中には登場人物のセリフが書き込まれている（これを「画中詞」と呼ぶ）。しかも絵は白描といって墨線のみで描かれており、その形態はさながらマンガである。この物語には、中流貴族の家の三人の娘が登場する。両親が娘たちに将来の希望を尋ねたところ、長女の大君は出家して尼になりたいと言い、次女の中君は宮中に出仕して華やかな生活を送りたいと言う。ところが三女の三君は男になって走り歩きたいと言うのである。そうして、ついには男装して蔵人として出仕する。兄も蔵人であったので、区別するために三君は「新蔵人」と呼ばれた。ちなみにこれが題名の由来である。その後、帝に正体を暴かれ、新蔵人は男装のまま帝の寵愛を受けることになる。やがて新蔵人は懐妊し、若宮を産むが、帝にはすでに何人もの若宮がいるため、新蔵人の生んだ子どもが帝位につくことはない。先に出仕していた中君にも勝る寵愛を得た新蔵人は、おごり高ぶった態度を見せるよう

になるが、やがて帝の愛は薄れていく。そして彼女は大君のもとへ行き、出家して尼になる道を選ぶのである。最後は姉妹で成仏を果たし、両親と中君も、往生が約束される。

　今でもマンガやドラマなどの趣向として愛好されている男装ものは、物語としても古くは平安末期成立の『とりかへばや』まで遡ることができる。その系譜に連なる男装の姫君の物語が『新蔵人』絵巻である。ただし、『とりかへばや』や『在明の別』など先行の物語を意識し、あえてずらすという趣向も凝らされている。その最たるものが、主人公の姫君の男装の動機である。先行の『とりかへばや』や『在明の別』では、基本的には主人公の意向で男装をしているものの、天狗の呪いであったり、家の後継問題であったりと、男装を正当化するやむを得ない事情も用意されていた。ところがこの『新蔵人』絵巻の主人公の男装は、ほとんど本人の意向のみで行われる。「普通」の姫君なら思いもしない願望を口にし、実際にその通り実行する主人公は、室町時代にあってしても間違いなくはみ出し者であっただろう。『新蔵人』絵巻に出会った私は、このはみ出し者の主人公に夢中になった。なぜなら、彼女はまさに私が探し求めていた自分の仲間であったからである。

　『新蔵人』絵巻が成立したと考えられる室町後期、天皇家も貴族も経済的に困窮していく中で、正妻である后妃は立てられず、後宮は女官ばかりであった。そのため、天皇の世継を産むのは、天皇に仕える女官たちであった。ちょうどこの物語において播磨内侍として出仕し、姫宮と若宮（本当は新蔵人の子）を設けた中君の姿こそが現実であったのである。このような一夫多妻制とも言える環境において、宮中で働く女房たちの最高の好運とは、帝の寵愛を受け、世継を産むことであった（脇田 1992）。正妻が立てられない天皇家で働くということは、見方を変えると寵愛さえ得られれば誰にでも国母になる可能性があったということである。そうなれば、やはり宮中における処世術が女房たちには重要になってくる。帝に愛されること、同僚の女房たちに妬まれることなくそつなく振る舞うこと、これらのことが宮廷女房の最大の関心事であっただろう。そのような背景の中で、女訓書と呼ばれるジャンルの書物が流行する。女訓書とは女性向けの教訓書であるが、そのはしりとなるのが鎌倉時代、阿仏尼が女房として出仕している娘、紀内侍に宛てて教訓をしたためた『乳母のふみ』である。中世の貴族女性の規範とも言

える『乳母のふみ』で述べられている教訓と『新蔵人』絵巻における主人公の振る舞いを比較すると、彼女がいかに規範から外れた人物として造形されているかがわかる。

　例えば、『新蔵人』絵巻では、冒頭で両親が一家の教育方針を披露する。それは「いづれもありたからむままに、ただ心にまかせて過ぐし給へ。親の掟をも従へぬものは人の心なり。終には我が心の引くに任する習ひなれば」（第1段、詞書）というものであった。この物語では子どもは「親の掟」でも従わせられないものであるから、心のままに好きに生きよと、自由に娘たちに将来を選ばせる。しかし、実は女訓書の中ではまったく逆のことを教える。「窓の内一つに傅かれて、親の掟に従ひて、世を過ぐす程は、多くの咎ももて隠され易く候」（第13段）と子供は「親の掟」に従うことが善しとされ、また「心のままなるが、返す返す悪しき事にて候」（第2段）と「心のまま」に振る舞うことを否定されているのである。

　そして、このような両親の言葉を受けて、「心のまま」に将来を選んで生きたのが『新蔵人』絵巻の娘たちであった。その最たる女性が新蔵人である。中世の中下層の貴族の娘にとって、将来の選択肢は皇族か目上の貴族の家へ女房として出仕する、対等の家格の男性の妻になる、出家して尼になる、の3通りしかない。1番目は中君の選んだ道であり、3番目は大君が選んだ道であった。そして、新蔵人が選んだ生き方は、非常識にも男装をして出仕するというものであった。しかし、男装をして「女なりとも男になりて劣らず振る舞」（第5段、詞書）う新蔵人の生き方は、能力を発揮する場が限られていた当時の女性読者に、憧れすら伴って受け入れられたのではないだろうか。

　私がこの物語をとりわけ興味深く思うのは、結末が異性愛的ハッピーエンドではない点である。女性を主人公とする多くの物語は、結婚して子孫繁栄する結末をもってハッピーエンドとする。しかし、この物語では主人公は出家をして尼になる。これが男性の主人公であれば、いわゆる出家遁世譚、つまり、男性が愛する人を失った哀しみで出家する、という悲恋の物語になったであろう。ところが、『新蔵人』絵巻の中では主人公はただ出家をするのではなく、仏道修行の末に女人成仏を果たすのである。これがどれほどすごいことかお分かりになるだろうか。中世において、女性は生まれつき「五障」があるため、成仏が難しいという言説があった。『法華経』由来のこの

言葉は、日本的な解釈が進む中で、女性の抱える罪障を意味するようになっていく。では、女性が成仏をするためにはどうすればよいか。これもまた『法華経』にその方法が示されている。「変成男子」と言って、男性の身体に変身することで、女性でも成仏が可能になるのだ。この「変成男子」を実現する方法はいくつかあるが、『新蔵人』絵巻では光明真言を唱えることが選ばれたようだ。『新蔵人』絵巻の最後の絵は、仏道修行に励む三君（元・新蔵人）と大君の様子を描いている（図1）。一見、順調に修行をしているようであるが、画中詞を読むと、そうではないことが分かる。三君は顔立ちが男性的であるため、周囲から男性の僧と勘違いされ、「尼たちが男の僧と一緒に住んでいる」と噂されているらしい。そこで大君は、妹に尼らしく頭巾を被るように促すのだが、それに対する三君の返答が痛快である。「変成男子とこそ言へ、生きながら変成女子になりたる心地ぞする」、つまり「変成男子」を目指しているのに女性らしくしろだなんて、「変成女子」をしている気分だ、というのである。その上で三君は女人成仏を果たし、さらに一家往生という仏教的ハッピーエンドを迎えるのである。これほどアナーキーな女性主人公が他にいるだろうか。『新蔵人』絵巻は間違いなく、世間一般の秩序に一石を投じる作品である。

図1　『新蔵人』絵巻　第16段（大阪市立美術館本）

　ここで注目したいのは『新蔵人』絵巻の伝称筆者である。この作品はサントリー美術館に上巻が、大阪市立美術館に上下巻が所蔵され、この2本以外には伝来していないのであるが、そのうち大阪市立美術館所蔵の本には伝称筆者として「後柏原院卿内侍」の名が残されている。江戸期の鑑定によるものであるが、女性が物語の筆者として名が残されているのである。後柏原院卿内侍（1483〜1543）は後柏原天皇に仕えた女房で能筆家として知られる。伝称ではあるものの、『新蔵人』絵巻という、女性を取り巻く社会の現状に対してきわめて挑発的な作品を作り、それを享受したのは女性であると

いう可能性は、私をたいそう勇気づけるのである。

3. 海外における日本研究との出会い

　さて、諸事情があって修士課程修了後は高校の教員として働くこととなったのだが、恩師のおかげで研究との縁が切れることはなかった。『新蔵人』絵巻の研究成果を輪読会のメンバーと共にまとめ、大学の研究室年報として発行した後、新たな作品の輪読に取りかかり始めた。次なる作品は、女装の少年が主人公の『児今参り』である。この作品もまた『新蔵人』絵巻と同様に、文・挿絵・画中詞で構成されている。『児今参り』は比叡山の児が、一目惚れした姫君に近づくために女装をするという物語である。先に紹介した『秋夜長物語』では僧に垣間見され、恋心を寄せられる対象であった児が、この物語では姫君を垣間見し、主体的な恋愛の行為者になる。途中、児が天狗に誘拐されるなど、『秋夜長物語』の影響が多分に見られる作品である。

　ところで、これまでに挙げてきた『秋夜長物語』『風に紅葉』『新蔵人』絵巻は、一般的にはほとんど知られていない作品であり、日本における研究もごく限られたものである。そして、『児今参り』も、同じく知名度の低い作品である。そのため、そのようなマイナーな作品が海外で研究されているということを知った時は、大変驚いた。2009 年にシュミット堀佐知氏（現・ダートマス大学）が『児今参り』を紹介するとともに全文を英訳し、2012 年には『児今参り』に関する論文をメリッサ・マコーミック氏（ハーバード大学）が発表していた。偶然にも同じ時期に同じ作品に関心を持ち、研究をする仲間がいたということだけでなく、それが海外の研究者だったというのは、当時の私にとって、非常に意外なことであった。恥ずかしながら、それまで私は日本文学研究をするからには海外留学する必要はなく、英語も不要であると考えていた。ところが、『児今参り』という、そもそも日本語でも先行研究のあまりない作品が海外で研究され、英語で論文が書かれているという現実を目の当たりにし、日本研究は日本国内だけでやっていれば良いというかつての考えは、全くの誤りであったことに気がついた。

　『児今参り』輪読会のメンバーでマコーミック氏の論文を日本語訳する作業を通して、日本の研究との差違を感じることもしばしばあった。日本の文学研究はテキスト分析が中心で、精読によって新たな事実を明らかにすることが多い。しかし、マコーミック氏の論文では、テキストの読みも踏まえた

上のことであるが、やはり中心となるのは、物語を構造分析し理論化することだ。もちろん、マコーミック氏が美術史専門であるがゆえの手法の違いも存在するのだが、積極的に海外の日本研究に触れていく中で、やはり日本と海外の研究手法の差というものが確実にあるということを確信した。そして、この違いが私の目には大変新鮮に映ったのである。日本国内だけで研究を続けている間に、私は日本の「当たり前」の研究手法を踏襲し、そのことに気づくこともなかった。海外における日本研究に触れることで初めて、日本における日本研究を客観的に眺めることができたのである。

　2015年3月、『新蔵人』絵巻の輪読会メンバーらで、シカゴで開催されたAAS（Association for Asian Studies）の年次大会に参加した。AASはアジア研究では世界最大規模の国際学会である。『児今参り』を通じて交流を持つようになったマコーミック氏をチェアに迎え、『新蔵人』絵巻をテーマにパネルディスカッションを行った。これが私の最初の国際学会体験である。AASでは、まず学会の規模の大きさと雰囲気のあまりの違いに驚いた。シェラトン・ホテルの本館と別館が貸し切りとなり、4日間で322ものパネルが発表を行うのである。自分の興味があるパネルに行って自由に発表を聞くことができる。パネルではペーパーは配布されない。発表よりもディスカッションが重んじられる。そして全体的にお祭りムードで、終始一貫して和やかな雰囲気に包まれたイベントなのである。こうして私は、日本における学会が世界の「当たり前」ではないということを実感させられた。

　海外の日本研究に触れ、学会にも参加したことで、日本の良さと海外の良さを知ることができた。そして、これから自分が研究を進めていく上で、日本と海外の研究交流は必要不可欠であると考えている。双方に刺激を与え合いながら研究することが、世界での日本研究の進展につながると考えるからである。しかし、言語の壁というものが国際的な研究交流を妨げる要因となりうる。そこで参考になるのが、シュミット堀佐知氏の取り組みである。

　2020年と2021年に、シュミット堀佐知氏が主催したワークショップにオンラインで参加する機会があったのだが、このワークショップの最大の特徴は英語と日本語の併用である。つまり、参加者は各自が得意とする言語を用いて発表、質問をしてよいのである。そして、議論を活性化することを目的として、発表者は事前にフルペーパーを提出する。主催者がフルペーパーをイベント用のウェブサイトにアップロードし、すべての発表者とディス

カッサントは、パスワードを使ってそれらをダウンロードし、事前に目を通しておくことを求められた。実際、ワークショップでは原稿をそのまま読み上げることは禁じられており、（他の人がすでに読んだ）ペーパーの最重要項目だけを要約することになっていた。自分にとって、英語での発表を理解する上で、要旨だけでなくフルペーパーを事前に読んでおけるのは非常に有効な方法であった。

　奇しくもコロナ禍は、デジタルアーカイブや電子書籍の活用、研究会やカンファレンスのオンライン開催を促進した。その結果、世界のどこにいてもデジタルアーカイブを用いて、国内外の論文を縦横無尽に検索しながら研究ができる時代になりつつある（言葉の壁の問題は残るのだが）。世界で活動する研究者同士が幅広く対話や交流を行い、互いに批正しあうことができる時代が、もうそこまで到来しているのだ。

4. おわりに

　私は「変」じゃない。「今」「ここ」の「当たり前」も絶対的なものではない。それらを証明することが自分の研究動機にもなっているのは、最初に述べた通りである。しかしながら、自分の研究活動を通じて、私自身もまた多くのことを「当たり前」として内在化させている、という事実に気がつくようになった。自分の中に内面化してしまった「当たり前」を可視化し、1つ1つ検証していくためにも、異なる文化との交流は、私にとって必要不可欠なものである。そもそも、私にとって古典研究自体が、「今」を相対化させる試みだったのである。見えない何かに押し付けられる「当たり前」は決して普遍的なものではないし、押し付けられた「当たり前」に抗った人々は、どの時代にも存在した。それを常に確認し続けることで、私は安心して生きていくことができる。

　私は修士課程修了後、13年間高校の教員を勤めた。教師として働きながら博士課程に進学し、博士号を取得した。そして今は高専で働いている。高校から高専へと環境は多少変われど、10代後半の子どもたちに教育者として関わっている点では同じだ。修士課程を終えて高校の教員となったとき、心に決めていたことがあった。それは、かつての自分と同じように生きづらさを感じている生徒がいたら、その子にとっての「窓」になろうという決意であった。「今」「ここ」ではない場所を覗くための「窓」である。私は学ぶ

ことによって生きていく上での安心感を手に入れた。それを社会に還元したいと思ったのである。時間的・空間的に視野を広げていくと、「今」「ここ」の「当たり前」など些末な問題であることが分かる。それを生徒たちに授業を通じて伝えたい。また、同じことを研究を通じて、たくさんの人々に伝えることができればいいと思う。

第2部

エンパワーメントとしての知の創造

アメリカ人障害者として日本で暮らすこと
インターセクショナル　バリア　インクルーシブ
複合的な障壁と非排他的な想像性

マーク・ブックマン（東京大学）

渡辺哲史 & シュミット堀佐知 訳

　今も昔も、「アクセシビリティ」という言葉は、日本に住むさまざまな人々にとって、それぞれ別々の意味をもつ。東京で暮らし、働く、アメリカ人の車椅子使用者として、僕はこの事実を実感してきた。2018 年、日本に移住するにあたり、インターネットで賃貸物件を探してみたところ、24 万件のうち 900 件が「バリアフリー」の住まいとして登録されていた。しかし、誰かにとってのバリアフリーが、僕にとってのバリアフリーではない。その 900 件のうち、僕が暮らせるアパートは皆無だった。玄関にある段差、狭いバスルームのドア（車椅子で入れない）、カスタマイズにかかる高額な費用など、理由は色々だ。最終的に、住まいは見つかったものの、それで僕の生活がバリアフリーになった訳ではなく、一歩その外に出れば、見知らぬ一般の人々に、色々手伝いをお願いしなくてはいけない生活だった。善意ある人々が、日本でよく見る小型の車椅子と同じような感覚で、僕の 300 キロある電動車椅子を、僕ごと持ち上げて階段を上ろうと試み（もちろん無理）、僕もその親切な人々もあわや大けがの一歩手前、なんてことは何度も経験済み。アメリカでは、専門知識のある介助者が障害をもつ人々に付き添うのが普通だが、日本は急速な高齢化・少子化・労働人口の減少による人手不足のため、介助者を見つけるのは至難の業だった。自治体の担当者は、僕が法で保障されているはずの、24 時間体制介護サービスを、1 日 5 時間に削減した上、食事や入浴などの介助は、交換留学生として日本に滞在中の、僕の婚

約者の役目だと言い放った。その理由は、「あなたの婚約者は、同居家族で すし、今は介護者不足ですから」というものだった。日本で生活している と、さまざまな場面で疎外感や排他的な制度に直面する。僕が日本人ではな いという事実もその起因の1つではあるものの、実は、日本で生まれ育っ た障害者すら、高齢・貧困・女性性などの社会的に不利な条件と障害が重 なって生じる「複合的な障壁」のために、僕と同じような問題に直面してい たのである（Crenshaw 1989）。

　地域的または世界的な視野で障害学研究に携わっている専門家の多くは、 普段見過ごされがちな「アクセシビリティ」という問題に人々の関心を向け させ、さまざまな障壁を取り除くために、障害者が自身の個人的な体験を 綴った文章に注目し、その中にアクセシビリティを実現のヒントを見出して きた。本稿では、先行研究をふまえた上で、2008年から今日まで、アメリ カ人の車椅子使用者として2つの国を行き来してきた、自分の経験を振り 返ろうと思う。まず、子ども時代の僕が、身体上の障害と免疫不全をきっか けに日本のアニメと出会い、やがて日本文化にも興味をもつようになった、 という話から始めたい。次に、僕が、日本で暮らす中で、教育・雇用などの さまざまな生活面において、障壁にぶつかるのだが、それがたまたま日本で 経験した出来事だったため、自分の障害者としてのアイデンティティに気づ く契機となり、さらにその後、研究テーマの着想にもつながった、という経 緯について述べる。そして、日本研究と障害学という2分野の関係性を理 解することが、いかに自分の教育法や、大学教員と政策コンサルタントの二 足わらじを実践する上で有効であるか、という点についてお話し、それに関 連して、今後のアクセシビリティ関連のリサーチやアクセシビリティ向上の 指針になり得るアイディアを提供しようと思う。そして、最後に、社会の構 成員である読者のみなさん1人1人が、障害者のアクセシビリティを向上・ 拡大する上で大切な役割を担っていることを述べ、すべての人々が自分の居 場所を見つけられる、非排他的な社会を、僕と一緒に実現しようと呼びか け、本稿を締めくくりたいと思う。

1. 障害がきっかけで出会った日本

　今僕がこうして、このエッセイは執筆しているのは、ちょっとした奇跡だ と言っても過言ではない。なぜなら、僕は出産予定日より16週間も早く生

まれてしまい、体中の至るところがまだ未完成で、両親は医者から、僕は30年はおろか、30日も生きられないだろうと宣告されたからだ。しかし、未発達の眼や、機能の衰えた肺や、父の結婚指輪が太ももにすっぽりおさまるほどの、小さくて弱弱しい体もなんのその、どうにか危険な状態を脱することができたのだ。僕のその後の成長も順調で、早産の後遺症は次第に解消され、身体的にも認知能力的にも、他の子どもたちに追いつけるかのように見えたそうだ。しかし、僕が4歳になる頃には、年齢相応の筋力や敏捷さの基準との開きに拍車がかかり、筋肉の発達に問題があることが明らかになった。そして、8歳の誕生日を迎えるまでには、主治医たちはこの筋肉の衰えの原因が、超未熟児として誕生したことだけではない可能性を疑い始めた。いくつかの検査を受け、最終的に下された診断は、「糖原病IV型」という、進行性の筋力低下を特徴とする、世界で6人しか症例のない神経変性疾患だった。この病気のために心機能が低下した僕は、心臓移植が必要になった。数か月の待期期間を経て、10歳で移植手術を受けることができたものの、移植後は免疫抑制薬による治療を受けねばならず、そのため、家の近所の公園で友達と遊ぶこともできなくなってしまった。この時に経験した疎外感や孤独こそが、のちに僕が哲学に関心を抱き、さらに日本文化に巡り合うきっかけとなったのである。

　今でも鮮明覚えているのは、校舎の窓から友達が外で遊んでいるのを眺めながら、やりきれない思いを抱いていたこと。どうして自分だけが仲間に入れないないのだろう、どうして、僕の身体は他のみんなと違うのだろう、どうして、僕だけが、何度も何度も病院で痛い検査を受けなくちゃいけないのだろう——このような疑問が次々と頭に浮かんだ。そうこうしているうちに、やがて実存主義に関する本を片っ端から読むようになった。やはり、僕のような、不安感と反抗心でいっぱいの11、12歳の少年たちにとって、心の代弁者となってくれる人物はニーチェ以外に存在しない——と思いきや、それが、いたのである。それは他でもない、日本のアニメの登場人物たちだった。そして、外出が許されなかった僕は、終日テレビのアニメに没頭した。

　ちょうど2000年代の頭、つまり、僕が室内に籠りっぱなしの生活を徐々に受け入れ、哲学への興味を抱き始めた頃、アメリカでは日本アニメのルネッサンスとも言うべき現象が起きていた。1990年代のバブル崩壊後、い

わゆるインターネットブーム時代に生まれたアニメや漫画などは、悩めるサイボーグを主人公にしたディストピア的な物語で溢れており、僕は、夢中になってそのようなアニメを観続けた。『攻殻機動隊』（2002〜05）や『鋼の錬金術師』（2003〜04）など、最先端の科学技術で身体改造を実現した主人公たちが、その超人的な身体能力を以って偉業を成し遂げながらも、異端者としての孤独や不安と葛藤する姿には、心から共感した。そして、草薙素子やエドワード・エルリックなど、登場人物たちが遭遇する架空の冒険を通して、自分自身の経験や、障害とともに生きることの意味を考える上でのヒントを得たように思う。しかし、僕が日本のアニメから学んだのは、障害に関連することだけではない。日本のアニメを見続けているうちに、この遠い外国に過ぎなかった国に関する、さまざまな情報・歴史的人物・物語なども自然と吸収することになったのである。

　そのうち、アニメには、多様な日本のイメージが描かれていることに気づいた。でも、僕が16歳になる頃には、そのいずれが正しいのかは、いつか日本に行って自分の目で確かめてから決めよう、と考えるようになった。幸い、その「いつか」は意外にもすぐ訪れた。17歳の誕生日を迎えたばかりの2008年夏、僕は日米青年交換留学奨学金というスカラシップをもらって、早稲田大学での短期留学を果たすことができたのだ。その頃はまだ、軽く足を引きずってはいたものの、歩行が可能だったので、同じプログラムで日本に行った他の学生たちとそれほど変わらない文化体験ができた。ホームステイをしながらキャンパスで日本語を学んだり、剣道を習ったり、カラオケボックスで歌を歌ったりした。そして、新しい友人を作り、日本への関心と知識を深めた。その2ヶ月間の旅があまりに楽しかったので、翌年の秋、アメリカの大学に入学したら、絶対に2度目の日本留学を実現させようと心に決めた。

　残念ながら、2回目の来日までには、数年を要することになった。授業の履修や、その他諸事情のためだが、その最たるものは、車椅子生活に突入したこと。徐々に歩行が困難になってきたことが、自分でもちゃんと自覚してないうちに大きな精神的打撃になっており、次第に、自由がきかなくなってきた身体を庇うことで頭がいっぱいになり、一時的に学問に対する意欲をすっかり失ってしまったのだ。僕と自分の身体との戦いは3年ほども続き、2012年の春、友人と家族による必死の説得によって初めて、一体自分がど

ういう状況にあるのかをやっと理解し、受け入れるに至ったのである。それから程なく、僕は再び日本に短期留学することに決めた。

上智大学での４ヶ月間のプログラム準備は、アメリカを拠点とする非営利団体である国際教育交換協議会（CIEE）がいろいろ手配してくれた。CIEE は、「障害をもつアメリカ人法」によって定められた、障害のある学生が必要とする一定の配慮に関わる規則・規制に精通していたので、彼らが今回の滞在を、可能な限りスムーズなものにしてくれると信じていた。実際、CIEE は、車椅子対応の住まいの確保、電車やバスなどの乗り換えルートのマッピング、授業中にノートを取ってくれるボランティアの斡旋など、あらゆる面で素晴らしいサポートをしてくれた。今思えば、2016 年に障害者差別解消法が施行されるまで、日本の法律では、このような取り組みは義務付けられていなかったので、僕のような障害をもつ学生が、日本に着いてすぐに利用できる施設やサービスを事前に手配してもらえたのは、特筆すべきことだ。

快適な留学生活のため、学生１人１人のニーズに合わせ、最善を尽くしてくれた CIEE であったが、彼らにも到底予想しえなかった状況に僕が陥ってしまったのも、１度や２度ではない。友人と出かけたり、夜遊びしたりして、キャンパスを中心とした、僕にとっての安全圏から一歩外に踏み出したときは、やはり、しっぺ返しを喰らった。例えば、バーやレストランに入ろうとしたとき、その入口にたった１つ段差があるだけで、あきらめなくてはいけなかったり、一緒にいた友達も、別の店を探すために、僕に付き合って歩き回る羽目になったりとか、そんなことだ。しかしながら、そのような非常に苛立たしい事態が起きたところで、ダメージの程度もたかが知れているし、最終的には、CIEE による尽力のおかげで、大きなバリアをあまり感じるもことなく留学生活を送り、日本仏教哲学のカリキュラムも、無事修了することができた。

上智での留学を終えて帰国した僕は、2014 年にビラノバ大学を卒業したのだが、今度はなんとフルブライト・フェローとして、日本で仏教学の研究を続けるチャンスに恵まれた。このような名誉あるフェローに選抜されたことに興奮し、しかもすでに２回日本での滞在を経験していたので、アクセシビリティのことを深く考えず、快諾してしまった。この無知が災いし（見方によっては、無知のおかげで）、３度目の来日は、それまでとは一線を画す、と

んでもない困難に見舞われることになった。まず、フルブライト・フェロー
は、自力で所属先の大学を探さなくてはならなかったのだが、10校以上の
大学に断られてしまったのだ。僕のような障害者を受け入れる態勢が整って
いない、というのがその理由である。でもこれは、よく考えてみると、当然
のことだったのかもしれない。なぜなら、2014年当時だけではなく、これ
を書いている2022年現在でも、日本の大学生の中で障害者と認定されてい
る人はわずか1%で、大学側が障害者支援の経験を積む必要も機会もないか
らである（JASSO 2021）。それでも、日本の文部科学省の担当者の口から、
車椅子使用者の留学生は僕が初めてだから支援できない、という言葉を聞い
たときは驚いた。最終的に、何とか東京の東洋大学に籍を置けることになっ
たものの、バリアフリーの住居や車椅子でも利用できる交通手段を探すとい
う、新たなハードルが僕を待ち受けていた。適切なアパートが見つかるまで
の数か月間、僕は、ホテルを転々としながら仏教学研究を続ける、という生
活だった（もちろん、フィールドワークのために仏教寺院を訪ねようとしても、ほとん
どのお寺は、バリアだらけだった）。1年間のフェローシップも半ばを過ぎた頃、
こんな疑問が頭をよぎるようになった：「お坊さんたちは、車椅子使用者が
お寺の境内に入れないことなんて気にかけていない。なのに、どうして車椅
子使用車の僕は、お坊さんたちが何を考えているか、気にかけなくてはなら
ないのか。僕が進むべき道は、仏教学ではなく、障害学ではないだろうか」。

2. 日本を通じて障害を発見する

　仏教研究から障害研究への転向を決意した僕は、まず、自分が日常的に遭
遇する障壁を記録しておき、1つ1つの障壁の源を考え、探ることから始め
た。

　毎朝、僕はベッドで目を覚ますと、介助者の手を借りて起き上がり、それ
から、車椅子に移動させてもらう。その車椅子は、当然、エンジニアが設
計したものだ。それに乗ってアパート内を移動し、シャワーを浴びる。「バ
リアフリー」アパートを建築したのは設計士、「バリアフリー」シャワー室
を設置したのは医療機器の専門家。着替えを済ませてからアパートを出て、
都市計画家が設置した、視覚障害者誘導用ブロックで舗装された道路を通っ
て、最寄りの駅まで行く。政府発行の障害者手帳を見せて割引された切符を
買う。係員に乗車のために必要なスロープを持ってきてもらい、電車に乗

る。そして、ようやく目的地に到着。でも、到着した目的地でも、新たに人々の助けを借りながら、障壁を１つ１つクリアしていかなくてはならないのだ。

　僕の人生は、会ったこともない何百人もの人が完成しようとしている、パズルのようなものだ。でも、そのパズルのピースが、いつもうまくマッチするとは限らない。「アクセシビリティ」というピースを持つプレーヤーが不在だったり、外国人で車椅子使用者である僕のニーズとは関係のない「アクセシビリティ」のピースを当てはめようとしたりするプレーヤーがいるからだ。このようなミスマッチのため、３度目の日本滞在中は、自由に外出したり、学問や雇用の機会を得たりすることができなかった。既存のシステムに排除され、僕の頭は次々と浮かびあがる疑問でいっぱいになった。なぜ、アクセシビリティを阻む障壁が存在するのだろう。障壁は誰にとっての問題なのだろう。障壁にはどんな種類のものがあるのだろう。どうすれば障壁を解体することができるのだろう。これらの、障害学に関わる問いへの答えを見つけるため、僕は 2015 年、ペンシルバニア大学大学院博士課程に進学した。

　大学院では、歴史学・文化人類学・社会学・政治学・メディア研究などのリサーチ・プロジェクトを通して、アクセシビリティ概念が日本でどのように構築され、また、その構築過程において、互いに相容れない動機や思惑をもつ関係者たちが、どのような役割を担ったかを明らかにすることにした。まず、アクセシビリティを規定する法律について調べていったところ、それらが、均質な障害者のための理想的な基準を想定しており、障害者の実生活とはかけ離れたものであることがわかった。そこで、多様な背景やニーズをもつ障害者たちが、日本の法的枠組みの中で、どのようにアクセシビリティを享受したり、アクセシビリティの仕組みから排除されたりしているのかをより深く理解したいと思い、エスノグラフィや質的データ分析を応用した研究に目を向けてみた。しかし、そのような研究も、均質的な障害者グループを対象にする傾向にあるため、法整備に関わる人々が、なぜ障害者の多様性に無関心なのか、という僕の疑問には答えてくれなかった。

　次に、日本におけるアクセシビリティ概念の前身を探るべく、アニメ・漫画・小説・映画などのポップカルチャーにおける障害の表象を分析することにした。若かりし当時の僕にとって、日本に関心を抱くきっかけをくれた、自分の原点とも言えるメディアを取り入れたプロジェクトは、とてもエ

キサイティングであった。しかし、このような非常に限定された文脈に見られる障害の表象は、自分の最終的な研究目標とはまた別の問題であり、僕が最終的に博士論文のテーマに選んだのは、日本におけるアクセシビリティの歴史だ。幸い、この研究はゼロからの出発ではなく、特定の個人や組織の行動がその時代時代にもたらした影響が、いかに日本のアクセシビリティの歴史を形作ってきたか、ということが先行研究によってすでに明らかにされている。そこで、それらの過去の研究成果をもとに、自分が日本で暮らす上でぶつかった壁を分析・理解する上でのヒントになるプロジェクトを構想した。それが僕の博士論文「Politics and Prosthetics: 150 Years of Disability in Japan」（政治性と義肢：日本における障害の150年史、Bookman 2021）だ。

　僕が「Politics and Prosthetics」の中で展開した主要な議論は、以下のようなものだ。日本では、1868年から2021年までの約150年間、障害者のアクセシビリティを向上させるためのさまざまな動きが見られた。しかしながら、それらの多くは、メリットを享受できる人の数だけそうでない人がいるような、中途半端な内容であった。そこで、政府の公的文書・マスコミの報道・障害者擁護団体が収集した資料などの分析に基づき、アクセシビリティが優先された障害者グループの特徴や、その優先順位を決定した背景を探ったところ、現代日本におけるアクセシビリティの政治性が、経済的な事情に大きく左右されてきたという事実が明らかになった。つまり、近代日本の大規模な社会的変化（工業化・都市化・軍事化・民主化・少子高齢化など）は、常に経済的逼迫と背中合わせであるが、そのような状況下、アクセシビリティ普及の立役者である建築家・エンジニア・教育者などの専門家は、障害者のニーズではなく、費用便益分析に基づき、その都度もっとも財政的負担が少ないアクセシビリティの形を推進してきた。その結果、異なる障害をもつグループが、各時代ごとに、恣意的にアクセシビリティの中心に据えられてきたのだ。また、経済的思惑と同様にアクセシビリティの在り方を左右してきたのは、障害者福祉に関わる知識・物資・専門家の国際的な流れであり、海外の動向に触発されて、日本国内での政策方針を決定する政治家は多い。

　このような歴史的背景を述べたあと、僕は「Politics and Prosthetics」の中で、日本研究者が日本文化のさまざまな側面（軍事行動・行政・経済市場・技術革新など）を理解する上で、障害者のアクセシビリティ向上を目的とする

技術に目を向けることがいかに大切か、そして、いかに欧米での社会正義・道徳に携わる諸問題に関心を持つ研究者が、日本における障害の歴史と政治性にも分析の目を向けることが大切なのかを解説した。その理由は、日本が世界第3位の経済大国である上、世界で最も高齢化が進んでいる国であるため、事実上の介護技術革新大国になったことに関連する。当然ながら、日本の介護テクノロジーは、すでに諸外国に輸出されてきている。アクセシビリティ向上を目指す政策や秘術革新の成功例は、これまで他国にとっての模範となり、失敗例は教訓として役立ってきたのであり、これからもこの傾向は続くと考えられる。

「Politics and Prosthetics」は、主に日本のアクセシビリティ史をたどる内容の博士論文だが、それだけではなく、障害者支援運動に携わる団体や地方自治体にとって、実践的な情報を提供するプロジェクトでもある。例えば、アクセシビリティ向上のための政策や活動が、障害をもつ人・もたない人に利益をもたらす一方で、想定外の不利益ももたらしうるという事実。また、アクセシビリティの普及活動には、建築家・エンジニア・教育関係者・役人・当事者である障害者・一般市民など、常に多くの人々が関わっているため、すべての関係者たちにとって望ましい成果をあげようとするならば、グループ同士が常に互いに協力し合い、共通の目標に向けた、さまざまな活動をコーディネートしなくてはならないという事実。実際、日本をケーススタディとする僕の研究でも、市町村・県・国・国家間、さらには国境を越えた枠組みなど、多くの地域的レベルの活動が相互連携しなければ、アクセシビリティの向上や改善は不可能だということが明らかになった。そして、このような連携を可能にするための第一歩は、「バリアについて率直に語ることを阻止するバリア」に注意を向け、そのような風潮に自覚的になることだ、とした上で、現在の日本で、障害に関するオープンな議論を難しくしている要因について、関係者の人々に考えるよう提案した。それとともに、僕自身も、その要因の源を探し当てるべく、過去の事例を深く掘り下げた。

もちろん、この博士論文プロジェクトは完全無欠ではなく、色々な制限・制約の中で書かざるを得なかったものであるが、それでも、規模の大小にかかわらず、障害者・障害者支援を支援するグループが、平等に利益を享受できるような政策の実現に必要な議論を一歩進めることができたと思う。言い換えれば、このプロジェクトの目標は、日本におけるアクセシビリティを

ケーススタディとして分析し、最終的には、日本の国内外において、すべての人々にとって、それぞれの居場所がある社会を実現するための指標を提示することだ。しかしながら、日本で暮らし、仕事をする上で、日々さまざまな障壁にぶつかっている障害者の1人として、他の人々がたどるべき道を提示するだけでは満足できなかったことも確かだ。僕が、大学教員とアクセシビリティ・コンサルタントの二足のわらじを履き、自分自身の手で問題を解決するための活動をしようと思い立った所以である。

3. 教育から実践へ

　僕が教育とコンサルタントの世界に初めて足を踏み入れたのは、ペンシルバニア大学大学院時代のことだ。2016年秋から2018年春にかけて、東洋言語文明学科でティーチング・アシスタント（TA）として、「日本の歴史と文明」や「日本のポップカルチャー」のような、学生たちに「日本」という概念を批評的・自覚的に捉えさせることを目的とする、イントロダクションの授業のディスカッションセクションを担当した。各ユニットの内容や教え方に関しては、TAはかなり自由を与えられていたので、僕は、通常の日本論にはあまり反映されない、女性・子ども・老人・障害者のような社会的弱者人々の声を掬い上げ、そのような人々が、さまざまな社会的・政治的・経済的・文化的プロセスによって、困難を強いられてきたという問題を、学生たちに考えさせるようなトピックや教材を選んだ。それとともに、学生たちがそのような問題を検討する際には、常に彼ら自身の歴史的立場を認識するよう促した。さらに、そのような歴史的立場の認識を生かし、学生たちが、自分たちの住んでいる町や地域にとって、有益な政策や改革案を提案する可能性についても、話し合った。

　僕自身も、博士論文のリサーチに入る直前の2018年、障害者として日本で暮らした経験をもとに、「アクセシビリティ・マッピング・プロジェクト（AMP）」という、僕のその後のキャリアの方向性を決定づけることになる、イニチアチブを立ち上げた。AMPは、障害をもつ人々の行動範囲や活動の質を制限してしまう障壁を特定し、事前に回避することを目的としたデジタル・クラウドソーシング・プラットフォームだ。これは、僕がのちに取り組むことになる、さまざまなプロジェクトに深く関わるので、以下にその構想・開発・実施・制約について簡単に説明しよう。

APM は、ペンシルバニア大学キャンパスの、アクセシビリティ・マップを改革しようという試みから始まった。それまでのアクセシビリティ・マップは、普通のキャンパスマップに、車椅子用のスロープやエレベーターがアイコンで記されただけのもので、改築などがあった場合、迅速な更新が難しい上、個人のニーズに対応しないという難点があった。例えば、既存のキャンパスマップの場合、ある建物の入口が「バリアフリー」だと示されていても、具体的にどのような障害や移動手段（車椅子・松葉杖・スクーターなど）に対応できるのか、詳細は記載されていない。これは僕が日本で暮らして実感したことだが、大学がせっかく設置した施設やサービスも、このような細かい情報が伴わなければ、それを多くの人に活用してもらうことはできないのだ。そして、それぞれの施設やサービスの最新情報を継続して提供するためには、実際に利用した人々の意見を随時収集することが不可欠だった。

　そこで僕は、学生・教員、そしていろいろな部署の職員と協働し、キャンパス内の施設を利用した際の個人的な意見（苦情から称賛まで）を、映像・音声・写真・文章のいずれかの方法で、誰でも閲覧可能なオンラインデータベースにアップロードできる、モバイルアプリを開発した。そして、AMPの認知度を高めるため、マラソンならぬ「マパソン（Map-A-Thon）」という、障害をもつ人ともたない人が一緒にキャンパス内を巡り、改善の余地があるバリアを見つけては報告する、というイベントを企画し、数回にわたって開催した。参加者たちは、Map-A-Thon を経験することで、押しボタン式の自動ドアから点字標識、授乳／搾乳スペースや祈祷室まで、「アクセシビリティ」にはさまざまな形態があることを知り、イベントを楽しみながらも、問題意識を深めたようだ。このようなやりとりを目の当たりにし、僕は、AMP をキャンパスマップ作りの道具としてだけでなく、僕たちが普段気づくことのない障壁についての対話の場を提供する、啓蒙的なプログラムとして捉えるようになった。そして、できるだけ早く日本でも同様のプロジェクトを始めよう、と固く決心した。

　2018 年 8 月、僕は国際交流基金フェローとして、博士論文を完成するためのリサーチを行うため、4 度目の来日を果たした。それまでの渡航で培った、国内の障害者コミュニティとのつながりのおかげで、僕はすぐに適切な滞在先を見つけ、東京大学で、アクセシビリティ研究を再開した。すると、日本に到着して 1 ヶ月も経たないうちに、さまざまな依頼が舞い込んでき

た。それは、東京 2020 パラリンピックの準備のために、僕が当事者であり研究者として蓄積した障害学の専門知識（日本のアクセシビリティ史や AMP プロジェクトなど）を貸してほしい、というものだった。一般向けの活動の中で最も露出度が高かったものは、おそらく 2019 年 3 月に行った TEDx 講演「可能性としてのパラリンピック：アクセシビリティの過去・現在・未来」で、その中で僕が論じたのは、「複合的障壁」のことだ。これは、自分が日米間を行ったり来たりした経験の中で気づいたことだが、日本でもアメリカでも、多くの障害者が、高齢・貧困・ジェンダー・セクシュアリティ・宗教など、障害以外にも差別の対象となりうる条件を抱えており、その「負の相乗効果」の結果、複合的なバリアに直面しているという問題である。そして、東京 2020 パラリンピック競技大会では、AMP のようなアプリを通じて、来場者のデータを収集することによって、こうした複合的バリアを事前に特定し、改善するチャンスになりうることも強調した。この講演を終えたあと、パラリンピックに関する相談が、以前にも増して政府関係者から寄せられるようになった。

　障害者支援政策コンサルタントとしての、僕の最初の大きな取り組みは、パラ大会に備え、ホテルやタクシーなどのアクセシビリティ向上に関わる、新ガイドラインを作成するための調査委員会に参加したことだ。メンバーのうち、外国人が自分 1 人だったことに、居心地の悪さを感じたのを鮮明に覚えている。「大会のために来日した、外国人障害者の宿泊施設は、和室と洋室どちらの方がいいと思いますか」のような、すべての外国人障害者を十把一絡げにする質問を受けたときは、特にそのように感じた。僕は、自分と異なる国・文化・障害などの背景をもつ人々はおろか、他のアメリカ人車椅子利用者の要望すら、断言できないというのに。それでも、開催地のホスピタリティ関係者のために、何かしらの具体案を提出する必要があったので、「日本型と欧米型をベースに、カスタマイズ可能な選択肢をたくさん用意することで、ユーザーの多様性に対応するのはどうでしょう」と勧めた。さらに、どのようなニーズが求められているのかを詳しく知るためには、AMP のようなクラウドソーシング技術を活用し、来場者に事前アンケートを行うのが有効であるという点も付け加えた。幸い、僕の提言は好意的に受け止められ、委員会は僕以外の当事者からもフィードバックを求めるなどしつつ、活動を充実させていった。残念ながら、障害をもつ人々からの多様な意見を

収集する仕組みづくりは、時間的・コスト的な制約のため、パラ大会開催に間に合わせることは叶わなかった。しかし、僕の提案が、2020年大会におけるアクセシビリティの多様化にある程度貢献できたことは、自分自身の精神的な報酬となったし、コンサルタントとしての活動を、さらに幅広く継続していこうという意欲にもつながった。

　僕は、障害者支援の社会的役割を担う、さまざまなグループ間の連携と協働を呼びかけるとともに、日米の公的機関や民間団体の代表者とも、「複合的障壁」や、自分自身が経験した「パズルのような人生」に関わるディスカッションを頻繁に行うようになった。海外からの旅行者にアクセシビリティ関連の情報を提供するサイト「アクセシブル・ジャパン」で、僕がいくつかの観光スポットに行ってみて、それぞれの場所のアクセシビリティについてレポートした、ブログ記事を考えてみよう。これらの記事は、鎌倉の山々から秋葉原のメイド喫茶まで、それぞれのスポットが、車椅子利用者にとってどれくらいナビゲートしやすい（しにくい）のか、僕個人の見解を述べた上で、他の観光客（障害の有無に関わらず）にも意見を求めたものだ。読者は、ブログのコメント欄で、写真や体験談をシェアすることで、照明環境・おむつ交換台の有無・感覚障害のある人々が不快に感じる臭いなど、僕が知り得なかった多くのバリアについて指摘してくれた。このようなフィードバックのおかげで、僕は、アクセシビリティ・コンサルタントとして仕事をする上で、より広い視野をもつことができ、アジア協会・商工会議所・国連などと協働した、教育・公共交通機関・災害リスク管理関連のプロジェクトの中で、その見識を生かすことができたと思う。

　2021年6月に東京大学の博士研究員として着任して以来、僕は今日まで、研究・教育・実践に従事してきた。その中で、過去に存在した日本社会の「複合的障壁」や、現代社会に暮らす障害者のエンパワーメントに、クラウドソース技術を生かすことの可能性などについて、僕の学生やワークショップ参加者たちに意見を交換してもらってきたのだが、そのようなディスカッションが、さまざまな分野の研究者と障害者支援活動家たちにとって、差別や障壁のない社会を築いていくためのヒントとなるのだ。

　例えば、2022年春に担当した「非排他的社会に向けて」という授業を考えてみよう。このコースでは、障害学の関連分野（建築・工学・教育・医学など）の学生を集め、彼らに、障害をもつ人々が現在直面している問題につい

て調べ、その解決法を考え、提案してもらった。学生たちは、まずグループでアクセシビリティ・マップを作り、この活動を通して、自分たちが想像するところの「アクセシビリティ」という概念には限界があることに気づき、障害をもつ当事者の人々から、より正確な認識を学ぶことの重要性について、互いに学び合った。また、学生たちは、このグループ活動やディスカッションを通して、実はアクセシビリティが、非常に身近な話題であるということに気づいたようだ。なぜなら、老齢・怪我・事故・病気などのために身体が不自由になるのは誰にでも起こりうることであり、彼ら自身や、その家族や友人も、例外ではないからだ。そして、この授業の中で、学生たちが、普段から見慣れた景色を、「アクセシビリティ」という新しいレンズを通して見直し、自分たちの生活圏にあるバリアの存在に気づくようになったということが、彼らの発言から察せられた。彼らが、これからも「複合的障壁」という見識を通して、各自の専門分野を発展させ、さまざまな文化的文脈におけるアクセシビリティの向上実現に貢献してくれることを、心から願う。そうすれば、近い将来、障害をもつ人々は、僕が初めて日本に移住したときのような苦労を、経験せずにすむかもしれないのだ。

4. おわりに

　この短い自伝的エッセイでは、過去13年間、障害をもつ者として日本とアメリカを行き来した経験を振り返りながら、日本という国／社会を研究することが、より平等で、誰もが自分の居場所を見つけられるグローバル社会を実現するための、1つの足掛かりになり得ることを述べた。自分の身体性を研究・分析の主軸とし、社会に存在する「複合的障壁」というものの実態を明らかにすることで、日本研究と障害学の対話が有効である点にも言及した。アクセシビリティを二重・三重にも妨げる「複合的障壁」という概念は、大学教員と政策コンサルタントの二足のわらじを履く僕の、教育・実践理念の核を成すものだ。

　障害は、僕が日本と出会い、その後日本で暮らすきっかけになった。さらに、日本で遭遇した数々のバリアが、僕が自分の障害者としてのアイデンティティを「発見」する契機になったということは、先述のとおりである。でも、「障害者」というのは、僕が日本での生活を通して「発見」した多くのアイデンティティの1つに過ぎない。年齢・人種・経済階級・ジェ

ンダー・セクシュアリティ・宗教などのために、日本で苦労したとか、逆に得をしたという経験について、このエッセイを書き直すことも容易だ。僕がこれまで享受してきた教育・雇用の機会や、満喫することのできた娯楽なども、このような外的要素に左右されてきたのだ。そのような事実について考えることも、日本国内外で障害者支援活動に従事するグループをはじめ、さまざまな関係者・当事者にとって意味深い対話を始める契機になると思う。

　僕という人間は、たくさんの要素から構成されているものの、研究の対象としてフォーカスするのは、やはり特に思い入れのある、障害者としてアイデンティティなのである。このアイデンティティの多面性という点を、読者のみなさんにつなげるため、いくつか質問をさせていただき、本稿を締めくくろうと思う。みなさんの中には、足を骨折したり、妊婦として交通機関を利用したり、自転車を押して移動したり、高齢の家族と暮らしたりしたことがある人が、大勢いると思う。そして、そのような場合、アクセシビリティが、すべての人々にとってメリットである気づいたのではないだろうか。だとすると、みなさんのその経験は、障壁・差別・排他的システムのない社会を実現するためのディスカッションに貢献できるのだ。なぜなら、一般の人々が、家を探したり、公共交通機関で移動したりする際に経験した苦労や成功体験を、周りの人たちに伝えることが、将来的に他の人のアクセシビリティにつながる可能性があるからである。自分の経験を友人の１人に話したら、その人はまた別の人にその経験を伝えるだろう。その輪がどんどん広がり、そう遠くない将来、みなさんの住むコミュニティ全体が、その障壁を取り除くために行動したり、みなさんの提案を実行に移したりするかもしれないのだ。本稿では、たくさんの人々が協働して問題解決をするという取り組みの１つの形として、僕自身の経験をみなさんにお話した。次は、みなさんの番だ。是非、自分の経験を話し、他の人たちと分かち合い、すべての人々がアクセシビリティを享受できる社会を一緒につくっていこう。

　第 2 部　エンパワーメントとしての知の創造

アカデミアの暗黙の特権を批評する

白人性と日本研究

セツ・シゲマツ（*カリフォルニア大学リバーサイド校*）
シュミット堀佐知 訳

洋の東西を問わず、人種差別の問題に関しては、一切沈黙を貫き通すというのが、戦後日本の学術的言説の特徴である。〜酒井直樹

支配と搾取が交錯する構造が、社会に蔓延するさまざまな疫病となり、その表面はひび割れ、亀裂が急激に広がっている。〜シェリル・ハリス

◆パートⅠ：「白人性」と日本研究におけるその機能

　2020年6月15日、アメリカを拠点とする、世界最大のアジア研究学会であるAAS（Association for Asian Studies）に、会員1410名の賛同署名付きの嘆願書が提出された（McLaughlin & Wang）。この嘆願書は、AASに「アジア研究分野に蔓延する、黒人に対する人種偏見・差別を公に認める」ことを要求するものであった。この嘆願書の筆頭人となったのは、日本の宗教を研究するジョリオン・バラカ・トーマス氏（現・ペンジルバニア大学准教授）と、当時ハーバード大学大学院博士課程で日本のメディア学を研究していたキンバリー・サンダース氏であり、その呼びかけの契機となったのは、警察官による黒人市民の殺害・致死事件（ジョージ・フロイドさんやブリオナ・テイラーさん他多数）に続く、全米そして世界各国で巻き起こった抗議運動である。嘆願書が提出された翌日、AAS実行委員会は回答声明を発表した。しかし、そ

の内容は、反黒人主義や、アジア研究分野に蔓延する白人性もしくは白人至上主義と反黒人主義との関係への言及を避けた上で、「多様性と平等」へのさらなる取り組みを約束するものであった。このような状況を受け、日本研究分野における反黒人主義の提起・分析・解体への第一歩として、筆者は本稿を執筆することにした。

　80〜90年代以来、「ホワイトネス・スタディーズ」は史学・文学・社会学・地理学・建築学・美術・映像学・法学などのサブフィールドとして定着してきた。日本研究も例外ではなく、過去20年の間でも、日本文化という枠組みのなかで「ホワイトネス・スタディーズ」がいかに展開されているかということが論じられてきている（Bonnett 2022, Fujikawa 2007, Russell 2017）。とは言え、日本研究の構成要素として、日本研究の構造論理と方法論にまつわる知の創造の問題として、そしてアカデミアという場で展開される「競技」の規則に組み込まれている暗黙の特権としての白人性は、まだまだ十分には検討されていないのが現状だ。

　シェリル・ハリスによる「財産としての白人性」という画期的な論は、白人性を単に人種的なカテゴリーやアイデンティティ（つまり外見的な特徴として現れるもの）として理解するだけでなく、それが形而上学的なものであり、さらに、法制度や組織によって保障された経済的恩恵にあずかるための特権として概念化されたものだ、という事実を明らかにするための礎を築いた。「財産としての白人性」の中で、ハリスはこう述べている：

> 人種に基づくヒエラルキーを前提とする社会では、白人性は非常に価値のある所有物であり…白人という身分によって得られる様々な特権や利益は、白人たちが擁護し、また、白人として通用する外見を持つ非白人は、必要とあらば虚偽の申告をしてでも獲得しようとしてきた、貴重な資産なのである（1713）。

　白人性とは、歴史的・社会文化的な文脈で構築された近代の産物であり、かつ制度的人種差別・非白人の非人間化を契機として機能する、言説的な構築物であるとともに、概念と実質の両面を併せ持つものである（Du Bois）。白人性は、歴史的には「白人種」とみなされる人々に付与されてきた属性であるが、時にはそれ以外の人々にも当てはめられる。それは、単に色素の薄

さや「白人種」の外見的特徴だけを指す概念ではなく、白人であることを表象する一定の規範・行動・シニファン・記号を指す、重層的で常に変化し続ける記号体系なのである。

　植民近代の白人至上主義と反黒人主義が形成する、人種的連続体において、白人性は権力・自由・統治権・支配体制の覇権的構成要素となり、その理論・象徴・表象と不可分の存在となったのだ。白人としての人種アイデンティティを持つことにより、白人性という特権を獲得するものもいれば、富・社会階級・教育・職業・言語能力・国籍・宗教（とくにユダヤ‐キリスト教）などの属性によって、さまざまな度合いの白人性を獲得するものもいる。したがって、本稿は白人を自認する日本研究者だけについて述べているものではなく、白人性がいかに論理として、人種資本として、社会経済的・文化的・言語的特権として、地政学的・空間的・組織的権力として展開しているか、という点について論じるものなのである。さらに言えば、ジョアオ・コスタ・バーガスが、著書『アンチブラックネスの否定』の中で解説しているように、「反黒人主義」と「アンチブラックネス」は、同一概念を指す言葉ではない（Vargas 2018）。

　白人性を特定の人々の財産とするハリスの論は、アメリカ社会を前提としたものであるが、この概念を日本研究に当てはめることも可能である。なぜなら、東西の帝国主義が争った太平洋戦争（いわゆる第二次世界大戦）前後の時期から 1945 ～ 52 年のアメリカ軍による日本占領までの日米関係の歴史を鑑みると、アメリカ政府が戦後日本社会の形成と、日本研究分野の創設過程に及ぼした影響は、計り知れないからだ。その創設以来、日米関係は、日本研究分野によって管理・（再）解説され続けてきているのだ。史学者タカシ・フジタニは以下のように述べている：

> 戦時中に築かれたこれらの基盤を踏まえると、アメリカの戦後秩序は、日本とその天皇制という「部下」を積極的に視野に入れた構造によって保たれることになっており、**日本研究は、この日米間の上下関係を作り上げ、維持するために必要な知を創造するという役割を果たす**。…アメリカの日本研究は、その潜伏期間とも言える第二次大戦中には、すでに人種思想に染まっており…戦後まもない時期、日本研究に携わったのは、白人または内部情報提供者の役割を頻繁に強いられた、多数の日系

アメリカ人研究者たちであった…（Fujitani 2001:391、太字はシゲマツ）。

　フジタニ（2001）の指摘に従うならば、彼がこの議論を提示した時点においてすでに戦後半世紀以上もの間、アメリカの日本研究分野は白人の学者たちによってほぼ独占され、その間、地政学・人種・ジェンダー上の日米関係史を象徴するかのように、彼らが既存の序列構造を維持すべく努めたことが伺える。それから20年経った現在も、白人男性が多数派を占めている点と研究方法論において、ほとんど変化は見られない。例えば、アメリカ国内で最も権威のある日本研究の学術誌『*Journal of Japanese Studies*』（JJS）は、編集委員会にも諮問委員会にも日本人／日本出身者のメンバーは僅少。論文・新刊書評の寄稿者はともに圧倒的に非日本人によって占められており、ホームページに掲載されている、JJS が推薦する日本研究文献も、日本の研究者による著作はごく最近まで皆無であった。日本人ではない西洋出身の日本研究の専門家たちが、先行研究に精通し、深い専門知識を有しているという前提は、決して疑われない。このような白人男性主導の日本研究分野の構造は、現在そうであるというだけではなく、これからもそうであり続けようとしているように見える。一般に学者は、批評精神が旺盛だとされているにも関わらず、なぜ、ほとんどの（白人の）学者たちは、彼らの所属する分野における、人種・ジェンダー権力構造を問題視しないのであろうか？
　本稿は、白人性という概念が、人種的優遇措置を受けている白人の研究者によって当然視され、活用され、新植民地主義的特権としても機能する一方で、自らを準白人視する日本人研究者たちにも、ほぼ看過されている状況を批評するものである。人種的ヒエラルキーを前提として生み出された知が、日本人にもたらしうる言説的・実質的損害に充分な関心を持たないまま、日本や日本に関わる事象を語ってしまう白人研究者たちの尊大な態度は、問題視されるどころか、しかるべきであるかのように考えられている。他者を搾取し、その他者の代弁者となることが、白人に付与されたネオリベラルな権利であるかのような、このような普遍的な感覚は、21世紀の現在にも引き継がれているが、改めてその意味を真剣に考える時が来たのではないだろうか。

1. 白人性と（非）西洋としての日本

　スチュアート・ホールの "the West and the rest"（西洋とそれ以外）という有名な韻を踏んだ文句があるが、日本の場合、その帝国主義・植民者としての歴史を鑑みると、この二項対立の後者に属するだけではない、複雑な立場を考慮しなくてはならない。日本の近代化の過程は、東洋であり続けながらも、西洋の制度・法的枠組み・科学技術などを積極的に取り入れ、「西洋に追いつく」ことを前提としていたため、日本は西洋と東洋のハイブリッド式近代化を果たすこととなったのだ。19世紀末から20世紀前半にかけて、日本の指導者たちは、帝国国家イデオロギーと日本帝国の拡張を通して、ステファン・タナカが言うところの「日本にとっての東洋」を繰り返し構築し、それによって人種に基づくヒエラルキーを（再）生産した（Tanaka 1995）。白人至上主義は、史学者ジェラルド・ホーンらが詳細に記録・実証したように、世界共通の人種構造であるが、近代日本はそれを撲滅するどころか、歴史上に繰り返し現れた人種や性別に基づく植民支配の在り方を模倣・再生産したのである（Horne 2004）。日本がナチス政権と同盟を結んでいた時代、東洋の国としては唯一の枢軸国となったことを受け、帝国政府の官職にあった者の中には、日本人は他の有色人種よりも優遇されるべきだと主張する者もいたという（Gerhard 2015）。このような、自らを白人と同一視しようとする、日本人の模倣アイデンティティの仕掛けは、日本が日本以外のアジアを「東方の彼方」という他者に仕立てあげ、植民化した点にも伺える。西洋由来の、帝国・植民主義に根差した人種・ジェンダー構造を拡大解釈することにより、日本人は、日本の国力と、海外在住の日本人が一等国民であることを、白人帝国主義者たちに認めてもらおうと目論んだのだ。

　21世紀の現在でも、「西洋」という、地球上の特定地域を指す語が、政治文化的なキーワードであり続けているものの、本稿はその関連語である「白人性」に注目する。なぜなら、今日「白人性」こそが、全世界で認識される権力・財産・人間的価値の表象となってきたからだ（Wynter 2003）。例えば、人種隔離政策を施行していた南アフリカにおいて、東洋人であるにも関わらず、その西洋に匹敵する経済力によって、日本人は「名誉白人」の称号を与えられた（Osada 2002）。日本人が準白人身分を獲得しえたのは、「原因は結果である。白人だから金持ちなのであり、金持ちだから白人なのだ」（Fanon 2007:5）という、ファノンが的確に指摘した法則のおかげだ。この「植民地

支配による白人化」の法則は拡大し、万国共通の法則になり、今や白人性という概念は、西洋・東洋という二項対立に還元できない人類の分類・区別方法なのである。

　前近代の日本にも、貴族の身分階級的な特権と直結した「色白の肌」という概念と、それを獲得するための美白行為は存在したが、それと近代の白人性とは別のものである。色白の肌を美の基準とする前近代日本では、その価値観がおのずと言説的・美学的に表象されるのに対し、現代日本に見られる白い肌の理想化は、ミコ・アシカリが指摘するように、近代国家日本の成立過程において、日本人が自らを「日本人種」として構築した過程と結びついている（Ashikari 2015:88–89）。近代の産物である白人性という概念は、前近代の色白概念とは機能が異なっており、その違いを考慮せずに両者を並べると、近代日本が自らを準白人的存在とみなしてきた事実が、「日本独特の伝統」として正当化・強化されてしまう恐れがある。この近代・前近代の比較検討は、今後もさらなる考察が必要であるが、本稿の目的はそこではない。筆者の関心は、白人性が白人の日本研究者によってどのように利用され、制度化された特権と知の生産を司る、地政学的構造という日本研究の重要な部位として、どのように機能しているのか、という問題なのである。

2. 日本研究の形成

　1999 年、アジア研究学術誌『positions: east asia cultures critique』に掲載された対談の中で、酒井直樹とハリー・ハルトゥニアンは、冷戦下（1945–1991）という文脈で形成された日本研究分野と、その植民地主義的構造について語っている。その対話では、2 人は地域研究の構造を植民主義的なものとみなし、それがアメリカで誕生した日本研究分野の形成過程で実現した、アメリカにとって有用な知を生産する装置である、と批判している（Harutoonian and Sakai 1999:595–598）。ハルトゥニアンによれば、地域研究に不可分の、国家利益としての知と暗黙の了解とは、以下のようなものである：

　　いったん特定の地域を研究するためのシステムが整い、国家の利益とその関心を満たすための、地域研究という分野が成立してしまうと、その背景に存在した、様々な思惑をさらに検討する必要はなくなってしま

う…西洋にとって、日本は常に未分析の生の情報で満ち溢れ、原住民たちが観察・研究されることを待ち望みながら生活する、研究対象であった。われわれのような西洋人たちは、外の世界からやって来て、西洋の目線で原住民たちを観察し、その生活圏に意味づけをしてきた。…基本的な日本語さえ習得すれば、統一性のある全体性、そして一貫した文化としての日本を理解できると考えてきた…われわれは未だに日本をアメリカの部下の一種として観察しているのだ（597–599）。

　ハルトゥニアンと酒井は、冷戦下における日本研究形成過程の根本的な分析を行い、それを提示することにより、地域研究の目的がいかに国家の思想に直結しているかということを明らかにした。ハルトゥニアンと酒井の対談のように、冷戦時代の政治的背景を発端とした日本研究の成立を批判する論は、かなりの数にのぼるが、それと比較して、日本研究の成立を人種とジェンダーという視点から分析する声は少ないのが現状だ。筆者は本論の中で、ハルトゥニアンと酒井の対話が、日本研究分野の主要構造・方法論・暗黙の了解・傾向に対する批評としては、大きな改善の契機とはならなかった事実を踏まえ、2人の基礎的な批評をさらに掘り下げていこうと思う。非日本人の日本研究者の多くは、日本研究分野のネオコロニアル体制と、それに付随する人種・ジェンダー傾向の問題について認識することを拒絶している状態なのだから。

　さらに付け加えたいのは、これまであまり議論されてこなかったことであるが、日本研究分野における不均衡は、人種だけでなく、ジェンダー（つまりシスジェンダー）の偏向にも関わる、という点である。日本研究者は白人男性の割合が最も多く、次に白人女性、というパターンが歴史的に継承されてきた。そしてわれわれは、それを当然で普通のことだと受け止め、批判するどころか、それについての指摘すらしてこなかった。また、日本研究に顕著な傾向は、白人男性である学者が日本人と結婚しているか、結婚していない場合であっても、親しい日本人を情報提供者として利用することであり、これは白人女性の学者にも見られる傾向である。このパターンが当然視されてきたという事実は、日本研究分野に内在する、人種・ジェンダーのみならず、（通常、私的な事柄だから、という理由で問題視されてこなかった）性愛にも基づく関係性を象徴する。もちろん、筆者のこの指摘は、日本人のパートナーを

持つ特定の個人を糾弾することが目的なのではなく、ジェンダーと人種の重層的な権力関係が、いかに地政学的な知の創造に関わっているかという事実への認識を促すものである。

　白人の研究者は、日本人の配偶者やパートナーを持っていない場合でも、自分たちの白人性や、白人が優勢的な立場にある社会の現状に概して無頓着であり、自分たちの研究を可能にしてくれている環境と、自分たちの人種的特権の関係性について、あまり考えたことのないような人も多い。白人研究者の中には、人種的特権を与えられている社会に背を向けたがる人々も存在し、そのような心理も、わからなくはない。しかし、そのような人たちさえ、自分が専門とする地域研究分野において、白人の覇権を無意識に再生産している可能性もあるのだ。

3. 搾取する権利としての言語能力

　日本人ではない日本研究者が、高い日本語能力を習得し、人種的学術資本を得ると、日本に関わる事象についての情報にアクセスするに充分な権利としてみなされる。非日本人の中でも、日本語能力の高い白人は（白人性と言語能力の相乗効果として）特に称賛される。言語能力の習得は、大抵階級的特権に支えられているものだが、それはさらに「生の知識」とされる一次資料/当事者の経験にアクセスする権利としてもみなされる。当事者としての日本人からの許可は義務化されていないのだが、後述するように、研究者が許諾を乞うまでもなく、日本人はたいてい喜んでそのような情報を提供してくれるのだ。日本文化に関する情報や日本研究関係の知識の量は、非日本人研究者の場合、同じ分野を専門とする日本人研究者のそれには及ばないことが多く、従って、彼らは日本人研究者の情報提供に依存せざるを得ない（その恩義を返したり、情報源を開示したりしなくてもよいのであるが）。このような、搾取者的で新植民主義的な知識探求モデルは、ごく普通の研究方法として確立され、非日本人研究者の比較的高い言語能力は、日本に住む情報提供者へのアクセスと、彼らの知識を搾取する契機となり、さらにそれは、日本に関する事象の重みや価値や意味を解釈する自明の権利に転換される。親日的な好奇心や欲望は、外国人研究者たちにキャリアと経済の両面で報酬をもたらし、その結果、日本人の提供する情報を消費・蓄積せんとする彼らの心理に拍車をかけるのだ。

日本と西洋の文化・言語・人種的特徴を併せ持つ、様々な日系の学者もまた、白人中心的な組織の承認を得ようとし、その結果、日本研究分野の既存構造を維持・再生産する行為に加担してしまう場合がある。一方で、そのような日系の日本研究者たちは、この分野の人種構成を変えうる、白人にとっての脅威的な存在であり、日本研究の競技ルールを変革できるほどの言語的能力を持ちあわせている場合も多い。しかし、他方では、そのような能力を発揮するには、まず自身の準白人的な身分を放棄し、その上で、分野に存在する人種差別主義や植民主義を撤廃すべく、積極的に努力しなくてはならない、という現実もある。

　白人の日本研究者が日本研究に対し真摯であり、分野に貢献しているという事実は、彼らが人種的特権を再生産していないとか、研究対象となる日本人に対して人種的偏見を抱いていないということを意味しない。レイシズムというものは、個人が他の誰かを人種差別したり、人種的偏見や嗜好を抱くことというよりは、システム上の問題なのである。近代と呼ばれる数世紀の間、白人性の存在自体や、知の創造者としての特権的立場は、客観的かつ中立的なものとして看過され、権力の装置として問題視されることはなかった。ジョージ・リプシッツが述べているように、白人性というものは「決してそれとして呼ばれる必要はなく、社会的・文化的な関係性を司る法則として認識されることもない」（Lipsitz 1995:369）、透明な存在なのである。そして、白人性は、客観的・人間的・公正・無性・非政治性の代名詞として機能してきたため、日本研究を含む学術分野において、その妥当性を問われることは、ほとんどなかった。言い換えれば、白人性というものが、あまりに人類普遍の立場として君臨することに長けていたため、それ以外の視点こそが特殊で、人類普遍ではなく、政治的な思惑に染まっており、そのために客観的ではなく、感情的なものだとみなされてきたのだ（Wynter 2003）。「標準的人間性」という言説に支えられてきた白人性は、いわゆる中立性と客観性の独占権を常に要求してきた。そして、自己批判的視点の欠如と他者を排除する横暴さを咎める声や、人種的特権への自覚を求める声には耳を貸さず、ひたすら自己防衛に勤しむ。日本研究分野の歴史上・制度上の成立は、白人性のもつ透明性を以て、白人の支配権と人種的特権を（再）生産してきたのである。

4. 白人による非西洋の解釈とその引用義務

　一部の例外を除き、日本研究分野において、知を創造する主要な方法は、西洋由来の理論や解釈の枠組みを援用しつつ、日本在来の事象に意味づけする、というものだ。学者たちは、アカデミアに所属し、アカデミア特有の訓練を受けてきたことを証明するために、権威ある白人男性たち——つまりマルクス、ウェーバー、ヘーゲル、カント、ハイデガー、フロイト、ベンヤミン、フーコー、デリダ、ドゥルーズ、ジジェク、アガンベン、シュミットなどのことだが——の論を引用する。彼らは、筆者が学部生・院生時代に受けた教育の基礎を提供した哲学者たちであり、様々な古典的・規範的思想や理論の一部を書いた人々。様々な植民主義的・人種主義的・性差別的な国家ぐるみの暴力を正当化し、暴力に加担してきたという事実にも関わらず、彼らは確立された権威の象徴であり、白人に付与された妥当性を証明する材料となってきた。権力と権威の象徴として白人男性の論を引用する事は、「承認の政治」に進んで参加する行為だ。そうすることによって、研究者たちは、既存の秩序を尊重する正統的な知識人だと認めてもらえるのである。この手続きを受け入れ、それに従うものは、職・フェローシップ・助成金・昇進などの報酬を得ることができ、白人が特権的立場を独占するアカデミアという世界で、学者として認識される。逆に、このお決まりのプロセスに従わない人々は、分野から疎外されるかもしれないというリスクを背負うことになる。

　確かに、日本研究者のための必読書リストには、非白人による文献も多少含まれている場合がある。しかし、分野自体が、白人男性の著作ばかりを正典としてきた伝統を疑問視しないかぎり、非白人の著作は「マイノリティも仲間に入れてあげよう」という多数派のジェスチャーとして扱われてしまう危険性がある。このような、凝り固まった知の創造回路は、批判されるべき人種・ジェンダーの序列を、逆に擁護・継続させるものなのだ。誰もが白人知識人の論を、半ば強制的に引用させられてしまうアカデミアの伝統は、「正統な知識の白人化」ともいうべき法則を再生産し、白人の権威がしっかりと認識・維持されることを永遠に保証するための装置として機能する。

◆パートⅡ：「準白人」として共謀する日本人研究者たち

　日本研究分野には、様々な度合いの白人特権を持つ研究者と、準白人としての恩恵を受け、その地位の存続を望む日本人研究者との共謀関係が存在する。この仕組みの中で、日本人研究者は、白人研究者にその価値を認めてもらおうと努力し、白人研究者たちは、自分たちが築き上げた解釈・批評・研究体系を通して、日本人研究者たちの成果を評価する。日本人研究者たちは、概して自らを白人の研究対象と同一視してしまうため、自分たちの日本に対する理解が正しいかどうかよりも、白人の同業者からの承認が得られるかどうかを気にする。日本が西洋人にとって研究に値する国で、アカデミアで日本が解釈の対象になりうるということは、日本人にとっての名誉であり、西洋の白人世界で分析・解釈の対象として表象されることは、すなわち日本が価値のある文明国だという証明なのだ。実際、日本文化は芸術・演劇・映画・建築・デザイン・ファッション・食・技術・武道などの分野で西洋人にとってのインスピレーションと模倣の材料となってきたのであり、白人・西洋人が日本人を模倣することは、日本人にとって非常に（時には最も）重要な関心ごとだ。なぜなら、日本人は、白人の（帝国主義的）権威者たちが、自分自身の価値基準をもとに作り上げた近代文明の門番であり、同時に近代文明の最終的な基準決定権を持つ仲買人であると信じているからだ。ある地域が西洋人によって「未開」だとみなされることは、日本がそのような国々を征服し、人々を虐殺する際に、それを正当化するための材料となった。

5. 白人性へのあこがれ＝レイシズムをはらんだ愛＋反黒人主義

　日本人が白人性に抱く尊敬やあこがれは、先述したように、人種と性別の序列概念を内包した日本の近代化プロセスの産物として理解することができる。ジョン・ラッセルは、90年代半ばから2016年にかけて自ら行った調査に基づき、日本における白人性の表象は、「多くの日本人が目指すべきだと信じている白人性テンプレート」を提供するものだ、と指摘している（Russell 2017）。願望・羨望からあこがれに至るまで、日本人の自己と白人性との関係には、両義性・矛盾・恨めしさ・苦々しさ・嫌悪感さえ入り混じることがあるものだ（このような複雑な感情は、不平等な権力関係にはつきものだ）。日本人

に見られる白人性尊重は、確かに西洋中心的な近代化プロセスの結果なのだが、その愛情の度合いは過剰なほどである。そして、日本人の過剰な愛情は、白人を自認する人々の間に、日本愛好心を引き起こし、助長させる。このプロセスを通過することにより、白人は、日本人に帝国主義的な愛と準白人としての承認を与え、両者の相思相愛関係が継続される。われわれは、このような白人の人種資本と白人至上主義を拡張・蔓延させる地球規模の枠組みを露呈し、批判しなくてはいけないのだ。

　海外に住む日本人の日本研究者の多くは、白人の配偶者やパートナーを持っている。この事実は、彼らが、パートナー以外の白人（と非白人）に「心配はご無用です。私たちはあなたがたの白人性を、深く、とことん、愛しています」というメッセージを、送っていることを示唆する。私自身も、白人男性と結婚していた経験があり、自己批判の重要性を認識するとともに、その居心地の悪さもよく承知している。しかし、そのような「同意に基づく親密性」は、ジェンダーと人種の複合的な権力構造を正当化する可能性を秘めており、私たちはそのような重層的な権力が、白人性への投資として機能する事実を疑問視し、それによって白人のパートナーをもつ日本人の「準白人」としての立場を相対化すべきである。自身の「準白人」としての特権を自覚している日本人たちは、白人性を最も端的に象徴する人々の特権に追従する。そして、彼らにとって、白人至上主義を解体することは、世界中で認識されている人種ヒエラルキーにおけるナンバー２の地位を失うことを意味する。

　日本人はしばしば、自分たちが抱く白人性への敬意やあこがれの存在を否定するが、それだけでなく、彼らは自分たちの白人性嗜好が「反ブラックネス」を歴史的・地理的に再生産している点についても、深く考えようとしていない（Jung and Costa Vargas 2021）。もし白人性という概念が、日本研究の一角を占めてきたのであれば、研究者たちは、白人性が人種的価値の序列であるという事実に対して、より自覚的になると同時に、それが反ブラックネス・反ブラウンネス・反アジア性・反先住民性などの概念を前提として成り立っているという事実にも、改めて向き合うべきである。言い換えれば、日本人が自らの白人性への愛情を自省することが、非白人へのレイシズムを自省することなのだ。そのような内省は、日本が沖縄民族・アイヌ民族・コリアン・中国人・台湾人・フィリピン人・インド人・タイ人・褐色の肌の

移民労働者たちなどに対して行った人種政策と歴史的・植民主義的な制度化されたレイシズムについて認識することにつながるだろう（Koshiro 1999; Lie 2009; Hirano 2022）。日本人が、自分たちの抱いている、有色人種蔑視に基づく視点や価値観に向き合おうとしない時、それは日本における白人至上主義を恒常化させる行為につながる。日本人研究者が、白人との相思相愛関係を通して、地球規模の白人至上主義の維持に貢献し続け、また、自分たちが加担してきた制度的レイシズムに無頓着であり続ける限り、われわれは、白人と日本人が一丸となって生み出すレイシズムの根深さ・規模・威力・影響力について検討し、分析し、発言し続けていかなくてはならないのである（Shigematsu 2021）。

　白人と認識される人々と日本人は「承認の政治」に関わる無言の協定を結び、さまざまな度合いの白人性を再生産する、複雑な人種資本の回路を作り出している。白人社会からの承認欲求と、白人の承認を得るための努力を放棄しようと呼びかける、グレン・クルタードの「承認の政治」批判論に倣い、筆者もみなさんに考えていただきたいと思うことがある。それは、日本研究に携わる人々が、既存の研究モードや方法を用いることによって（詳細は後述）、白人性という人種資本の再生産に寄与してしまっているという事実についてである（Coulthard 2014）。一方で、この問題に光を当て、議論することによって、準白人身分の日本人研究者が、その人種的特権を喪失する可能性があるという事実は、日本人が白人性の獲得・維持欲求に関して、口を閉ざしてしまう原因となっている。他方で、「自分は白人性を超越した」と信じている白人研究者に関しては、以下の点について考えてもらいたい。

6. 白人性の方法論：アカデミアのルール（支配／規則）

　ここで言う白人性の方法論とは、言わば、学術探求のフィールド（分野／競技場）におけるルールのことで、研究者たちは、彼らがこの競技に参加する権利を持つということを暗に表明するために、このような決まり事を自明の理として受け入れ、アカデミアへの帰属性を表明するように訓練されてきている。ルールを作り上げたのは主に白人の男女たちで、彼らの地位は、非白人研究者が、白人への承認欲求を抱き、白人の権威者を引用することでアカデミアへの所属を表明するというしきたりによって、保護されている。アカデミアの競技ルールには様々あるが、代表的なのは以下のようなものであ

る：

1. 白人の研究者／専門家が、非白人である研究対象の代弁をしたり、彼らについて語るという、主体・客体の人種関係について、疑問を持ったり、批判したり、意義を唱えたりしてはいけない。日本研究における新植民主義的な知の生産構造は、日本（人）という客体／他者を研究対象とし、人種的特権を付与された白人の主体／研究者によって、解釈・評価されるという、人種関係性と人種別役割分業を内包するものである。研究対象となる「日本的なもの」は、文学・映画・美術・哲学・宗教・歴史・文化だけでなく、日本人の行動・思想・心理・セクシュアリティなども含まれる。

2. 西洋発祥で、西洋に帰属し、白人性の優位を強化する理論に基づく、解釈パラダイムを疑問視してはいけない。先述のように、日本研究の専門家らは、欧米発祥・ヨーロッパ中心主義的・西洋由来の理論を、権威的な知の体系として、日本の解釈に援用している。このような人種的な知識の特権パラダイムは、知の創造者としての白人が、日本に関するさまざまな事象の中で、一体何に価値があるかを決定し、語り、それを他の白人の研究者が、英語などの西洋言語で書かれた研究の中で引用することにより、白人による知と権力の独占体制が維持される仕組みを持っている。日本人研究者の著作が研究の中で引用される場合も皆無ではないが、日本人が日本研究分野で最も価値のある思想家のうちに数えられることは、ほとんどない。この人種的役割分業に基づく日本研究の方法論は、地球規模の地政学的知識と権力が形成されるプロセスを通して、白人視線の学問体系を拡大再生産していくのだ。

3. その創設以来、白人男性と、白人男性の方法論をほぼ受け継いできた白人女性が過半数を占めてきた日本研究分野の、人種的・性別的に偏った歴史と研究者の比率に異議を唱えてはいけない。日本人・日系人・若干の黒人、そしてそれ以外の非白人研究者も、日本研究分野に存在するには違いないが、彼らも、既存の人種的・性別的な序列を維

持するためのルールを守ることになっている。

4. 「革新的・人道的な立場からの改革」という枠組を超えた国家批判を
行ったり、国家の正当性や国家利益を疑問視したりしてはいけない。
日本研究者の任務は、男性支配的・異性愛的・家父長的な植民主義体
制の国民国家の利益に貢献し、政府の軍事的な国境警備体制を正当化
し、近代以来の植民地主義構造を引き続き正常視するための材料とな
る知識を、拡大再生産することなのである。

5. 日本人や日本人コミュニティへの責任を負わずに、情報提供者である
日本人に関する知識を創造するという、日本研究の搾取的方法論に異
議を唱えてはいけない。通常、人を対象とする研究は、被験者への損
害を防止するためのプロトコルが規定されているものの、研究によっ
て生成された言説が、被験者とそのコミュニティにもたらしうる損害
を、プロトコルによって防止することはできない。他者は、英語で書
かれた研究報告の中に自己が表象され、認識されていることに感謝さ
えしていればよいのである。他者とは、主体が研究する客体なので
あって、主体の共同研究者でもなければ、研究成果が客体の利益にな
るわけでもない、というのが、正しい「客観的な学術研究の姿勢」な
のである。

6. 研究者が本人の知的財産を資本として経済的利益を得る、という個人
主義的な知識所有論に、異議を唱えてはいけない。研究調査を実施す
る過程において、学者は多くの人々の援助に依存するのだが、その最
終的な研究成果は、書籍・学術雑誌・論文集などに所収される研究論
文の形をとる。さらに、その成果は、資本主義体制下の商品生産活動
の一環として、研究者個人の知的財産になるとともに、執筆者・非営
利の大学出版会・民間の出版社のいずれかによって、その著作権が所
有されるのだ。

7. 欧米の名門大学出版局から刊行された、英語で書かれた研究にこそ最
高の価値がある、という言語的序列の仕組みに異議を唱えてはいけな

い。日本に関する事象が英語の研究論文や書籍で扱われているということは、日本が帝国主義的な白人性を表象する言語で描写されているということであり、それは、日本がそれだけ価値のある国だ、という証明なのだ。

◆パートⅢ：何をすべきか

　白人・準白人研究者の中には、自分たちが人種的特権の恩恵にあずかっており、また、確立されたアカデミアの決まり事を遵守することにより、白人の人種資本を再生産している、という事実を認めない人々もいるであろう。しかしながら、それ以外の白人・準白人の研究者たちが、逆に自分たちの性別・人種による特権的立場を使って、白人至上主義の解体に貢献することも可能なのである。一般に、日本研究に携わる人々の多くは、あからさまな白人至上主義や反ブラックネスは標榜しない。とは言え、先述のような損得勘定に基づき、自分たちが白人性の獲得に意欲を注いでいることや、制度と権威ある組織に支えられた白人至上主義の存続に貢献している、という事実に目を向けようとしない人々も少なくない。地域研究に関わる欧米系の学者たちは、オリエンタリズムに内在する人種的枠組みという問題をいまだに解決できないでいる。なぜなら、そのような枠組みを、1つ1つ完全に解体しようとするならば、新植民地主義な搾取の仕組みと、知の生産に関わる方法論が作られた過程で形成された、実際的な状況を変えることが、まず必要だからである。言うまでもなく、筆者がここで論じていることは、白人・準白人の日本研究者たちが、これまで創り出し、積み上げてきた膨大な量の知識を否定するものではない。本稿は、彼らがそのような素晴らしい業績を重ねることができた背景には、日本研究分野に内在する、人種・ジェンダー上の構造が関わっているかもしれないという事実に気づいてほしい、という呼びかけなのである。

　このエッセイが提示した論点の一部もしくはすべてを、批判したり、否定したりする人々は、大勢いるかもしれない。もちろん、筆者は自分の主張が完全無欠であるとか、問題点や矛盾点が無いなどとは思っていない。本論の意図は、研究者たちの間に、様々な意見の相違や対立が生じるであろうことを承知の上で、あえて対話のきっかけを作り、そうすることによって、

白人性の優遇と反黒人主義という、日本研究に内在する人種的序列について
の議論を推し進めることなのである。われわれが、制度化された白人至上主
義に加担する行為について内省し、声を上げていかない限り、現行の「改
革主義・多文化主義」版の白人至上主義を、地球規模の反黒人主義制度の中
では「まだマシな方」だとして、許容・継続させてしまうことになるのだ
（Rodriguez 2021:35–58）。われわれが、日本研究分野内の人種的特権制度を自
覚し、その責任を負うためには、まず、コミュニティ全体としての対話と行
動を起こすことから始めなければならない。人種的特権を持つ研究者によ
る、個人的な罪悪感の表明は、対話をシャットダウンしてしまう無用なジェ
スチャーで、日常的な人種的偏見から残忍な暴力行為まで、自分たちがさま
ざまな形の制度的・組織的な反黒人主義に加担しているという事実について
考えることを放棄する行為なのである。

　コミュニティとしての対話と、実現可能な行動の第一歩として、日本研究
内の制度的白人性に異議を唱えようという人たちに、いくつか提案したいこ
とがある。それらは、学者または学生として日本研究に携わる人々に、分野
の改善のために検討してもらたいたい行動と指針である。

1. 問題を認識しよう：自分の研究が非政治的・客観的・中立的であり、
   ゆえに正統的なものだと思い込むのはやめよう。アカデミアは、社会
   への実際的な影響と目に見えない損害をもたらす、権力と権威主義の
   競技場として機能しているものなのだ。

2. 内部から改革しよう：人種・ジェンダーによって付与された自分たち
   の特権を利用し、制度的・組織的改革の契機にしよう。特定の人種や
   ジェンダーを自認する人々が、日本研究の知の形成において支配的で
   いる現状を、文書・行動などを通して公にしよう。また、所属する学
   部やプログラムなどの規定や慣習を根本的に再検討・分析し、問題提
   起をしていこう。

3. 政治性を帯びた知：国家権力の助言者・情報提供者として活動する日
   本研究者の責任や義務を検討しよう。権力に内通するジャーナリスト
   が存在するように、学者の中には、（国家）権力に懐疑的になるどころ

か、それに追従・迎合することにより利益を得ようとする人々も実在するのである（Matsumura 2022）。

4. 引用という政治：人種・ジェンダーの特権に基づく権威を再生産する「引用の政治」を攪乱しよう。引用の政治に関しては、サラ・アーメッドがその問題点をはっきりと指摘している（Ahmed 2016:17）。

5. 翻訳という政治：レイシズムや植民主義に対抗する、非白人の理論家・哲学者・思想家・作家たちによるテクストを積極的・継続的に翻訳し、そのようなテクストの翻訳プロジェクトに労働提供や援助をしよう。その成果が日本研究を改善する新しい枠組みの一部になりうるのである。

6. 資金援助：日本研究を改革するための経済的投資をしよう。学部・プログラム運営費用の一部や自分たちの収入の一部を、翻訳活動や反レイシズムのための活動に寄付し、支援しよう。

7. 個人主義から集団主義へ：これまで標準視されてきた、ネオリベラルで個人主義的な知の生産体系を批判・改善するための行動をとろう。周辺化されてきた声や視点に照準を合わせた共同研究や共同執筆などを積極的に行おう。

7. おわりに

　本稿は白人性批評であり、日本研究に関わる人々の、コミュニティレベルの内省と、日本研究が反黒人主義を助長している事実へのさらなる認識を呼びかけるものである。日本研究関係者は、分野における人種・ジェンダーの不均衡を看過することにより、この不穏な問題や追及の重要性を否定したり、責任を回避しようとしたり、人々の声を掻き消そうとしたりするかもしれない。しかしながら、筆者は、内省と対話と行動を呼びかけたい。日本研究者同士が対話し、コミュニティとして行動を起こし、人種・性別に基づく序列構造について率直に話し合い、そのような現状を改善する努力をすることを願う。そうしなければ、これからも白人性は、誰にもその正統性を疑わ

れないまま、最高権威として横行し続けるだろう。そして、われわれは知ら
ず知らずのうちに、組織的・経済的・心理的・象徴的・物質的・肉体的な反
黒人主義の継続に加担し続けてしまうのだ。

第3部

周縁的なものに光をあてる

世界とつながる 日本古典文学

物語の継承と再創造から

末松美咲（名古屋学院大学）

1.「日本古典文学」のイメージ

　「日本古典文学」と聞いて、古い、閉じたものだと感じる人は多いだろう。遠い時代の難しい言葉で書かれた「古典文学」は、日本で生まれ育った人々でさえ、自分とは何ら関わりのないものだと考えがちである。中学生や高校生であれば、古典文法を必死で暗記する授業を思い浮かべるかもしれない。大学生であれば、日本文学を専攻しない限り、ほとんど触れることのなくなった分野だろう。そして、社会人になればなおさら、日本の古典文学については「学生の頃に授業でやったな」と懐かしく思い出す程度のものではないだろうか。

　私は現在、そうした「日本文学が専門ではない」大学生に、「教養」として古典文学を教えている。と言っても、この科目を教え始めて 2 年しか経っていない、まだまだ試行錯誤中の新米講師である。受講するのは、単位が必要だから、という学生が大半である（これは教養・専門の別に限らず、どの科目であれ同様かもしれない）。実際に、授業のコメントには「日本文学には興味がないけど、単位が必要だから」とか、「時間帯がちょうどよかったので」などと、正直に履修動機を書いてくれる学生もいる。

　そのような学生たちに、初回の授業で「古典文学と聞いて、頭に思い浮かぶものは何ですか？」と質問する。すると、多くの学生が、『竹取物語』・『源氏物語』・『枕草子』・『平家物語』など、自分たちが中学・高校で習った

ことのある作品の名を挙げる。また、古文の読解に苦しんだことを思い出す学生もいれば、面白い先生に当たって古典が好きになった、という学生もいる。いずれにせよ、「古典文学」のイメージは、中学・高校の授業によって形成されることが多いのだと分かる。

　私は「日本文学」という科目のなかで、平安時代から江戸時代前期までの古典文学を取り上げている。その理由は、もちろん、自分の専門分野が古典であることと、授業回数との兼ね合いによる。しかしそれ以外にも、私が古典を教える理由がある。それは、今後おそらく「古典文学」には触れないであろう大半の学生たちに対し、彼らが抱いている「古典文学」への固定観念を変えたいと思っているからだ。近年は、サブカルチャーをきっかけに歴史ものや古典作品に興味を持ったという若者も多いものの、まだまだ「日本古典文学」には固定化されたイメージが付きまとっており、自分と関係のある、決して特別ではない分野だと認識している人は少ないように感じる。

　本稿では、このように「日本古典文学には興味がない」と言う私の学生たちを仮想読者と設定し、わずかながらの講義経験を通して得られた実感をもとに、彼らに伝えたいことを書き留めようと思う。そして、「日本古典文学」は「閉じたもの」「古びたもの」「堅苦しいもの」というイメージを持つ人々に、日本の古典文学は、私たちが想像するよりもずっと身近なものであり、現代にも世界にもつながりうる可能性を秘めた分野であることを知ってもらえたらと思う。

2. 物語の継承と再創造

　さて、まずは、私が主にどのような研究を行っているのかについて、簡単に説明しておきたい。私の研究対象は、室町時代から江戸時代前期にかけて制作された物語である。現代でも一般に知られている『浦島太郎』や『一寸法師』など、「お伽草子」と呼ばれる作品類を中心に、成立や享受のあり方について考察している。とりわけ、従前の作品が改作されたり、同じ物語の異本が発生したりする場合に、その「再創造」の背景にはどのような欲求があったのか、という点に関心を持っている。

　お伽草子作品には、現在400編以上が数えられており、多くが絵巻や絵本といった視覚的要素のある形態で伝わっている。現代の私たちが漫画やアニメを楽しむように、昔の人々も絵と物語が織りなす世界を楽しんでいたの

である。そして全54帖ある『源氏物語』のような長編の物語とは異なり、1巻から3巻の長さで完結するものがほとんどである。

お伽草子の特徴としては、絵入りの短編物語であることのほかにも、様々なジャンルの作品が存在するという点が挙げられる。公家の恋愛を描いたもの、武家の活躍を描いたもの、仏教のご利益を説くもの、庶民の立身出世を描くもの、異世界を描いたファンタジーのようなものや、動物や植物を擬人化したものまである。描かれる時代も、舞台も、登場人物も、多種多様である。こうした物語の多様性は、物語を読むことが、中央の貴族だけでなく、地方の武士や庶民など、様々な階層の人々にまで広まるなかで生じたと言われている。つまり、物語内容の多様化には、読者層の拡がりが関係しているのである。その一方で、お伽草子作品は非常に類型的でもあり、相互に深く関わり合う作品群だとも言える。絵入りの物語で、いろんなジャンルがあり、そして似通った内容のものがたくさんある、と言えば、現代の漫画やライトノベルにも通じるので、そのように考えてもらえれば分かりやすいかもしれない。

お伽草子が多様なジャンルや設定をカバーしながらも、非常に類型的であるのはなぜか。それは、お伽草子が、先行作品の要素を下敷きにしたうえで、その時代や地域の求めに応じた物語として制作されたからである。すべてのお伽草子が、王朝物語・軍記物語・説話などの先行作品を引用し、本説の影響を受けながら成立していると言ってもよいだろう。現代では、似通った作品をすぐに「パクリ」と断じてしまう傾向もあるが、著作権という概念もなく、物語と作者が今ほど強く結びついていない時代のことである。そもそも、作者や成立背景がまったく分からない作品も多い。そのなかで、物語は自由に作り変えられ、受け継がれていった。同じ物語であっても、本文表現が大きく違うものがあったり、舞台・登場人物・展開から、なんと結末まで異なるバージョンの本が作られたりしたのだ。

しかし、こうした再創造や翻案が顕著なのは、お伽草子というジャンルに限ったことではない。『源氏物語』は、早くから「古典」として権威付けられたために、物語内容の改変は少なかったものの、中世王朝物語では『源氏物語』を模倣するような作品が多く生まれ、さらには後日譚や物語の空白を埋める補作まで生まれた。能やお伽草子にも、『源氏物語』の登場人物や作者の紫式部を物語内に登場させ、原作とは別の新たな作品として仕立てられ

たものがある。原作を共有する読者のコミュニティから、原作には描かれな
かった物語が創造されたり、原作とは別のストーリーが誕生したりすること
は、現代の漫画やアニメのファンによる二次創作にも似ている。

　このように古典文学が継承され、再創造されるサイクルは、現代にも引き
継がれている。現代社会の文化や技術が、それ以前の歴史を礎として成り
立っているように、文学作品も、それが成立した時代のみに開かれた産物な
のではなく、時代を超えて読み継がれ、新たに享受されていくものでもある
のだ。現代においても、古典作品が新たなメディアとして再生産されること
は、決して珍しくない。例えば、大和和紀の漫画『あさきゆめみし』を読ん
で、初めて『源氏物語』の詳しい内容を知った、という人も多いだろう（私
もその一人である）。2013 年には『竹取物語』を翻案した高畑勲のアニメ映画
『かぐや姫の物語』が公開されたし、2022 年の冬には古川日出夫の現代語
訳を原作としたアニメ『平家物語』も放送され、話題を呼んだ。これらの視
覚的な作品は、原作をそのまま引き継いでいるのではなく、作者による独自
の解釈や、新たなテーマが付与された、いわば再創造された作品である。現
代文化のなかにも、継承され続けてきた古典文学の軌跡を見出すことは可能
なのである。

3. 古典文学の記憶

　物語の継承と再創造による、古典文学の軌跡の極端な例は、特定の視覚的
構図を繰り返し引用することによって作られる「古典の記憶」ともいうべき
ものだ。例えば、単著の連載漫画として、2014 年と 2022 年に発行部数世
界一をギネスブックに認定された漫画『ONE PIECE』のワンシーンを取り
上げてみよう。『ONE PIECE』は異世界の海賊を主人公とした物語で、ファ
ンタジー色の強い作品であるが、日本をイメージした「ワノ国」を舞台とし
たシリーズには、随所に日本の昔話や古典作品のモチーフが引用されてい
る。ワノ国では、「牛鬼丸」というキャラクターが、僧兵の出で立ちで剣士
たちの刀を奪う「刀狩り」を行っている。牛鬼丸は、主人公の仲間の剣士に
勝負を挑むが、その姿を一瞥すれば、この人物が源義経（牛若丸）の従者で
あった弁慶をモデルとしていることが分かる。さらに、二人の戦闘シーンの
背景には橋の欄干が描かれており、キャラクターたちが橋の上で戦っている
ことがうかがえる。ここには、お伽草子や能などに見られる「橋弁慶」のモ

チーフが引用されているのである。

　義経と従者・弁慶の出会いの物語は、数多くある「義経もの」のなかでも、最も有名なエピソードのひとつである。「橋の上で刀狩りをする弁慶が、千本目の太刀を求めて牛若丸に挑みかかるが、打ち負かされて従者になる」というモチーフは、現代でも様々なメディアに繰り返し登場する。そこで描かれる義経は中性的な美少年、対照的に弁慶は大男の荒くれ者、というのが定型である。子どもの頃に読んだ絵本、あるいはビデオゲームや漫画を通して、二人の典型像を知ったという学生も少なくない。

　「美少年の義経」と「大男の弁慶」という人物像は、『平家物語』には見られず、『義経記』や義経を主人公とした室町期の物語のなかで生まれ、以来人口に膾炙したものだ。『義経記』には、稚児時代の義経（遮那王）が、楊貴妃や李夫人などの世界的な美女にも劣らないほどの美貌の持ち主として設定されている。また、『義経記』のなかでは、義経と弁慶の対決は清水寺や五条天神が舞台となっているが、お伽草子『弁慶物語』や『橋弁慶』、能「橋弁慶」などでは、二人の対決の場は五条大橋とされる。このような、室町期に見られた舞台設定の揺れは、五条大橋という空間の境界性とも相まって、次第に後者のイメージとして定着していく。この構図は一定の型を保ちながら連綿と継承され、絵巻や絵本だけでなく、奉納絵馬や浮世絵の画題としても描き続けられてきた。こうした人物像や場面設定の固定化は、物語が視覚情報を伴って伝わったからこそ可能になったものだろう。ビジュアルイメージとともに享受されてきた義経・弁慶像は、現代にも引き継がれ、児童向け絵本のみならず、様々な小説・ドラマ・ビデオゲーム・漫画に至るまで、その影響力は一目瞭然である。この二人が登場する作品は枚挙に暇がないが、大衆文化・ポップカルチャー・メディアのなかで、彼らの固定的な像が繰り返し再生産されることによって、その文化的記憶が、世代を超えた人々に共有され続けるのだ。

　一方、人口に膾炙した義経・弁慶像をそのまま引用・再生産するのではなく、敢えてそれをずらすことで、新しい物語を再創造するという試みも見られる。20年以上前の作品になるが、1995年から1999年まで、少女漫画雑誌『マーガレット』で連載されていた上田倫子の『リョウ』は、義経・弁慶のイメージを大きく転換させ、新たな物語を作り上げた作品である。この漫画の冒頭では、時代は現代に設定され、義経はリョウという女子高生として

登場する。そこに、源平合戦が起きた 12 世紀後半からタイムトラベルして
きた弁慶が現れ、主人公・リョウを平安時代に連れ帰るのであるが、ここで
も二人の出会いは五条大橋の上である。弁慶は大男ではありつつも美男子と
して描かれ、やがて二人は恋に落ちる。このように義経が女性として大胆に
性転換され、「義経－弁慶」の主従関係が「女－男」の恋人・夫婦関係に変
化する背景には、「中性的な美少年」と「命をかけて義経に仕えた大男の従
者」という、先行する義経・弁慶像が存在する。「義経もの」に限らず、少
女漫画の「歴史もの」ジャンルに「性別越境」的なモチーフがまま見られる
ことはすでに指摘されているが（藤本 2010）、歴史上の人物の性別を転換した
作品は珍しい。『リョウ』の主人公である義経を女性として設定するという
発想は、やはりこれまで継承されてきた中性的なイメージを下敷きとしたも
のであろう。作者は、室町時代以来の人物像を踏襲したうえで、今度は義経
の物語を女性の視点から作り変えたのである。

　このように、「古典の記憶」は、現在でもなお大衆文化のなかで継承され
ているだけでなく、敢えてその記憶をずらすことにより、新たな物語の創
作も試みられている。そのような作品は、研究者による現代語訳や子ども向
けの学習漫画のように、古典的物語の内容をできるだけ変えずに、現代の
読者に分かりやすく伝えようとするものではない。だからこそ、作者は自由
な発想を生かし、人々を楽しませる物語を紡ぎだせるのであり、それはある
意味、「生きた古典文学」の一つの形だと言える。私たちが生きる現代社会
も、中古・中世・近世などの時代から、繰り返し再創造されてきた物語で満
ちているのである。

　ところで、これまでに見てきた「橋弁慶」の物語は、京都の五条大橋に義
経と弁慶の像が置かれていることからも分かるように、もとは京都という土
地と不可分に語られるものであった（ただし、現在の五条大橋は、「橋弁慶」の伝
承が広まった室町時代の五条大橋とは別の場所にある）。しかし、時代が下り、様々
なメディアが社会全体に普及していく過程で、京都という土地やその地域性
を越え、「日本」というより大きな共同体に属する人々の間で、義経と弁慶
にまつわる「古典の記憶」が共有・再生産・継承されるようになる。

　それでは、グローバル化が進む現代社会においても、こうした日本古典文
学の継承と再創造のサイクルは、日本という地域レベルの枠組みに限定され
るものなのだろうか。その答えを考えるべく、最後に、地理的な枠組みとい

う観点から、日本の古典文学を見つめてみようと思う。

4. 国際化社会のなかの日本古典文学

　現代において、日本の文学が、日本という限定された地域でのみ享受されるものでないことは、『源氏物語』の国際的な知名度の高さなどを見てみても明らかであろう。『源氏物語』は、明治期に英語・ドイツ語・フランス語に翻訳されたのを皮切りに、現在では 32 の言語に翻訳されている。さらに2019 年の 3 月から 6 月にかけては、ニューヨークのメトロポリタン美術館で「The Tale of Genji: A Japanese Classic Illuminated」と題された『源氏物語』に関する美術・工芸品などの大規模な展覧会が開催されており、『源氏物語』に対する継続的な関心の高さがうかがえる。

　『源氏物語』とともに根強い人気を誇るのは『枕草子』であるが、こちらも 1930 年代にはアーサー・ウェイリーによる英語抄訳が発表されている。『枕草子』と言えば、2021 年 8 月に、フィンランド出身のミア・カンキマキ氏が『清少納言を求めて、フィンランドから京都へ』を日本で刊行し、話題となった。この本には、まったく異なる時代のまったく異なる文化を生きた清少納言という人物を、親しみを込めて「セイ」と呼び、深く理解しようとする著者の姿が描かれている。この作品はフィンランド国内で大きな反響を呼び、日本での出版以前に、エストニア語・ドイツ語・イタリア語に翻訳されたという。

　このように、平安時代の女性たちによる文学作品は国外でも高く評価され、多くの翻訳が出されている。また、これらの有名な作品が翻訳によって海外に伝わった例だけでなく、前近代の文学作品が、古典籍や絵巻などの形で物質文化として海を渡ったのも事実である。現在、国文学研究資料館は、「在外日本古典籍所蔵機関ディレクトリ」上で、国内外の日本古典籍所蔵機関についての情報を提供しているが、現在挙げられているだけでも、世界の165 機関が日本の古典籍を所蔵している。

　海外に渡った古典籍のなかでも、絵巻や絵本など、視覚的要素のある作品は多い。私は授業で、外国の美術館や図書館に所蔵されている絵巻を取り上げることがある。そうすると、学生からは必ずと言っていいほど、「海外に日本の絵巻があるなんて知らなかった」「なぜ、外国に日本の作品が伝わっているのか」という反応が返ってくる。現在、米・仏・独をはじめ、海外に

所蔵されている絵入り本のほとんどは、もともと、近代以降に海外のコレクターたちによって収集され、国外へ持ち出されたものである。絵入りの物語は、文字が読めなくとも楽しむことができるため、外国人に好まれたようである。昭和期の古書肆として有名な反町茂雄の『一古書肆の思い出』には、絵本好きの外国人の話や、欧米の図書館からの注文にまつわるエピソードなどが語られており、当時、前近代に作られた絵巻や絵本が海を渡っていく過程を窺い知ることができる。また、現在把握されている海外の古典籍の数や実態は全体の一部に過ぎず、今後、新たな伝本の発見も期待されている。このような在外絵巻・絵本は、それぞれの所蔵機関において、日本の文化や文学を知る資料として活用されることもあり、日本研究に携わる人々だけではなく、一般の人々にとって役立つもの、つまり、日本文化理解を促進するためのツールにもなりうるだろう。古典籍が、物質文化として海外に輸出されることで、その「物質」を契機とした異文化間交流も考えられるのである。

　さらに興味深いことに、国外に流出した前近代の絵巻や絵本が、海外文学の創作に影響を与えた可能性も近年指摘されている。例えば、1726年に発表されたスウィフトの『ガリバー旅行記』が、『御曹司嶋渡り』や『蓬莱山』などのお伽草子作品から着想を得て執筆された可能性があることが、石川透氏によって報告されている（石川2019）。『御曹司嶋渡り』は、源義経が秘伝の兵法書を手に入れようと、上半身が馬の姿をした馬人の島、女性ばかりの女護島、小人の住む小さ子島など、様々な島を旅するという話である。『ガリバー旅行記』との類似性は以前から注目されていたが、スウィフトが日本の絵入り本を目にしていた可能性があることから、『御曹司嶋渡り』から『ガリバー旅行記』への、より直接的な影響が検討されはじめているのだ。多くの在外資料は近代以降に海外へ渡ったと先述したが、スウィフトが絵入りのお伽草子に触れていた可能性を考えると、日本の古典文学は、もっと早くから海外で享受されていたのかもしれない。

　このような国際的な物語再創造の例は、『西遊記』などの古典中国文学が、東アジアの文化的ネットワークを背景とし、中国国内だけでなく、日本や朝鮮半島でも愛読されたことからもわかる（『西遊記』もまた、現代に至るまで様々に再創造されている作品である）。なお、先述した漫画『ONE PIECE』には、『ガリバー旅行記』の引用と考えられるシーンも描かれている。『御曹司嶋渡り』が『ガリバー旅行記』に影響を与えているのだとすれば、日本の古

典文学が海外に渡って享受され、そこから再創造された物語を、さらに現代の日本の漫画が取り入れるという、創作の連鎖が起きていることになる。この現象は、国境を越えた文化の流れを背景とした、世界的規模での物語の再創造と言えるだろう。時代や地域という境界を越え、自由に再創造されてゆく物語のサイクルは、テクストや視覚芸術のデジタル化が進むなか、今後一層、世界各地に広がる可能性を秘めている。ちょうど、写本から版本への転換期に、読者層が飛躍的に拡大したように。

　あるいは将来、「日本古典文学」というジャンルの位置づけが見直される日も来るだろう。ハルオ・シラネ氏は、「世界文学」を「翻訳され、他の国や地域の文学作品と一緒に並び、世界で読者を獲得し、他の国や地域の文学や文化に影響を与える作品」と定義し、村上春樹作品や『源氏物語』などをその例として挙げているが（シラネ 2012）、世界中どこからでも互いに情報を分かち合うことが可能になりつつある現在、様々な形態の文学作品が、新たな文化を創造していくうえで有効な世界的な知の財産として、多くの人々に共有されていくことになるであろう。

5. 世界とつながる日本古典文学

　さて、ここまで「継承と再創造」という視点を切り口として、日本古典文学の時間的・空間的な広がりについて述べてきた。このように俯瞰すると、日本の古典文学が必ずしも時代的・地域的に閉じたものではなく、現代文化に繋がるとともに、国際社会に向けても開かれたものであることがうかがえるだろう。古典文学は、新しい文化の創造や、国際交流の可能性を切り拓く土壌ともなり得るものなのである。

　私は本稿に、「世界とつながる日本古典文学」という表題を冠した。しかし、ここで言う「世界」とは、現代国際社会のことだけを指しているのではない。文学テクストの内に広がる小宇宙も、一つの「世界」である。文学作品は、自分の「世界」と知らない誰かの「世界」を媒介してくれるものでもある。そして、古典文学作品は、それが作られた時代と、それを享受する今という時代をつなげる、懸け橋のようなものだ。

　しかしながら、異なる時代を考察するうえで、継承されてきた知の遺産と同様に重要なのは、取捨選択の過程でこぼれおち、継承されることのなかった知である。例えば、現代でも人口に膾炙している『かぐや姫』や『浦島太

郎』などの昔話も、それらが初めてテクストとして成立した平安時代・室町時代のバージョンを読むと、様々な相違点に気づく。物語は継承されていくプロセスで、テクストの制作者・享受者、または時代の要請に合わせて変化していくものである。同じ物語の時代ごとの変化や、私たちが馴染みのある昔話の原作を読んだときの違和感のなかに、当時の文化や思想を知る手掛かりがある。その手掛かりに対峙し、「なぜこのような変化が起きたのだろう」「どうしておかしいと思うのだろう」と考察することは、昔の文化や思想を知る契機になるだけでなく、普段私たちが気づかない、現代の価値観を映し出す鏡にもなるのだ。そして、そのように自分の真実を相対化する作業は、時代を異にする他者だけでなく、自分とは異なる背景を持つ、同時代の他者を理解するためにも有効な手段である。

　日本古典文学は、作品内の世界、作品を生み出した世界、現代日本という世界、国際社会という世界など、多様な世界をつなぎ、読み手を新しい世界に誘ってくれる存在なのである。

テクストと物語をつなぐ
日本文学

クリストファー・ローウィ（カーネギーメロン大学）
陳元鎬 & シュミット堀佐知 訳

　身も蓋もない言い方だけれども、日本語の表記体系は、変だ。3つの異な
る文字体系（漢字・平仮名・片仮名）が常に同時に使われているだけでなく、
英語にあたる orthography ＝正書法という概念は、ほぼ無きに等しいので、
表記法に限って言えば、書き手に信じがたいほどの自由が与えられているこ
とになる。もう1つのすごい特色は、後述するように、「行間註釈」と呼ば
れるもののおかげで、頭注や脚注に頼らずに、同じ文の中で言葉に注釈をつ
けることができるという点だ。あまりシンプルな説明になっていなくて、申
し訳ない。とにかく、物語の作者たちが、その何世紀にもわたる発達過程と
密接に関係する日本語表記のさまざまな特色を、視覚的表現手段として活用
し、ストーリーの背景にある文脈を補完するのも納得の行くことである。そ
の効果が最小限の場合もあれば、文字の果たす役割を考慮せずには語れない
ような、文学的効果を発揮する作品もある。

　ご想像通り、後者の類の小説は、非常に興味深い視覚性を伴うテクストに
なっている。そのような作品世界で、読者は、馴染みのない形状を持つ馴染
み深い語彙や、特別な振り仮名付きの漢字や熟語、斬新だけれども、ちょっ
と違和感を覚えるような記号などに遭遇する。このような文学作品は、僕が
呼ぶところの「テクストの視覚性」に溢れている。また、非標準的な日本語
を前面に据えている文学は、近代に成立した「標準日本語」の覇権に対して
批判的な傾向があるが、その多くが、テクストの視覚性をふんだんに活用し

ているのも、偶然ではない。

　テクストの視覚性がもたらす効果には二種類ある。1つは、言葉の意味をはっきりさせること。特に非標準的な日本語を多用する作品の場合、馴染みのない物語世界を巡る読者にとって、特殊表記は水先案内人のような存在だ。もう1つは、問題提起。特殊表記のおかげで、読者自身と、彼らの眼前にあるテクストとの隔たりが、一層明らかになるのだ。逆の言い方をすれば、読者が慣れ親しんできた類のテクストには、案内人となる注釈は要らないのである。しかしながら、一体何故、日本語の表記法には、これらの多様な機能が備わっているのだろう。そして、それらは一体どのようにして生まれたのだろう。

1. すべての道の行く先は？

　僕が表記体系というものに興味を持ったのは、日本に関心を抱く以前のことだ。子どもの頃の僕は、解読不能なもの、つまり、自分以外の誰かにとって意味を持つけれども、自分には理解できない書物・文字・言語などに非常に興味を覚えていた。友人や家族は、僕が「難解な文字らしきもの」に心を奪われているのをよく知っていて、実際、僕の両親は、ある年の誕生日に、僕のその後の人生を変えることになる本を、プレゼントしてくれた。それは、エドワード・モーンド・トンプソンの『An Introduction to Greek & Latin Palaeography』と、ピーター・ダニエルズ＆ウィリアム・ブライトの『The World's Writing Systems』だった。両親が、文字について書かれた数ある書物の中から、なぜこの2冊を選んだのかは分からない。本屋の店員さんに勧められたのかもしれない。まあ、とにかく、僕は数え切れないほどの時間を費やして、この2冊を読みふけった。その内容を深く理解できるようになるのは、それから何年も経ってからのことだが（実は、今でもギリシャ語やラテン語の文章は読めないし、手書きであれば、尚更である）、両親からの贈り物のおかげで、僕の文字熱は一層高まった。

　現在、世界で使用されている主要な表記体系の中で、最も複雑だと言われる日本語に関心を抱き、独学で勉強し始めたのは、ちょうどその「熱中時代」のことだ。多くの日本の作家たちが、文字を1つ1つ意識的に選択しながら執筆しており、それが彼らの創作において、しばしば重要な役割を果たすということが分かった時は、小躍りした。僕が、芥川の『歯車』や谷崎

の『鍵』などを読んでいて、ハタと気づいたことだ。でも、僕が独学で知りえたことが、日本語の表記システムという、巨大な氷山のほんの一角に過ぎないことを、当時は知る由もなかった。

このような興味が高じて、大学では、1年生から正式に日本語の学習を始め、3年生の時には、1年間の日本留学も果たした。まず、早稲田大学での夏期短期プログラムを終え、それから宮城県での1年間の留学生活が始まった（これは、まだ東北大震災が起きる数年前のこと）。表向きは「語学留学」だったけれど、本当の目的は、日本文学を学ぶためだった。ちんぷんかんぷんでもいいから、絶対に近・現代日本文学の授業を聴講しよう、と心に決めていた。

ある晩、友人が冗談半分で、こう言った。クリスは近・現代文学よりも、さらに上の難関を目指すべきだ。古典中国語を日本式に読んだり書いたりする学問に挑戦してみたらどうか――僕はその話に飛びついた。仙台のあのキャンパスの一角で、まだ覚束ない日本語を駆使しながら、古典中国語を学んでいた時に感じた、圧倒的な荘厳さのような空気は、今でも鮮明に記憶している。これが、古典中国語との最初の出会いであった。

僕の留学先は、小中学校の教員を養成するための教育大学だったので、厳密に言うと、この漢文との最初の出会いは、漢文の授業ではなく、小中学校で漢文を教えるための教授法を習う授業であった（この科目が必修であることを不満に思う学生は、とても多かった）。しかしながら、漢文そのものの授業だろうが、漢文教授法の授業だろうが、僕にとって、大差はなかった。まだ2年間しか日本語を勉強していなかった自分にとって、唐詩の講釈や、その教授法に関する説明は、どちらも同じくらいちんぷんかんぷんだったのだから。

それでも、2つのことは理解することができた。1つは、漢文テクストに、送り点・振り仮名・助詞などを書き入れることで、中国語の語順や文法を日本語のそれに変え、（やや不自然さは残るけども）十分に解読可能な古典日本語テクストに変身させることができる、ということ。この、書き込み付きの漢文を、日本語の語順に書き直したものは、書き下し文と呼ばれるが、ある学者はこれを「書き直されたテクスト」と読んでいる（Crawcour 1989）。この「書き直されたテクスト」は、漢字と仮名が混在している点で、現代標準日本語の書き言葉とそう違わない。

もう1つの発見は、書き下し文は、しばしば書き下す人の主観に左右さ

れるため、同一の白文から、複数の正しい書き下し文が生まれることがある、ということ。ある漢文テクストを、2人の注釈者が書き下せば、2つの異なる書き下し文ができあがり、どちらも決して間違いではないというのは、ごく普通の現象である。その理由は色々あるが、おそらく最も一般的なのは、注釈者の好みによって、漢字の訓読みを採用する場合と、音読みの場合との差であろう。例として、杜甫の「月夜」という詩の書き下し文の起句「今夜鄜州月／閨中只獨看」を見てみよう。これは、「今夜鄜州の月／閨中 只獨り看るならん」（Suzuki 1928）とも、「今夜なる鄜州の月を、閨中にては只えに獨り看るならむ」（Yoshikawa 1952）とも、読者に読ませる（音読させる）ことができる。この2種類の起句の音読を聞いた人は、同じ詩だと気づかないかもしれない。

　ここで強調したいのは、鈴木と吉川の書き下しを、「同じ詩の異なる翻訳」だと捉えてはいけない、ということだ。例えば、スティーブン・オーウェンによるこの起句の英訳（"The moon tonight in Fuzhou / she alone watches from her chamber"）（Owen 2015）は、鈴木・吉川どちらの書き下しの英訳としても適切である。つまり、この2種類の書き下し文は、互いに競合する杜詩の日本語訳ではなく、それぞれの注釈者が、よかれと思う漢字の発音を提示する、原文と翻訳との中間的段階にあるテクストなのだ。もちろん、このような注釈の伝統には長い歴史があり、注釈者がどのような書き下しをよしとするかにも、歴史的な根拠がある。ただ、あの頃、仙台のあの教室の席に座って、漢文教授法の授業を聴講していた僕にとっては、このような文字体系の言語を使って創作する作家には、無限の創造の可能性が与えられているという事実が、ただただ衝撃で、以来、ずっとそのことで、頭の中が一杯になってしまったのである。

　ここで、数年後に早送り。ある日、腹ペコの僕は、東京にいて、まあまあ有名なラーメン・チェーンの、もう今は無くなってしまった店で、季節限定メニューを見ていた。でも、僕の目が釘付けになったのは、メニューのアイテムではなく、カウンターの後ろの壁に貼られたポスターの紙幅一杯に書かれた文字の列だった：「旬を！〈^^〉！しむ。♡温まる」。現代日本語の3つの文字体系の1つである平仮名が、「！《^^》！」と「♡」の振り仮名＝注釈に使われていることに驚いたのである。絵文字に平仮名の注釈を付けるという技は、それまで見たことがないものだったからだが、それと同時に、この

変則的な文字の使い方は、僕が仙台で遭遇した漢文の注釈と、何となく関係があるようにも見えた。このような注釈を可能にした日本語の仕組みとは、一体どんなものなのだろう。近代の文豪たちも、振り仮名を使った注釈機能を活用したのだろうか。それとも、これは単なる現代的な現象なのだろうか。次々と疑問が浮かぶ。そして、この瞬間、僕のそれまでの人生における、最大の研究プロジェクトの種が蒔かれたのである。

2. 文学？　言語学？　それとも…？

　日本文学の道を志していた僕は、日本語の文字体系が文学作品において果たす役割を研究しようと心に決めた。と、そこまではよかったのだが、それをどのように実行するか、というのは、また別の問題だった。すぐにはっきりしたのは、僕の学術的な関心は、文学と言語学という、ほとんど接点のない２つの分野のちょうど境界線上に位置する、ということ。まあ、紙に書かれた文字や、活字になった言語に対する無関心という点では、両分野一致しているのだが。

　文学研究を行う上で、テクストの内容に重点を置き、形式には注意しないことのメリットは明白だ。例えば、夏目漱石の『こゝろ』だったら、抽象概念としての『こゝろ』（作品の中に現れる言葉や考え）を、目の前にある特定のテクストとは切り離すことにより、初出の新聞連載、さまざまに書籍化されたもの、ネットで無料提供されている青空文庫版などなど、その形式の異同を気にすることなく、スムーズにこの作品について論じることが可能になり、その上、オリジナル・英訳・中国語訳など、別々の言語バージョンを読んだ人々が、『こゝろ』について考えたり、議論したりすることさえ可能になるのである。問題なのは、このような研究方法は、個々のテクストのもつ独自性ともいうべきものを、必然的に抹消してしまうことだ。ここで言う独自性には、テクストの視覚的特徴（レイアウト、文字の大きさ、フォントなど）・媒体の種類・使用言語など、あらゆるものが含まれる。

　文学研究者たちと同様に、言語学者たちも、文字というものには、ほとんど関心を払わない。文字言語は、彼らの研究対象である音声言語を記録するための、不完全な道具に過ぎないからである。さすがに、わざわざ文字を侮辱しようという言語学者は、最近では少なくなったものの、「自然界」で使われている、音声言語のありのままの姿を知る上で、文字言語など役に立た

ない、と考える言語学者は今なお顕在だ。思うに、昨今の音声録音技術の普及が、このような考え方に、さらに拍車をかけているのではないだろうか。

　文字言語の敵視とまでは言えないとしても、文学研究者や言語学者たちが、文字にまったく関心を示さないということは、結果として、言語のそれ以外の要素を特権視しているに等しい。彼らがこのようなポーズを取りがちな理由の1つは、比較的最近まで、双方の分野が、文献学という、幅広い分野の傘下に置かれていたためであろう。文献学は、漢字文化圏では長い伝統を誇る学術分野で、いろいろと思うところがあるのだが、僕の研究との関連で言えば、文献学は、音声言語と文字言語を正確に理解するという目的のために文学テクストを研究する学問であり、もともと、文学も言語学も、文献学に従属する並列的な準学問分野だった。文学と言語学は互いに交わらないので、僕が文学創作において文字が果たす役割について研究しようと思い立っても、その現象自体を説明するための用語すら存在しなかった。つまり、この研究に着手するためには、僕がまず日本語の表記体系のさまざまな特徴を把握し、描写・解説しなくてはいけないということだった。この時の、努力と分析の成果は、僕が「書記日本語のアーキテクチャー」と呼ぶものとして、実を結んだ。

3. 文字体系のアーキテクチャー

　書記日本語のアーキテクチャーの話に入る前に、「文字体系」という用語が指し示す範囲を確認しよう。文字体系というのは、もっとも広い意味では、言語を表象するための大まかな規則に従って機能する、文字・数字・記号などの有限の集合体だ。それは、単一の言語と結び付く場合もあれば、そうでない場合もある。例えば、セム系言語のヘブライ語という「言語」を表記するのに使われる「文字」はヘブライ文字だ。しかし、ヘブライ文字は、ヘブライ語だけを表記する文字ではなく、ロマンス系言語のラディーノ語・ゲルマン系言語のイディッシュ語・イラン系言語のユダヤ＝ペルシア語などの、非セム系言語を含む、さまざまな言語の表記に使用されているのだ。これらの非セム系言語は、ヘブライ語よりも、それぞれスペイン語・ドイツ語・ペルシア語にずっと近いものである。

　ここで重要なのは、ヘブライ文字とヘブライ語の関係は必然的なものではない、という点だ。ヘブライ文字が、ロマンス系言語の表記にも容易に応用

できるということは、文字体系を特定の言語とは独立した存在として考えなくてはいけないということだ。もちろん、特定の言語を表記する際に、それに最も適した文字体系が存在するのも事実である。しかしながら、決して簡便とは言えない文字と言語の組み合わせが、前者に新たな機能をもたらしうる、というのも事実である。例えば、漢字は、中国語を表記するのには適しているが、ベトナム語・日本語・朝鮮語など、異なる系統の言語を表記する場合には、その言語の文法・語彙・音声を表現するために、その漢字に手を加える必要があった。日本語は非常に用言の語形変化が激しい言語であるが、その無数の語形を漢字のみで表現しなければいけなかったため、表語文字としての漢字とは別に、表音文字としての漢字（万葉仮名）が誕生した。そして、万葉仮名はさらに変身を遂げた。漢字の草書体や省略形など、さまざまな過程を経て、平仮名と片仮名が誕生したのである（Frellesvig 2010）。

　言語構造の特徴が文字体系の発展に影響を与えるという考え方は、類型論モデルと呼べるもので（Handel 2019）、漢字がさまざまな言語環境において、どのように、そして、なぜ変化したのかを事後的に説明する場合、非常に有効である。しかし、文字体系と文学との関係性を分析する場合は、それほどでもない。なぜなら、現代の作家たちが文字を用いる文脈は、その文字体系が発展した歴史的背景から、ほぼ切り離されているからである。ある文字体系を生じさせた歴史的条件と、その結果である文字体系を応用する様式は、別々の史実なのである。後者を検討するためには、その文字体系の限界、つまり、理解可能な表記とそうでないものとの境界を見極める必要がある。その「文字体系の限界」を言い換えたのが、「アーキテクチャー」という概念だ。それは、特定の文字体系で書かれたテクストが、標準的な読み手に理解されるよう、書き手が守らなくてはいけない規則や習慣の集合体だと言える。例えば、ヘブライ文字は右から左へ書くのが、そのアーキテクチャー的特徴である。そのため、ユダヤ＝スペイン語は、ヘブライ文字では右から左へ書くのだが、ラテン文字を使用する際は、左から右へ書くのである。テクストの方向性を決めるのは、文字体系のアーキテクチャー的構造である。

4. 書記日本語のアーキテクチャー

　書記日本語のアーキテクチャーという概念が分かると、日本語の文字が、どのように文学テクストの中で機能するかを分析できるようになる。注目す

べき書記日本語のアーキテクチャーの特徴には、少なくとも8つある。

1. 3つの基本的文字体系
2. 符号
3. 書字の2方向性
4. 予測可能な空間配置
5. 行間註釈
6. 本文の存在
7. 互換性
8. 漢字体系の拡張性

　このうち、文学と文字の関係性を考える上で特に重要なのは、(1)3つの基本文字体系、(5)行間註釈、(6)本文の存在である。

　「3つの基本文字体系」と言うのは、もちろん、漢字・平仮名・片仮名を指す。平仮名と片仮名は、47の基本文字を含む2つの集合体（5つの母音、40の子音と母音の組み合わせ、単独子音の「ん／ン」）で、それぞれ漢字から派生したものだが、どちらも漢字とは異なり、互いにも独立した機能をもつ。漢字は、簡単に言えば、現在日本で使われている中国由来の文字体系を指す。平仮名は、ジャネット・シバモトが、文字体系のレファレンスとして非常に価値のある（しかも、子どものときに両親がプレゼントしてくれた本！）、『*The World's Writing Systems*』（Daniels and Bright 1996）の項目としても書いているように、助詞・助動詞・活用変化を表す接尾辞など、文中で文法的な役割を果たす語を表記する文字、という風に説明されることが多い。もちろん、そのような説明は、決して間違いではないのだが、現実には、この解説よりも、はるかに多様で複雑な機能を果たしていることを、覚えておいてほしい。実際、日本語の文字体系のアーキテクチャー的機能を利用する際には、たいてい平仮名が用いられるのだ。最後に、片仮名は、主に外来語・動植物の学名、擬音語・擬態語などを表記するのに使用される文字である。

　「行間註釈」と言うのは、縦書きの文章では漢字の右側に、横書きの文章では漢字の上部に表示される注釈のことで、その中で最も重要なのは、振り仮名である。振り仮名の主要な役割は、意図された読みを読者に明示することである（先述した杜詩の複数の読み方も、これによって可能になった）。この場合、

表記には平仮名が用いられることが多い。しかし、漢字にどの読みを当てるかは、書き手の判断によっても大きく変わり、同一のテクストの中に現れる同じ漢字であっても、読みが統一されているとは限らない（Konno 2009）。また、振り仮名の役割もさまざまで、後述するように、同じテクストの中で、8種類もの異なる機能が観察される場合もあるという（Shindō 1982）。日本語の文字体系に潜在する表現機能を、書き手が最大限に発揮するためのカギは、この柔軟性である。そして、行間註釈に用いられる文字は、漢字、片仮名、そして、平仮名はもちろんのこと、場合によって、アルファベットを含む非日本語の文字も使われる。

　最後に、「本文」とは、すべての行間註釈を取り払った後に残るテクスト本体を指す。多くの場合、本文さえあれば、作品の内容を読み手に伝えることができるので、振り仮名やその他の註釈は、添加物のようなものだ。また、日本語で書かれたテクストに必ず本文があるのに対し、行間註釈は絶対的に不可欠な要素ではないので、行間註釈は本文に従属する関係だ。

　書記日本語のアーキテクチャーは、一見ややこしく見えるが、このシステムが分かれば、さまざまな文学作品に現れる、以下のような文が、どうして可能になるのかを、理解することができる。

1．吉里吉里人と非吉里吉里人ば識別するんでがすと。（Inoue 1981）
2．厚い茶封筒は、膝の上に置かれたままだった。茶封筒を見つめ、指先でその上をなぞった。―우・리・나・라（母国）
　　小さく声を出しながら、茶封筒の上に四文字のハングルを書いた。（Lee 1988）
3．だからあんた、なーんにも心痛ミすることじゃないんだよ。（Sakiyama 2006）
4．「像てきたね」/「なにが？」/「側脸が你のお爸さんに」/「はあ？像てねえよ」（Yokoyama 2014）

　これらの引用文から振り仮名を取り除いたら、おそらく、読者は文や言葉の意味を理解することも、ましてや、読み上げることもできないであろう。

　上記のテクストにおいて、著者たちは、非標準日本語を、平均的な読者に伝えたり（1と3）、日本語以外のことばを取り入れたり（2と4）する目的

で、書記日本語のアーキテクチャー的特徴である、本文と行間註釈を活用している。注目してほしいのは、彼らの採用した振り仮名は、単なる「発音の表示」という、振り仮名の一般的な役割をはるかに超えているという点である。

5. 抵抗としての文字：井上ひさしと『吉里吉里人』

　非標準的な文字の使い方をする、上記のような文学作品を、遊戯的とか例外的だとして軽んじるのは簡単だが、そのような態度は、実を言えば、日本研究分野にとって致命的なものだ。例えば、非標準的な文字を活用することが、現代の標準日本語と日本国家のヘゲモニーに抵抗する場になりうる、という事実について、未だに本格的な学術的考察が行われていないのも、日本研究者が、テクストの形式に関心を払わないことと、無関係ではない。日本国外で活動する日本文学の専門家が、テクスト形式を研究対象にしたがらない理由の１つとしては、非標準的な文字の使い方をする作品は文章が読みにくく、翻訳しにくいということが考えられる。もう１つ考えられるのは、日本語の文字体系に付与された独特な特徴に注目する研究は、日本語の「特殊性」や、最悪、日本人の「特殊性」を論じる研究と同一視される可能性があり、研究者が躊躇いを覚えてしまうことだ。もちろん、テクストの形式に注目することと日本人論は、まったく別のものであり、その２つが混同される可能性が皆無ではないからといって、文字が文学創作において果たす役割を軽視してよい訳ではない。実際、日本語のこのような側面を無視することは、僕たちが最も耳を傾けるべき声——書記日本語のアーキテクチャー的特徴を逆手に取り、画一的な日本人・日本語のアイデンティティという概念に抵抗を試みる、周辺化された声——を掻き消すことになってしまう。研究者が、日本の均質性という「物語」に抵抗しようとする作家たちの抵抗手段に目を向けようとしないということは、彼らの努力を無にするも同然なのだ。

　ここで、２人の作家が、彼らの作品の中でどのように日本語のアーキテクチャーを活用したのかを、より詳しく検討してみよう。まず、井上ひさしは、現代日本有数の劇作家で、小説家としても非常に活躍した人物だ。井上の作品は、文壇に蔓延するエリート主義を揶揄したり、東京の文化を日本文化と同一視するような官僚を批判したりすることで知られている。演劇であ

れ、小説であれ、井上の主要な関心事の１つは、言語と地域性、そして、この２つがどのように地域の人々のアイデンティティに関わるのか、という問題であった（Rimer et al. 2014）。彼が、生まれ育った東北の言葉や文化に対して抱く、強い想いは、井上の創作活動において、非常に重要な位置を占めている。

　井上の地域性へのこだわりがもたらした、残念な結果の１つは、彼の作品群に真摯に取り組もうとする、英語の研究があまりにも少ないことである。現代標準日本語（即ち東京の日本語）を読み慣れている研究者たちが、難解（そう）な井上の作品を敬遠する可能性はあるし、井上がこだわり、その作品に偏在する、生粋の東北弁で交わされる会話文は、たとえ翻訳不可能ではないにしても、潜在的読者・研究者の数を限定してしまうだろう。その典型は、井上の代表作である大長編『吉里吉里人』である。同書は、宮城県と岩手県の県境に近い、吉里吉里と呼ばれる架空の村に住む、貧しい住民たちの生活と、吉里吉里人による日本からの独立宣言を描いた小説だ。そこで展開されるのは、抑圧されてきた周縁（吉里吉里）による、中央（日本）への反撃や、村人たちが、中央の専売特許である官僚制度・教育・公務、そしてもちろん、言語を巧みに利用することにより、権力の拡大と維持に奮闘する物語である。

　『吉里吉里人』における言葉の表象は圧巻である。振り仮名をフルに活用することで、井上は読者を非標準日本語の渦に巻き込み、その行間註釈の視覚的インパクトによって、中央（東京）と周縁（東北）との隔絶を実感させる。繰り返すが、『吉里吉里人』の振り仮名を消してしまったら、この作品は、ほぼ解読不能になると言っても過言ではない。もうひとつ、圧巻なのは、振り仮名が果たす機能の多様性だ。前述したように、『吉里吉里人』の中だけでも、８種類もの用法が見られることが、言語学者・進藤咲子によって指摘されている。また、一見無秩序に見える井上の振り仮名が、実は非常に綿密な意図のもとに展開されていることも、進藤が明らかにした事実である（Shindō 1982）。

6. 横山悠太とバイスクリプタル・アイデンティティ

　井上ひさしが、振り仮名を駆使し、中央と周縁の隔絶を際立たせたと作家だとすると、横山悠太は、２種類の文字体系を巧妙に用いて、１人の人物の

中に共存する2つの文化・言語アイデンティティと、その相互関係性を描き出している作家だ。具体的に言えば、振り仮名は、横山にとって、日本語と中国語の間、そして、それぞれの表記体系の間で揺れ動く心理状態を視覚化するための、有効な手段なのである。このような心理状態、即ち、「バイスクリプタル・アイデンティティ・クライシス」ともいうべきものは、横山が『吾輩ハ猫ニナル』(2014) の中で用いた漢字の形式を通して具現化されている。

　『吾輩ハ猫ニナル』は、日本と中国のアイデンティティに葛藤する主人公・カケルの物語だ。カケルは中国人である母親と中国で暮らしているが、ある時、父親の出身地である日本へ行って、ビザを更新するという難題に直面する。横山は、2つの祖国と2つの言語に愛着を抱くカケルの、バイリンガルでバイスクリプタルな心理を表現するために、（彼が想定する標準的読者にとって）馴染み深い漢字の読み方と馴染みのない漢字の形式や、馴染みのない熟語などをいろいろと組み合わせる。ベースは、日本語の文法に従って書かれている文章なのだが、語彙が現代中国語の言葉だったり、漢字が簡体字だったりするのだ。そして、その本文に振り仮名を付けることにより、現代中国語に馴染みのない日本語使用者にも理解できるテクストに生まれ変わるのである。これは、2つの母国・母語の間に線引きすることを拒否する、トランスナショナル・アイデンティティに根ざした文字表現を生かした作品だと言える。また、本作は、読者にある「文学的難問」を投げかけている——このテクストは、一体何語で書かれ、音読した場合は、一体どのように聞こえるのだろうか。

　例えば、「成田空港」が、「成田机場」と表記される様子を想像してほしい。最初の2つの漢字は同じであるが、最後の2文字である「空港」と「机場」は二重に異なっている。まず、横山が「空港」を表すために使った「机場」は、中国大陸で使われている簡体字で、これを日本バージョンで表すと「機場」（「飛行機の場所」の意）になる。第二に、「机場」（機場）という熟語に当てられた「くうこう」という読み方は、日本語の音読みによる「きじょう」とは一致しない。「机場」は、読者の大多数にとって意味を成さないため、「くうこう」という振り仮名が不可欠なのである。

　横山が、『吾輩ハ猫ニナル』を通して達成した快挙は2つある。1つは、カケルの揺れ動く心理状態を反映する文字システムを確立したこと。もう1

つは、日本語では一般的ではない漢字の形状や読み方の組み合わせを読者に慣れさせたこと。言い換えれば、『吾輩ハ猫ニナル』を読み終えるころには、読者は、カケル式文字体系のルールを習得しているということ。

　かくして、井上と横山という2人の作家は、行間註釈という日本語の表記体系のアーキテクチャー的特徴を利用し、斬新で、読むものをはっとさせるような「気づき」に溢れる文学空間を作り出すことに成功したのである。

7. 結論

　現在、日本研究分野は、多様化が進んでおり、かつて軽視されたような主題にも、徐々に考察の幅を広げつつあるため、研究者にとっては、刺激的で、歓迎すべき時代だと言える。そのような時代が到来したからこそ、近代日本の文豪を論じているだけではほとんど聞こえてこない、周縁的な作家の声に耳（あるいは目）を傾け、彼らの声を掬い上げる文字というツールの役割も、文学研究の一環として、分析できるようになったのだ。また、研究者にとってすでに馴染み深い作家を、新たな視点から考察したり、デジタル技術が文学に及ぼす影響に疑問を投げかけたりするための、さまざまな契機を与えてくれるのも、今という時代なのだ。

　すべての作家が、文字体系を表現の手段として活用しているわけではないが、文字を独創的に使用する書き手の作品を検討する際には、その仕組みを的確に論じるための語彙を考案していかなくてはいけないし、作者による文字の工夫が、物語との間にどのような相互作用を及ぼすのかを、正しく理解しなくてはならない。このようなテクストは、あえて実験的な表現に挑戦する、個性の強い作品が多いのだが、その中でも特別に実験的な書き方をする作品でさえ、日本語の文字体系のアーキテクチャーを遵守しているということは、強調しておきたい。

　最後に、今度、地下鉄の吊り広告に目をやったり、暇つぶしに漫画を読んだり、大好きな小説を読み返したりする時には、日本語の文字体系のさまざまな機能が、微妙な文学的効果をもたらしていることに注意を向けてみてほしい。それから、自分にこう問いかけてほしい——この日本語に特徴的な文字体系システムがなかったとしても、この広告や漫画や小説は、これらのテクストとして、同じように存在しうるのだろうか、と。

第4部

日本とアメリカのあわいで

なんでアメリカで
日本古典文学研究するの？

シュミット堀佐知（ダートマス大学）

1. はじめに

　今回、企画・編集者として、8人の友人たちに「なんで日本研究するの？」という質問に対する、彼らなりの答えをエッセイの形で寄せてもらった。本稿も、人生の半分をアメリカで過ごし、研究の成果を英語で出版し、日本についてほとんど何も知らない学生たちを相手に、アメリカの大学で教鞭を取ってきた自分の、自分なりの「なんでアメリカで日本古典文学研究するの？」への回答である。

　日本で生まれ育ち、教育を受けたのち、「よし、アメリカの大学院で日本文学を学ぼう！」と思い立つ人は珍しい。そういう人自体が少ないし、彼らの多くは卒業後、日本で就職する。私自身、研究者を目指してアメリカに渡った訳ではないので、「なんでアメリカなの？」と訊かれると、答えに躊躇する。正直に告白すると、「なんで古典なの？」と訊かれても、答えに窮する。もともと、日本語教育者を目指して大学院に入り、修士号は日本語言語学で取得したのだが、諸事情により、その後日本古典文学に転向したのである。

　1つ断言できるのは、もし自分が25年前、結婚のためにアメリカに移り住み、数か月間、某所で働いた頃に襲ってきた鬱病を経験しなければ、研究者、ましてや日本研究者にはなっていなかったということだ。この経緯を簡潔に説明するのは難しいのだが、強いて言えばこんな感じである：1997

年、長い遠距離恋愛に終止符を打つべく太平洋を渡った私は、アメリカ社会という、津軽海峡とマリアナ海溝とネス湖を足して3で割ったような過酷な環境を、西武園ゆうえんちの流れるプールか何かと勘違いして、無防備に飛び込んでしまった。溺れる1歩手前で岸に打ち上げられ、顔面から着地し、そのまま1年以上が過ぎた（あくまでも比喩）。いまの能天気な私を知る人が聞いたら驚くだろうが、新婚2年目の私は、食べることも笑うことも本を読むことも電話に出ることも外出することもできず、電源が切れた玩具のような状態だった。そのうち、何かしなくては、という気が湧いてきて、Graduate Record Examinations という、大学院のための共通試験の勉強を始めた。そして、それまで見たこともなかったような英単語を覚え、幾何・代数の復習をしているうちに、鬱から抜け出すことができた。

　なんで私は鬱になったのか。おそらく、当時の私のような、英語も流暢に話せず、アメリカの流儀も心得ていないアジア人が、白人マジョリティの組織に、のほほんと入ってきた時の針の筵状態と、ハリウッド映画やメディアが描く「多様性を愛する国」のイメージとのギャップに打ちのめされたからである。アメリカの主流社会は、アメリカナイズされてない非白人には冷酷だ。私が鬱になったのは、自分の能天気さと無知のせいだが、アメリカを理想化した言説やイメージが、これほど地球の大部分に浸透していなければ、もう少し心の準備もしていたはずである。

　では、なんで私は大学院受験を思いついたのか。それは、自分が全く無価値な存在じゃない、という証明が欲しかったからだと思う。人種や性別や文化背景は変えられないが、アメリカの大学院は、努力すれば、学費が免除されるだけでなく、ティーチング・アシスタントまたはリサーチ・アシスタントとして働くか、奨学金をもらい、生活費を稼ぎながら学位を取得できるのである。私は幸運にも大学院時代、1度も学費を払うことなく、研究と教育の経験を積み、卒業と同時にテニュアトラックの仕事に就くことができた。だから、夫に出会っていなければ、日本でのらりくらりと一生を送っていたであろう私が、こうして研究者の端くれになれたのは、この国の移民としてビシバシ鍛えられたおかげである。

2. 教育と研究のモチベーション

　偶然が重なって今の仕事に就いたわりには、研究も教育も私にとっては

天職だったと思う。そこで、「なんで日本研究するの?」を「なんのために?」という問いに解釈し、自分が研究・教育に関わる上でのモチベーションについて述べたい。私の意欲の源は、簡単に言うと、この国の人々をほんの少し「ハッピー」にすることである。こんなことを言うと、ちょっと頭のネジがゆるい人かと思われそうだ。でも、人文学の目的は「人間とは、人生とは何ぞや」という問いの答えを探求することで、しかも、その探求自体が「目的」なのではなく、人々の暮らしを少し豊かにするための「手段」である(と私は解釈している)のだ。

「ハッピー」が呑気すぎるなら、「この国の、短気な正義感気質をもうちょっと和らげたい」とでも言おうか。なぜ私が、こんな大きなお世話のようなことを感じるかと言うと、自分が4半世紀の間、この人類史上最も裕福な超軍事経済大国の人々を観察していて、国が超金持ちであることと、その国の人々の心が満たされてことは、あまり相関関係がない、という当たり前の事実を常に思い知らされているからである。言うまでもなく、私は日本古典文学がこの国の底辺で貧困や失業で苦しんでいる人々を助けられると思うほどクレイジーではない。私が研究と教育を通してメッセージを伝えたい相手は、狭き門を潜り抜けてこの大学にやって来た、エリート予備軍の学生たちと、アメリカで博士号を取得した同業者、特にフェミニストを自認する日本古典文学研究者である。

「世界の警察」というニックネームにも象徴されるように、アメリカ社会は、善悪に関して白黒はっきりさせることを美徳とする傾向にあり、正義感の強い文化であると言える (Haidt 2013, Henrich 2020)。そのような特徴は、毎年1月に行われる大統領の一般教書演説や、ハリウッド超大作アクション映画などにもよく表れている。そして、その「世界の警察」的姿勢は、アカデミアという、アメリカ発信の言説が圧倒的な影響力を持つ世界にも当てはまる。学生が日本古典文学作品の英訳を読んだ時の反応や、英語のフェミニズム批評には、彼らの正義感が満ち溢れている。正義感そのものは美徳であっても、矛先を誤れば、意味がない。この場合問題なのは、学生や研究者たちが、王朝物語などの中に表象される性や婚姻関係のうち、現代アメリカのリベラルな性道徳基準——抽象概念としての「男女平等」、ジェンダーステレオタイプの否定、成人と未成年間の性行為や明白な同意のない性行為をレイプと断じるような法概念、など——に当てはまらないことを取り上げ、

それに対する批判や、そのような状況に甘んじている（と彼らが考える）女性キャラへの苛立ちを述べる、という現象である。

「文学の解釈は人それぞれ」かもしれないが、「そんな風に読むなら、その作品を読む意味がない」と思える読み方もある。日本人がゴビ砂漠やマチュピチュや万里の長城に出かけて行き、そこにテントを建てて、その中で日本から持参したおにぎりを食べながらスマホで京都の寺社特集番組を観て「やっぱり大原三千院、最高！」と満足して日本に帰国して行ったら、それはその人の勝手かもしれないが、多くの人は「なんで？」って思うのではないだろうか。それと同じように、学生たちが、Netflix のドラマを観るように古典文学作品を読み、内容を消費者目線で評価するのを、「人それぞれ」でOKにしてしまうと、授業を通して新しいことを学ばなくてもよい、ということになってしまう。

例をあげよう。10 世紀ごろに成立した『落窪物語』という、ラブコメ調の作品があるのだが、主人公「落窪の女君」は、継母によって、屋敷の離れにある半地下の部屋に軟禁されている。自分には結婚なんて無縁だろうと思っていた女君だが、あることがきっかけで、道頼という、ハンサムで魅力的な貴族男性と獄中結婚（？）を果たし、道頼の活躍で屋敷を脱出し、紆余曲折の末、「めでたしめでたし」になる。さて、平安王朝物語のお約束として、現代人が好むと好まざると、ヒロインたちはほぼ 100％「奥手」で「純情」である。ということは、主人公の男女が初夜を迎えるシーンでは、女性は驚いたり、震えたり、涙を流したりする。しかしこれは画一的な常套句であり、ほとんどの場合、その趣旨は男性が性犯罪者だということではなく、女性が上品だとか、可愛らしいとか、そういうことを表現しているのである。『落窪物語』の場合、ナレーターはわざわざ「女君は、自分の着ているしょぼい単衣の肌着が、恥ずかしくて泣いた」と説明している。しかし、そんな重要なポイントも、学生たちの頭には入ってこない。「勝手に女性の部屋に入っただけでなく、性行為にまで及ぶなんて、犯罪！」と、みんな口々に言う。そう、その通り。もしこれがフィクションじゃなくて、現実の出来事で、それが現代社会で起きていたら。

当然のことだが、私は学生たちが古典文学作品の読み方を知らなくても、叱ったりしない。知らないことを教えてあげるのが私の仕事である。教える際には、What（情報）よりも、How（方法）を伝授するよう心がけている。

学期中、私が何度も繰り返して言うポイントには以下のようなものがある：「それは、このクラス取らなくても言える事なので、この授業で新しく発見したことを取り入れた発言をしましょう」「そのコメントは物語の内容じゃなくて、現代の常識に関することなので、テクストに戻りましょう」「その解釈を裏付ける証拠は何ですか。その解釈とは矛盾する証拠もたくさんありますよ」「これは一夫多妻制社会だから、『不倫』じゃありません」「女性キャラが夫の薄情を嘆いていることと、作者は一夫多妻制反対、は理論の飛躍が過ぎます」「平安王朝物語には、相思相愛の独身同士の性交渉はあまり描かれません。物語の関心は人間関係につきものの葛藤だから」。

　もう１つ、私が学生に何度も説明するのは、書き手（筆者）と、書き手が想定する読み手（読者）との関係性のことである。よく考えれば（よく考えるまでもなく）、日本古典文学は、21世紀アメリカの大学生のためには書かれていない。通常、書き手と読み手は色々な情報を共有していて、書かなくても分かることは書かないものだ。例えば、姉と弟が、LINE上のやりとりで、大好きなお母さんのことを冗談でからかった場合、他人がそのメッセージだけを読んだら、ただの親不孝な子どもだと思うだろう。漫才のネタも、漫才師の性別・年齢・出身地・容姿などによって、気の利いたジョークにも差別発言にもなりうる。だから、言葉を語彙レベルだけで解釈するのは不毛である。文学作品も同じことである。

　このようなことを授業で話しているうちに、学生たちは日本古典文学のよき読者に成長していく。私が毎回楽しみにしているのは、『蜻蛉日記』の中で、道綱母（厳密に言うと道綱母の分身的ナレーターだが）が、夫・兼家に「病気で心細いからお見舞いに来て」という内容の手紙をもらうシーンである。平安貴族の夫婦は基本的に別居しており、夫が複数の妻のもとに通って来ていた。妻が夫に呼ばれたからと言って、のこのこ出かけて行くと、「召人」という「お手つきの女房」並みの扱いになってしまう。だから、道綱母の女房たちは「奥様、だめです！」と諭すのである。私と学生たちは、「好きな男性に呼ばれた場合、女性はリスクを背負ってでも行くべきか」というディベートで盛り上がる。ご存じのように、『蜻蛉日記』の中では、道綱母は女房たちの制止を振り切って、兼家のもとに駆け付ける。史実か否かは別として、「感情 vs. 理性」で感情が勝つという、私も学生も共感できるエピソードである。

さて、問題は同業者である。私は、他の日本文学研究者（大多数は目上の方々）に向かって、「こういう風に作品を読んだらどうですか？」と言えるほど無神経な人間ではない。しかし、この国の日本古典文学研究の将来に一抹の不安を感じていることも確かである。日本文学の博士号をアメリカの大学院で取得し、王朝物語を専門にする研究者の多くは、学生たちの条件反射的反応とさほど変わらない、作品の現代的・アメリカ的解釈を英語の研究論文・書籍として出版しており（『源氏物語』のフェミニスト・クィア批評だけでもField 1987, Bargen 1997, Sarra 2020, Childs 2010, Jackson 2021 など多数）、学会の発表などを聞いていても、この傾向はこれからも続くと思われる。

3. フェミニズムは誰のため？

アメリカはフェミニズム発祥の地だとよく誤解されている。そのせいか、「マルクス主義・フェミニズム」とか「ブラック・フェミニズム」のように特定しない限り、「フェミニズム」という用語は「アングロ・アメリカン・フェミニズム」（AAF）を自動的に指すのが現状だ。これは由々しき問題である。なぜなら、「フェミニズム」という概念語が、あたかも人類に普遍的な理想であるかのような印象を与えている一方で、内実は特定のグループ（主にエリート白人女性）の権威が尊重される仕組みになっているからである。英語で書かれた日本古典文学のフェミニズム（AAF）批評は、アメリカの物語研究界では、決してニッチなものではなく、主流の一角を占めている。そのような物語批評が、日本文学研究の主流の1つであることと、学術界におけるアメリカの覇権は無関係ではない。しかしながら、自らの言語的・政治的・民族的・経済的特権に自覚的な、物語研究の論考にはお目にかかったことがない。

もし、日本古典文学研究分野の目的が、分析対象となるテクストや、そのような作品が成立した歴史的・政治的・文化的・宗教的背景をより深く理解することなのであれば、テクストをあたかも現代小説か人類学の研究ノートであるかのように読み、そこに描かれた人物やモチーフやプロットが現代西洋の道徳基準に見合わないという理由で批判し、そのような批判を文学批評として認めるという現行の習慣は、分野の目的に反するのではないだろうか。現代アメリカとはまったく違う文化・歴史・宗教・政治的背景のもとで創作された文学を、フェミニズムという自分たちの「真理」と「正義」で裁

く姿勢は、「世界の警察」に通じるものがあるだけでなく、主体的で聡明な自己（＝研究者）が、物語世界の登場人物を、「オリエント」に棲息する不可解な他者・客体として、評価・批判・軽侮・啓蒙・援助するという、近代以来の洋の東西における序列関係を踏襲している。だから、日本文学のフェミニズム批評の逆バージョン、例えば、シェイクスピアの戯曲を、仏教の無常観や儒教の仁・義・礼・智・信に当てはまらないという理由で批判するような日本語の論考は、シェイクスピア研究として認識されないであろう。

　フェミニズムが（暗に）提唱する「男女平等」という概念も、普遍的で自明的な理想だとみなされることが多いが、それは幻想である。過去に実現されてもいないし、目指すべき完成形は常に変動している。だから、誰も「はい、これが『男女平等』のレシピですよ」とは言えないのである。では、仮にこの世に万人が同意する「男女平等」の形が存在したと仮定しよう。その場合、フェミニスト研究者の仕事は、古典文学作品の内容を、その理想に当てはまるように書き変えることなのだろうか。文学は常に「清く正しく」あるべきなのだろうか。「清く正しい」文学は、社会を「清く正しい」ものにしてくれるのだろうか。逆に、「清く正しく」ないものに対する耐性がさらに低下して、社会がますます不寛容になったりしないのだろうか。

4. アメリカ社会の性規範

　ここで質問。日本でもアメリカでも、たいていの人が「アメリカの方が日本より性に対して革新的」だと信じているのは何故だろう。「そんなの当たり前だ」と言う人もいるかもしれない。日本についてほとんど何も知らない学生たちも、「アメリカ：日本＝革新的：保守的＝男女平等：男尊女卑」という二項対立を、堂々と日本文学の読みに取り入れてくる。もちろん、これらは並列的な二項対立ではなく、近代以来の洋の東西における上下関係を継承するものである。つまり、「革新的」「男女平等」が「保守的」「男尊女卑」より優れているからその序列が帰納的に提示されるのではなく、学生たちは大学に入学する以前に、「西洋＞東洋」という図式を内面化しているので、それを演繹的にアメリカと日本に当てはめているのである。同じ特徴であっても、それは肯定的にも否定的にも解釈することが可能なので、このような論理展開は容易であり、私たちが無意識に、日常的に行っていることである。

日本の歴史や文化にあまり馴染みのない人々が、日本の「性の後進国」イメージを共有しており、逆に、アメリカの性規範をサンフランシスコとかニューヨークなどのリベラルな都市のそれと同一視しているのは、私が渡米以前に抱いていたアメリカ像と重なるところが多い。実際は、アメリカには性に保守的な共和党支持の州が多数存在するし、サンフランシスコもニューヨークも、決してユートピアではないのだが、人間は、直感や社会的言説に踊らされる生き物なのだ。エビングハウス錯視が目の錯覚であることを知識として学んでも、２つの円が同じ大きさに見えるようにはならないように、長年空気のように吸ってきた「真実」とか「常識」が、社会的構築物であることを知識として理解していても、先入観や偏見を完全に払拭することは非常に難しい。もちろん、私が言いたいのは、「無理だから諦めよう」ということではなく、先入観を減らすことの難しさを自覚することが、先入観を減らすための第一歩だ、ということである。そして、私たちは、自分たちの条件反射的反応に、より自覚的になり、直感を裏付ける客観的な証拠があるのか、反証はないのか、考える癖をつけなくてはいけない。文学を読むことによって、自分たちの直感を相対化する練習をするのは非常に意味のあることだ。

　「アメリカは性に対して革新的」という人口に膾炙した言説に戻ろう。私は、アメリカ社会における性規範の２大特徴は「過度な男性性」（hypermasculinity）と「性愛嫌悪」（erotophobia）であり、この２つは互いに補完・強化し合う、同じコインの表と裏だと思っている。以下に根拠を挙げる。まず、アメリカ社会は暴力という、男性性を付与された反社会行為に対して、概ね寛容であり、しばしばそれを「勇敢さ」「正義」「強さ」「カッコよさ」などと関連付け、美化する。その一方で、性という、女性性を付与された概念を敵視・罪悪視・タブー視する傾向にある。小学生高学年以上が対象の映画・テレビ番組・ビデオゲームなどでは、戦闘・爆発・破壊シーンは「カッコいいもの」として描かれ、そのような暴力の肯定的な表象には無頓着な親たちも、キスシーンや肌の露出には非常に敏感である。赤ちゃんの裸体も、アメリカではタブーである。また、アメリカ英語の全語彙の中で最も侮辱的な罵倒語は、女性器を指す言葉の１つである。それと対照的に、男女を問わず、度胸があることを褒める表現に "S/he has balls" という言い方もある。くだけた会話の中で、「殺す・殴る・蹴る・破壊する・虐殺する」

などの動詞は「大成功する」を意味する。面接の感触が良かったら "I killed that interview!" などと表現するのである。「暴力団員」を指す gangster は「めちゃくちゃカッコいい人」。スポーツチームの名前としては、「戦闘士」を意味する Fighters、Chargers、Knights、Cavaliers だけでなく、「強盗団・襲撃隊」などの犯罪集団を指す Raiders、Pirates、Buccaneers、Marauders、Vikings などもよく使われる。言うまでもなく、「過度な男性性志向＆性愛嫌悪」という性規範は、アメリカ建国の歴史・宗教・政治的文脈と切り離すことのできないものだ。市民の武装権を憲法で保障している先進国は、世界中でアメリカだけであるし、毎年多数の一般市民が無差別銃撃事件で亡くなっても銃規制は進まず、代わりに今年（2022 年）、女性の「産む・産まない権利の選択」が最高裁で違憲となった。

　もし、アメリカ社会が、性と同じぐらい暴力を嫌悪し、暴力と同じぐらい性を美化することに寛容な社会だったら、無差別銃撃事件で命を落とす無実の一般市民は激減し、セックスワーカーや性的少数者がヘイトクライムの犠牲にはならず、女性器の名前が最も侮辱的な罵倒語にはならず、女性の産む・産まないを選択する権利は保証され続け、性暴力の被害者は堂々と加害者を糾弾でき、リベンジポルノなどというものは、生まれなかったであろう。フェミニズムが暴力よりも性を嫌悪しがちなのは、非常に残念なことである。日本古典文学を専門とするフェミニスト研究者は、物語世界に描かれる性を「これを現代アメリカでやったら性暴力」という反実仮想に執着する一方、『平家物語』などの軍記物語に直接的に描かれる暴力には、まったく無頓着である。もし、フェミニズム（AAF）の妥当性や存在価値が、普遍的な正統性であるなら、フェミニストを自認する日本古典文学研究者は、物語に表象される性と暴力に対する二重基準をどう説明するのだろう。もちろん、私は、物語中の暴力を、性と同様に批判せよと言っているわけではない。古典文学の中の出来事と現代社会の問題を同じ地平で扱うことの不毛さを指摘したいだけである。不毛なだけでは終わらないかもしれない。私たちが、文学に現れる架空の人物の行動などを批判することによって、現代社会に実在する様々な不平等や搾取に対して何か行動を起こしたような錯覚を抱き、目の前にある問題や、困っている隣人に対しては何もしない、という事態を招く恐れもあるのだから。

5. おわりに

　自分の周りの友人や同僚の多くがそうであるように、私も忙しい毎日を送っており、目の前の仕事や家事を一通り片付けたら、1日が終わってしまう。立ち止まって、自分の過去を振り返る機会など、滅多にない。だから、本稿を書くために、過去4半世紀の出来事を回顧することができたのは、よい経験になった。バブル崩壊直後に大学を卒業し、自分にどんな能力があり、どんな風に社会に貢献できるのか見当がつかず、途方にくれていた私が、心から天職だと思える仕事に就けたことは、ありがたいことである。この恵まれた環境も、もとを辿れば、アメリカ社会という過酷な環境で疲弊し、病気になったことが契機になったのである。同じ出来事も、見方によって、幸運にも不運にも解釈できる。だから、何事も二項対立の一方だと決めつけず、複数の解釈を受け入れるのは悪いことではないと思う。

　最後に、「なんで文学研究するの?」という質問の、部分的な答えとして、自分が思う所の文学の存在意義ついて少し述べたい。巷では、数値化したデータを、客観的で信憑性のある学術的なエビデンスとして重宝し、ストーリーを主観的で信憑性がなく、非学術的なものとして軽視する傾向がある。しかしながら、データを数値化するのも、数値を解釈するのも人間であり、様々な分野の学術研究において、日常的にデータ操作が行われているということは、すでに指摘されているところだ（Ritchie 2020）。しかし、仮に「100%客観的で信憑性のあるデータ」というものが存在するとしてもそれは、主観的なストーリーが無価値であるということを意味しない。例えば、天災や人災が起きたとき、その被害を数値化することも必要であるが、同様の災害の再発を防ぐべく、世論や政治を動かすためには、生存者の生の声を聞き、その恐ろしさを人々が共有することが不可欠である。人間は、客観的なデータを客観的なまま、頭の中に保存することはできない。複雑な現象を理解するには、データをストーリーに変換し、理性だけではなく感情というフィルターを通さなくてはならない（ちなみに、記憶力を競うコンテストでは、参加者はランダムな情報をストーリーに仕立てることで、それらを短期記憶からより長期に近い引き出しに入れるのだそうだ）。そう考えると、歴史も神話も宗教も政治も音楽も、視覚芸術すら、一種のストーリーなのである。

　人は、物語（ストーリー）を見聞きすることによって、世界観を形成する。遠い過去や外国の物語は、登場人物と読み手の時間的・物理的な距離を縮め、読み手の世

界観を広げてくれる。もちろん、デマや偏見や差別も、ある種の強力な「物語」である。情報過多の今日、人々は自分の所属する「集団」（tribe）から発信される情報を無批判に受け入れ、別の「集団」の発信する情報を自動的に拒絶しながら、時間や思考に費やすエネルギーを節約している。言うまでもなく、帰属する「集団」の如何でものごとの価値判断をする人々は、思考力が脆弱になり、狭窄視野に陥り、「集団」間の亀裂をさらに深めてしまう。アメリカという、世界の頂点に君臨する社会でエリートコースを進む学生や、すでにエリートとして権力をもつ人々が、遠い過去や異国の文化や、そのような社会で創作された文学に真摯に向き合い、自分たちの特権や正義や真理に脚注をつけ、「世界のリーダー」としての肩の荷を少しばかり軽減できたら、それは人文学の目的に適うことである。自分の教育者・研究者としての仕事が、少しでもその目的に貢献出来たら、と思う次第である。

微妙に場違いな自分を肯定してくれるもの

根無し草たちの日本研究
知の大成としての書物・言語・国境の関係について

ディラン・ミギー（名古屋大学）

ジェイソン・セイバー ＆ シュミット堀佐知 訳

　数年前の夏、僕は、マンハッタンのアッパーイーストサイドからの小さいアパートの書斎に佇んでいた（アッパーイーストサイド「の」ではなく「からの」アパート、と書いた意味は、後述）。

　アパートの案内をしてくれた女性は、その書斎の床から天井までを埋め尽くす書架の、セロファン紙に包まれた本を、手に取って開いてみるよう、勧めてくれた。早速しゃがんで、最下段の辞書・事典類を手に取り、かの指が繰ったであろうページを見てみようとしたところ、セロファン紙から立ち込めた特有の匂いにはっとした。この匂いを嗅いだ瞬間、忘れかけていた記憶が、急に蘇ってきたのだ。プリンストン大学ファイアストン図書館の天井の低い地下書庫に始まり、コロンビア大学 C.V. スター東亜図書館の「サブマリン」、金沢大学時代の指導教官の研究室を埋め尽くした蔵書、そして、僕が学士を取った、閑静で緑豊かなアップステート・ニューヨークにある SUNY の、マーレイ・グレイヤー・ライアン・コレクションと呼ばれる、ピカピカの近代日本文学の英訳の数々まで。あのセロファン紙特有の匂いが僕の脳に伝わってからの数秒間、長年日本関係の書物を読み漁ってきた僕の日本文学研究者としての人生を彩る、懐かしい記憶の欠片が、次から次へと頭に浮かんできたのだ。

　僕は寄木張りの床に片膝をついて、エドワード・サイデンスティッカーとアイヴァン・モリスの作品が目の高さに置かれている棚から、廻り縁すれ

すれの最上段にある三島と安部公房の小説の初版にいたるまで、丁寧に蔵書のタイトルを眺めた。E・デイル・サンダースによる『第四間氷期』の初版は、ちょうど手が届きそうだけど届かない高さに置かれていた。1960年代から70年代にかけて、アメリカ人の文学愛好者にとって、日本文学とは、一体どんな存在であったのだろうかと想像してみた。ティール・グリーンとターコイズの、上品でモダンなハードカバーに包まれた、さまざまな日本文学作品の英訳本を通して、アメリカ人読者が日本のイメージを形成しつつあった時代のことである。

　僕が、それらの本を熱心に眺めてるのを見て、案内人の女性は、僕の出身地を尋ねた。「もともとは、ニューヨークです」と僕が答えると、彼女はにっこりして、身振りだけで僕にこう促した——どうぞ、こちらへ。今あなたが立っている方ではなく、こちら側、そう、本棚の反対側の端までおいでください。そして、外国風のラジエーターの隣に並んでいる、この背もたれが傾斜した椅子の所まで、移動して来てください。

　女性は、次に、「どうぞ、おかけになって」と、声に出して勧めてくれたが、僕は、笑顔で断った。そして、さっきまで日本海で泳いだところで、まだズボンの下に穿いている水着が湿っているかもしれないし、そのために椅子を台無してしまってはいけませんから、と説明した。

　「どうぞ」と彼女は言った。「どうか、お気になさらず、おかけになって下さい。キーン先生も、きっと、そうおっしゃったはずですから」。

1.「根無し草」という感覚

　そろそろ、この話の背景についてちゃんと説明すべき頃だろう。冒頭で述べたように、僕が訪れた場所は、アッパー・イースト・サイド「からの」アパートであって、アッパー・イースト・サイド「の」アパートではない。実は、このアパートは、日本文学の大権威にして名翻訳家としても名高い、ドナルド・キーン博士が住んでいた、マンハッタンのアパートの内装をそのまま移築したものなのだ。鴨長明が天災を避けて、かの方丈庵を解体して京都山麓に建て直したように、10年前、ドナルド・キーン宅も、新潟県柏崎市の小さな住宅街の建物の一角に、引っ越してきたのだ。このアパートは、色々な意味ですごいし、実は、柏崎という土地とのギャップもすごい。もし、読者のみなさんが柏崎を知らないのであれば、まず、潮風が吹き付け

る、海沿いの小さいを町を思い浮かべてほしい。次に、その町の日本海側には漁船用停泊場、内陸側には機械部品工場がずらっと並び、その両端の間を大型トラックの隊列が、1日中ひっきりなしに往復している様子を想像してみてほしい。柏崎というのは、そんな町だ。田中角栄式政治恩顧主義の全盛期に、町中に網目状に建設された、今はもう潮錆びた商店街を突き抜けて伸びた道路が、柏崎の目抜き通りだ。そこには、カラオケ・キャバレーや、夫婦経営の小さな洋品店や理髪店などが並ぶ。パナソニック専門の家電製品店のショーウィンドウには、1992年に発売されたファックス機の宣伝に使われた、色褪せた10代の松嶋菜々子の等身大切り抜きが、当時のまま飾られている。

　一体なぜ、かのドナルド・キーンが、自宅をこの無名の田舎町に移築しようなどという、突拍子もないことを思い立ったのだろうと、誰もが不思議に思うだろう。でも、その理由は、秘密でも謎でもなく、今でも柏崎のあちこちに、ひび割れた歩道のタイルや、土台が歪んでしまったプレハブの建物として残っている。2007年、柏崎の海岸17キロ沖で発生した、マグニチュード6.6の中越沖地震である。その余波で起きた土砂崩れが、市内の300棟以上の建物（そのほとんどは瓦屋根の古い家屋）を飲み込み、1000人以上の怪我人と11人の死者を出すほどの惨事となった。そして、その数週間後、柏崎市役所の（おそらく文化・観光を担当する部署）の電話が鳴った。それは、まだまだ市の職員たちが、瓦礫の撤去や建築物の再建に追われ、てんやわんやだった頃のことで、この時、たまたま電話を取った人は、どんなにか困惑したことだろう。なぜなら、電話をかけてきたのは、米国コロンビア大学名誉教授・日本文学の大権威のドナルド・キーン博士で、そのキーン博士が、14世紀に即身仏となった、弘知法印という高名なお坊さんの伝記を基にした、江戸時代の説教浄瑠璃の復活上演を柏崎で行いたい、と申し出てきたのだから。その『弘知法印御伝記』という古浄瑠璃は、1685年（貞享2）以来上演されていない幻の作品で、しかも、弘知法印のミイラ化した遺体が、柏崎から車で40分の新潟県長岡市の寺に安置されているというのが、柏崎での復活上演という提案の説明だった。僕の想像では、その職員は絶句して、長い沈黙のあと、やっとこう返事をしただろう：「…こ、古浄瑠璃、ですか？」。たとえキーン博士が、柏崎の人々はきっと喜んでくれるでしょう、と太鼓判を押してくれたとしても、その電話口の職員が、幻の浄瑠璃と柏崎市役所と

その他もろもろの繋がりを、その場でちゃんと把握できたかは定かではない。

　その繋がりというのは、もちろん、「リバイバル」（復活・復興）というコンセプトである。1963年、長年行方不明だった、『弘知法印御伝記』の絵入り浄瑠璃本が、大英博物館で発見されたものの、上演までにはいたっておらず、本作の復活上演は、被災地・柏崎の復興を促し、この地にさまざまな希望をもたらすことを約束するものであった。そして、2009年6月、新潟生まれの三味線奏者である、5代目・鶴澤浅造（越後角太夫）の協力を得て、上演会は現実のものとなった。この、被災2年目を迎えようとしていた柏崎での大イベントは、地方メディアだけでなく、全国の新聞・テレビ・雑誌などで絶賛された。さらに、よく知られているように、その2年後の2011年、キーンは、東日本大震災をきっかけに、日本人として日本の人々とともに暮らし、日本で余生を送ることを決意。その翌年、日本への帰化が正式に認められた（日本は二重国籍を認めていないので、同時に米国籍を喪失）。

　その頃までには、キーンのアパートをニューヨークから柏崎へ移築する計画が、着々と進んでいた。2011年8月を皮切りに、アパートそのものにくっついていない物（書籍・絵画・花瓶・絨毯・オットマン・暖房器具など）と、真鍮製のドアノブのように、くっついていても取り外せる物、総計2500点以上のアイテムが柏崎に空輸され、それらがひとつひとつ、マンハッタンのキーン宅を厳密に再現すべく、「新居」に再配置されたのだ。「新居」というのは、「ドナルド・キーン・センター柏崎」の2階に設置された「復元展示室」である。この一大事業に要する莫大な費用は、スーパーのお菓子売り場でおなじみの、ブルボン社の寄付によって賄われた。柏崎に本社を置くブルボンは、1923年の関東大震災直後に設立された製菓会社で、その使命は、自然災害などの非常時に非常食として活躍する、高栄養・高品質のビスケットを製造することであった。関東大震災という、近代日本でも異例の大災害を背景とした同社の成り立ちを考えると、キーンが中部沖地震・東北大震災という、2つの天災を契機として起こした行動と文化的貢献に、彼らが賛同し、援助を買って出てくれたのも、納得が行くことかもしれない。

　現在、「ドナルド・キーン・センター柏崎」では、来館者への特典として、復元展示室の「居間」から階段でアクセスできるギフトショップで、ブルボン社の全商品を提供している。そこで、日本文学ファンは、センターのロ

ゴ付小袋に入った「アルフォート」という濃厚なチョコレートや、「ルマンド」というサクサクのクレープクッキーを味わうことができる。ルマンドを一口食べた人は、アメリカが生んだ日本文学の最高権威と、日本が生んだ欧風クッキーの大人気メーカーのコラボが、意外に名案だと気づくはずだ──これは、僕が保証します。

　さて、読者のみなさんは、僕がただ、学者・地方自治体・製菓会社という、世にも不思議なトリオが一丸となり、この愉快で奇妙な展示を奇跡的に実現させたことを喜んでいるだけだと思っているかもしれない。でも、そう結論付ける前に、この時、柏崎のドナルド・キーン宅を訪れた経験が、なぜ僕にとって非常に印象深い出来事だったのか、そして、なぜ僕が、この経験を本稿のテーマにしたのか、説明させてほしい。

　それは僕が、「ドナルド・キーン・センター柏崎」の見学を終え、建物の外に出て、数秒間歩き、柏崎市という現実世界に戻ってくるまでの間のことだった。なぜか突然、自分が「ここ」にも「そこ」にも存在しないような、強烈な感覚に襲われたのだ。もちろん、物理的には、僕は確かに、セミの鳴き声が耳を突き刺す灼熱の新潟にいたのだが、本当は、自分が柏崎には存在していないような、そんな気がしたのだ。あれは、映画を観終えて、映画館を出てから現実に引き戻されるまでの、「軽い混乱状態」に似ていたかもしれない。まだ耳に残っているサウンドトラックが感情を揺らし続け、2時間ものあいだ目を釘付けにして、主人公に自分を重ね合わせつつ、培い、維持した心理状態が、突然その拠り所を失った、あの気分。そして、その後に残されたのは、自分もいつか、日本文学の権威になれるかもしれない、という幻想だけだ。いや、それだけではなかった。馬鹿げたことかもしれないが、僕は、ドナルド・キーンのアパートにいたとき、まるで自分が、自宅でくつろいでいるかのような気持ちになっていたのだ。彼の布張りの椅子に腰かけ、ハドソン川に沈む夕日と、ラベンダーと赤紫に染まった流れがところどころ混じり合う水面を眺めながら…。その景色は、実を言うと、窓を覆っている日よけのスクリーンに、かなりリアルにデジタル印刷されていたものだったのだけど。そのスクリーンの反対側に広がっていた、実際の柏崎の景色は、おそらく、誰かのハイゼットフラットベッドの軽トラックと、その隣で、広げた古新聞に積み上げられ、天日干しされている海草だったと思う。この地域は、「えご草」と呼ばれる赤紫色の海藻で知られているが、価格規

制がないため、海岸近くに住む一般市民の人々が、隣近所と協力してそれを採取し、激しい価格競争に勝つべく、しのぎを削っているのだ。「えご草」を元手に一攫千金を狙う話も悪くないけど、僕はそんなリアルな現実はしばし忘れ、ハドソン川の幻想に耽ることにした。

　この、「えご草」と「えご草色のハドソン川」のギャップは、「復元展示室」に関する僕の最後のポイント──やるせない現実──に繋がってくる。それは、つまり、柏崎と言う地方自治体が、書斎の壁一面を埋め尽くすキーンの蔵書（と、それらが象徴する偉大な業績）に、「新居」を提供してくれたという文化的遺産は、残念ながら、柏崎に住んでいる人々の生活とはほとんど接点がない、という現実だ。僕がそのことに気づいた時に感じた衝撃は、日本の某人気旅行サイトに掲載された、「ドナルド・キーン・センター柏崎」を特集した記事の見出しでもある、「何故、柏崎に？」という執筆者の不躾な質問に、見事に要約されている。ドナルド・キーンが自身の研究者人生を捧げた学術書や翻訳の数々は、同時に僕が過去30年間に渡って読み続け、何度も読み返したものであるが、柏崎とこれらの研究成果との繋がりは、「柏崎とサクサクのクレープクッキー」とか、「柏崎と地震」のそれと同じぐらい恣意的なものだった。例えば僕が、「ドナルド・キーン・センター柏崎」の近所にある「ウエルシア薬局」や「ヴィーム・スタジアム」というパチンコ店に行って、そこにいる地元住民にアンケートを取ったとしよう。その回答者の中で、ドナルド・キーンが浄瑠璃『国性爺合戦』を英訳し、その芝居を海外に紹介したことを知っていて、1秒以上その意義について考えたことのある人は、おそらく皆無だろう。

　英語で書かれた日本研究の成果は、何のために存在するのだろう。日本に住む、一般の人々、特に地震などで被災した人々にとって、どのような意味があるのだろう。僕の頭にあったのは、そんな疑問だった。実は、キーンのアパートが移築された場所が、新潟ではなく、もっと別の場所だったら、このような哲学的な問いに、頭を悩ませることはなかったかもしれない。実は、僕は義理の家族が、柏崎とはそう離れていない川口町という所に住んでいるため、昔からこの辺の土地に縁があったのである。そして、川口を訪れ、義理の家族と一緒に時間を過ごすうちに、僕は地元の価値観や振る舞いを吸収した。だからこそ、柏崎の人々が、「ドナルド・キーン・センター柏崎」に多少なりとも違和感を覚えたり、またはもっと辛辣に言えば、この

土地に住む人々の生活とは無縁の、お偉いさんの自己満足事業だと感じたりしていることに、僕はうすうす気づいていた。でも、その地元の人々の気持ちを強く実感したのは、「ドナルド・キーン・センター柏崎」での見学を終え、振り返って燦然と輝く建物を見た直後に、正門から数メートルしか離れていないナス畑――いわば、柏崎の「素顔」――が視界に入ってきた瞬間だ。その時、この２つの空間が、まったく相互に相容れない隔絶された世界で、僕はどちらにも完全には根を下ろしていない、根無し草のような存在だと気づいたのだ。

2. 壁の中の別世界

　初めて「ドナルド・キーン・センター柏崎」を訪れた日、あの「復元展示室」という空間が醸し出す、不思議な「根無し草感」というものの存在に気づいた。あの日以来僕は、日本の大学で教員・研究者として生計を立てている自分の微妙な立場の比喩として、「根無し草」であることを、受け入れられるようになってきた。いや、単なる比喩とは言い切れないかもしれない。僕は今まさに、名古屋大学の自分の研究室でこれを書いているのだが、床から天井まで、10メートルの壁を埋め尽くしてそびえる８段建ての書架の背表紙を見れば、その約半数は、英語で書かれた書籍だとすぐ分かる。ここにある本のうち、数箱相当は、僕が2011年４月に名古屋大学に就任した時に、ニューヨークから持ってきたものだ。僕の研究室の本と、キーンの書斎にある本は重なるものも多く、時には同じ小説の同じ版で、同じ順番で本棚に並んでいたりする。時折、それらのページを繰って、引用されている文献の情報や、授業で使う箇所を探したりしていると、現在進行形の物理的な手触りも感じつつ、過去の自分が行ったまったく同じ動作を、体が覚えていて、それを筋肉反射にまかせ、反復している感じもする。同じ本を同じような動作で扱っていても、前回とは違う新しい発見があり、それを新たに学生たちに教えてあげることができる場合も多い。そんな時、戦後以来積み上げられてきた、英語による日本文学研究と日本文学作品の英訳が、いかにこの日本文学という分野の、主要な一部分を占めているかということに、改めて気づかせられるのだ。

　だからと言って、僕は、これらの英語で書かれた日本文学の必読書を、無邪気に称賛している訳ではない。例えば、名古屋大学で、留学生たちを対象

に日本文学や日本文化のコースを教え始めた最初の数年間、英語だけで教えるように、という大学からの要請を遵守せず、原文にチャレンジしてみたいという意欲的な日本語学習者や、英語で日本文学について議論してみたいと思っているけど英訳は読みたくないという勇敢な他学部の日本語母語話者には、日本語の文献を読ませたり、日本語で解説をしたりもした。留学生だからと言って、注釈や現代語訳付きの『方丈記』というオプションは与えず、ドナルド・キーンの『Account of My Hut』を学生に読ませて、お茶を濁せばよいとは思えなかったのである。また、英語で行われる授業は、キャンパスを内側から国際化するだろうという、大学側の大きな期待を背負っていたものの、実際は、その逆の現象を引きおこした。つまり、英語だけで教えるプログラムを、それ以外のプログラムから断絶することにより、日本出身の学生と、そうでない学生の間に溝ができてしまうのだ。僕の担当している授業の様子は、「日本の大学に移築されたアメリカの大学のミニチュア版」という点で、柏崎のキーンのアパートに通じるものがある。例えば、僕がAというテクストの英訳を教えている時、その隣とか、2部屋先の教室を覗けば、同僚がAを日本語の原文で教えているかもしれないが、物理的に近くにいても、同じテクストを読んでいても、その2つの学生グループは、互いに交じり合うことがほとんどない。留学生たちは、物理的には、日本の大学に存在しているのに、日本の大学という空間に、しっかりと根を下ろしてはいないのである。

　本稿の残りの部分では、僕がここまで素描してきた「根無し草感」というテーマについて、モノとしての本をフラットな存在論的観点から眺めつつ、もう少し深く掘り下げてみたいと思う。本というのは、それ以外のモノ・人・場所とペアになると、びっくりするほど変テコな組み合わせを形成しうる物体なのである。それから、物質としての書籍やその内容だけでなく、本の物理的な所在（どんな場所にどんな本が配置されているか）やその空間的・時間的移動も同時に観察すると、日本研究という分野に関わる、知の形成プロセスが非常によく見えてくる。それはさまざまな政治性を帯びた、純粋無垢ではないもので、僕自身、必然的にこのプロセスの一端を担っているのだが。

　以下に述べることは、僕が名古屋大学に就任する前と就任してからの、日本文学研究者・大学教員としての経験も参考にしている内容だが、日本のアカデミアにおける我が根無し草性をちゃんと解説するには、ユーモアと少し

ばかりの自虐性を必要とするので、なにとぞご理解を。

3. 図書館と「！」事件と根無し草感

　2011年4月、名古屋大学に就任して取り掛かった最初の任務の1つは、日本文学に関する英語の図書館の蔵書を点検し、追加すべき書籍——それは、実際にたくさんあった——のリストを作ることだった。僕は小さなモールスキンの手帳とペンを手に、著者名・タイトル・出版年など、かなり具体的な情報を記録することを予想しつつ、仕事にとりかかった。しかし、僕を待ち構えていたのは、まったく予想だにしていない状況だった。それは、蔵書の一部が、「留学生用図書」として、それ以外の書籍（「非・留学生用図書」と言うべき？）とは別の開架に置かれていた、ということである。僕は手帳を開き、そこに巨大な「！」を書いた。もちろん、日本の市立図書館や他の大学図書館でも、同じような分類がまかり通っているのを知っていた。「外国人用図書」という滑稽なジャンルに分類された、ほぼ「英語で書かれた本」を指す書籍が、日本語の本（これは時々 Nipponese Books ／ Literature という馬鹿馬鹿しい英語のジャンル名として分類されている）とは区別して開架に置かれているのである。おそらく、このような分類法は、利用者の便宜とか、悪意のない理由で考案されたのだろうと思う。しかしながら、見るからに外国出身である人々にとって、「外国人用図書」コーナーに足を運ぶほど恥ずかしいことはないという事実を、日本中の司書にみなさんに知っていただきたい。そのような図書の分類法は、「外国人は、自分が日本語で書かれた本を読めるようにはならないという事実に屈した人々だ」とか、もっとタチが悪い場合、「外国人は、英語で書かれた書物の優位性を当然視し、英語以外の言語で書かれた本には興味のない人々だ」と決めつけているのも同然なのである。根拠がこのどちらであっても、またはそれ以外の理由であっても、あの「外国人用図書」というサインは、日本出身じゃない人々の自尊心を傷つけるものなのだ。この馬鹿げた図書分類法は、僕が2011年4月の「！」事件から数年後に柏崎のキーンの書斎を訪れた際に、とても自然でアットホームな気持ちになったことと関連がある。つまり、展示されていたキーンの蔵書は、セロファン紙で包まれ、見学者が本棚に寄りかかるのを防ぐスタンションが書架の前に設置されていたものの、少なくとも日本の図書館に行った時に感じる、外国人に対する先入観に気分を害されることはなかった。どの本も手に

取って開くことができ、知らない第三者によって、僕の一挙一動に関する文化的・政治的解釈を押し付けられることがなかったからである。

　もちろん、名古屋大学中央図書2階の、あまり人目に付かず、落ち着いた一角に留学生専用図書コーナーを作った人に悪意はなかったはずだ。それどころか、ユートピア的とも言えるようなイメージを思い描いて、そんな企画を思いついたのだと思う。美しく整えられたソテツが見渡せる、図書館内の癒し系スポットに、世界各国からやって来た学生たちが集まり、『ワイアード』のような英語雑誌の最新号を捲りながら、知的で興味深い会話を楽しむ、活気に満ちた文学サロン、とか、そんなところだろう。そのような大学側の意向が見て取れるのは、利用者のグループが好きなようにアレンジできるモジュール式シート（立体クッション）12個が、その特別スペースのために、新しく購入されていたことだ。残念ながら、名古屋大学中央図書館の「留学生用図書」に選ばれた書籍は、村上春樹のデビュー小説と第2作目の英訳、アーサー・ゴールデンの『サユリ』、森田昭夫が1988年に出版した自伝『メイド・イン・ジャパン』などに代表される、およそ知的な会話の契機にはなり得そうにない、思わず目が点になってしまうコレクションであった。

　少しがっかりした僕は、新入生のための基礎的な本がちゃんと揃っているのか確認すべく、図書館の他のエリアを探索することにした。4階の開架に到着し、誰からも忘れ去られた本たちが並ぶ暗い通路を頭に思い浮かべ、角を曲がると、そこで僕の足はピタッと止まり、手に持っていた手帳を落としそうになるほど、驚いてしまった。目の前に現れた日本文学関係の蔵書が、大学時代に慣れ親しんだ書物の数々（マーレイ・ライアン先生が、SUNYの中央図書館に作ってくださった日本文学コレクション）と、ほぼそっくり同じものだったからだ。思わず、エドワード・サイデンスティッカーの『Snow Country』（1956年に出版された、『雪国』の英訳）の初版に手を伸ばした。1996年にニューヨークを襲ったブリザードの真っ最中、SUNYの図書館で、喬松の並木を見下ろす巨大なパノラマ窓の前に座り、この作品を初めて読んだ記憶が蘇ってきた。僕はさっそく扉ページを開き、この本を担当した、明らかに仕事熱心な写植さんが施した装飾が、ちゃんとそこにあることを確認した。それは、雪華模様（＊）をアレンジして、あたかも雪がひらひら舞い落ちているかように見せるという、心憎い演出だ。次に、その雪華模様は、僕が越後湯

沢を訪ね、『雪国』の執筆中に川端康成が滞在していた宿屋を探して、歩き回っていた時の記憶を思い起こさせてくれた。その旅は、『Snow Country』を初めて読んだ時から、ちょうど2年後の冬のこと。僕は、偶然にも、越後湯沢から2駅の川口で生まれ育った女性と結婚し、その妻と一緒に、この小説の舞台である〈雪国〉を訪れていたのである。これは、書物と出会ったり、愛読書を読み返したりすることが、時に僕たちの人生という物語に、予言的なサブプロットを挿入してくれるという、不思議な事実を改めて思い出させてくれる出来事だった。

『Snow Country』のページをめくっていると、他にも次々と色んな記憶が蘇ってきた。この英訳を読み終え、どうしても原文が読みたくなったこと。数時間かけて、電車でアップステートからニューヨーク市のグランドセントラル駅まで行き、雪と霙の混じる中、ロックフェラーセンター内の紀伊國屋書店までの数ブロックを歩いたこと。新潮文庫版の『雪国』が1冊売れ残っていたこと。それが、定価の2倍以上で売られていたこと。初めて見る日本の文庫本のあまりの小ささと、あの小説が、この薄いペーパーバックに凝縮されている事実に感動したこと。しかし、無味乾燥な表紙のデザイン（青の背景に、雨の筋が描かれているだけ）と、英訳版のような写植技術を応用した演出がなくて落胆したこと。帰りの電車の中で、窓の結露に指を走らせ、人間の瞳が、『雪国』に書かれているほどはっきりとガラスに映るものなのか、実験を試みたこと。僕が指で作ったばかりのファインダーを覗いてみると、そこに現れたのは、僕自身の瞳ではなく、タリータウン郊外のトンネルの内側に描かれた、男根の落書きらしきものだったこと。それを見て、思わず笑ってしまったこと。

僕の日本語の先生だったマーレイ・ライアン先生は、親切にも、僕を毎週オフィスに呼んで下さり、僕たちはそこで一緒に川端の作品を原文で読んだものだ。ライアン先生が担当していた学部生の授業では、文学作品はすべて英訳を使うことになっていたので、原文を読みたがっていた僕を、先生は特別に個人指導して下さったのである。僕が丸1日かけて入手した『雪国』ではなく、『伊豆の踊子』から始めましょう、と先生がおっしゃった時は、ちょっとがっかりしたのだが。個人授業の中で、ライアン先生はよく、ドナルド・キーンの指導の下で日本文学を学んでいた、コロンビア大学院時代の体験談を聞かせてくれた。時間が経つにつれ、ライアン先生の解説の

多くは、キーン先生のゼミを受講した時のノートに基づいているのだと気づいた。例えば、ある時、僕が「雨足」という言葉を理解できなかった時、ライアン先生は、1960年代の初期にとったと思われる、緻密なノートの集大成を取り出し、その中から「雨足」についての長い説明を見つけて、解説してくれた。それが唐詩も出てくる「雨脚」という古典中国語から派生した言葉で、英語では正確に表せない、非常に特殊な雨の降り方を表現していると知って、僕はとても感心した。しかし、それ以上に驚いたのは、ライアン先生が、大学院時代のノートを30年近くも保存していて、しかも自分のオフィスのすぐに手の届く場所に、きちんと整理された状態で保管していたことだった。まるで、ドナルド・キーンのゼミと、ライアン先生の個人授業を隔てる物理的・時間的な距離が、大した問題ではないかのように。ライアン先生が、生き生きと、そして示唆に富むやり方で「雨足」について解説して下さった時、僕自身、1960年代のドナルド・キーンのゼミを受講しているかように感じた。これは、教師から学生への口伝という、文学に関わる知の継承の昔ながらの伝統を垣間見る経験だった。

　思いがけず、名古屋大学図書館の「秘蔵書」の棚の前で、小1時間も過去の回想に耽ってしまった。そして、まだ書籍リスト作りの方が全然進んでいないことに気づき、思いつくまま、20〜30冊ほどのタイトルを書き留めて、手帳をズボンの後ろポケットに滑り込ませた。そして、なぜだかよく分からないけど、これらの日本文学関係のコレクションをいじらず、僕をさまざまな時間的・地理的空間への魔法の旅に誘ってくれた現在の姿まま、温存しておけたらいいのに、と思った。しかし、そのようなノスタルジックな感傷は、新入生たちにとって、まったく有益ではないし、せっかくの蔵書が、滅多に日の目を見ないという現状が、よくないことも分かっていた。これらの本が、新たな読者と出会い、息を吹き返すためには、図書館の片隅で、貴重な骨董品のように保存されるのではなく、定期的な更新と調整を与えられる、現在進行形のコレクションでなくてはならないのだ。

4. 結論：日本文学はどのように世界に伝わったか

　ここまで、自分の過去を振り返りつつ、思う所を述べてきたが、「根無し草」という比喩に関わる、最後のコメントで本稿を締めくくりたいと思う。「ドナルド・キーン・センター柏崎」には、キーンが長年に行ってきた、さ

まざまな講演会の録画を鑑賞することができる小劇場が設置されている。その録画の中には、2012年2月11日に名古屋大学で行われた、「日本文学はどのように世界に伝わったか」という講演会のビデオも含まれている。それは、多かれ少なかれ、キーンが過去に行ったスピーチの焼き直しで、彼が60年間の研究人生において出版した、すべての回顧録・新聞記事・思考実験の記事・批評などを部分的につなぎ合わせ、リメイクしたものだ。それなのに、このような文化センターの小劇場という空間を媒介して鑑賞すると、このスピーチは突如として、厳粛な雰囲気を醸し出す。18歳の時にニューヨークの書店でアーサー・ウェイリーによる『源氏物語』の英訳と出会い、研究者人生がスタートした、というおなじみの逸話から始まり、その後、若き日のキーンが、いかにして日本語と日本文学を学んで行ったのか、という周知のストーリーが、改めて、厳かな畏敬の念を感じさせるものに生まれ変わる。

　実を言うと僕は、2012年のあの日、超満員の豊田講堂でこの講演を生で聴くことのできた1人だ。そして、会場の雰囲気は、ビデオで観るよりもはるかに生き生きとした、高揚感あふれるものだった。キーンは、前年の東日本大震災をきっかけに、日本に帰化し、同時に米国籍を失ったため、当時、一躍マスコミの注目を浴びていた。友人や同僚との会話を通じて分かったのは、多くの日本人（キーンの作品を読んだことのない人たちを含む）が、彼の行動に、深い敬意と感謝の念を抱いているということだった。当日、豊田講堂のメインホールの外には、テーブルが2つ並べてあった。1つには、日本文学の英訳や研究書など、キーンの著作の数々が展示され、もう1つには、彼の新刊が堆く平積みされ、それらは観客が購入できるものであった。入場を待って並んでいると、僕の少し前に、僕の文学の授業をとっている学部生が立っていた。大学全体の抽選会で、このイベントの入場券を獲得したその学生は、振り返って、無邪気な笑顔で「本物のドナルド・キーンを見ることができるなんて、信じられませんよね！」と言った。返事の代わりに、僕は、ただ微笑んだ。

　講演中、僕は、ドナルド・キーンのオーラや存在感に、と言うよりは、むしろ、彼の馴染み深い身振りや仕草に感動した。キーンがこの講演のために名古屋を訪れるまで、彼に会ったこともなかったし、日本語で話すのを聞いたこともなかったが、実は、僕は長年に渡り、勝手に想像したキーンの声と

話し方で、彼の著作や英訳を読んでいた。だから、彼が、ニューヨーク州に住む僕の親戚を彷彿させる、ニューヨーク訛りの日本語を話すのを聞いて、とても驚いた。でも、彼の話し方は、耳に心地よかった。また、マーレイ・ライアン先生の文学講義を思い出させる、微妙な言い回しや、雰囲気を感じ取ることができ、胸が熱くなった。だから、豊田講堂の満員の観客が一斉に立ち上がり、キーンに長い長い拍手を贈った時、僕のスタンディング・オベーションは、その日の講演への感謝だけでなく、30年の歴史に纏わる個人的な理由も含め、感謝の意を表明していたのだと思う。ドナルド・キーンが僕に教えてくれたこと——それは、日本に住んでいて、微妙に場違いな自分がそこにいても、堂々と日本のことを学んでもいいんだ、ということ。そして、自分が、時に根無し草みたいな存在だと感じてもいいんだ、ということ。

おわりに

シュミット堀佐知

　日米の日本研究者によるバイリンガル・エッセイ集を構想した時、友人で本書の寄稿者でもある江口啓子氏にメールを送り、どの出版社に企画を持ち込むべきか尋ねた。すると、すぐに文学通信の岡田編集長の連絡先を教えてくれた。啓子さん、仲人役をどうもありがとう。

　また、本書を編纂するにあたり、私の書いたエッセイを読み、忌憚のないダメ出しと助言をくれたのはセツ・シゲマツ氏である。今回の企画でシゲマツ氏と協働できたことは、私の研究者としての成長につながったと思う。セツ、愛の鞭をどうもありがとう。

　忙しい中、この本を一緒につくって下さった、日本研究者仲間の8人と文学通信・編集長の岡田圭介氏と編集者の渡辺哲史氏にも、深い感謝の念を表明したい。みなさん、本当にどうもありがとうございました。

　最後に、残念なお知らせがある。「アメリカ人障害者として日本で暮らすこと」を寄せてくれたマーク・ブックマン氏は、本書の完成を待たず、2022年12月16日、帰らぬ人となった。マークと最後に会ったのは、2022年の8月である。その日私は、ゆりかもめの「お台場海浜公園」駅に降り立ち、東京オリンピック・パラリンピックから1年が経過してすっかり閑静になった駅周辺を見回しながら、彼のアパートを訪れ、「スプリングボード・ジャパン」ウェブサイト上での企画について打ち合わせをした。窓を閉め切っているにも関わらず、蝉の声がアパート一面に鳴り響き、屋内で座っ

ているだけでも汗が滲んでくるような猛暑日だったことと、マーク、カメラマンのピーター・ウェルド氏、マークの介助者であるネパール人男性と私の4人の打ち合わせが、英語と日本語の混ざった会話で行われたことをよく覚えている。まさか、この日が、マークとの最後の対面になるとは、夢にも思っていなかった。この日から約4か月後、マークは31歳の若さでこの世を去ってしまった。さまざまな人々の期待と尊敬と憧れを背負い、研究・教育・社会運動のすべてにおいて、若きリーダーとして活躍し、家族と友人たちに深く愛されていた彼の急逝は、悔やんでも悔やみきれない。

Why Study Japan?

SCHMIDT-HORI, Sachi

SASAKI, Takahiro
HIBI, Yoshitaka
EGUCHI, Keiko
BOOKMAN, Mark
SHIGEMATSU, Setsu
SUEMATSU, Misaki
LOWY, Christopher
MCGEE, Dylan

なんで日本研究するの？

Bungaku-Report Co.,Ltd.

Preface

Sachi Schmidt-Hori

1. What is "Japan Studies"?

When I first suggested, for the title of this book, *Nande Nihon kenkyū suru no?*, a question that can be parsed as either "Why do you do Japan Studies?" or "Why do you study Japan?," my editor said that *Nihon kenkyū* (Japan Studies) might not ring a bell for many readers in Japan. Intrigued, I called up my childhood friend, F, and asked her if she had ever heard of the term and what she thought of it. F, who was born and raised in Japan and who rarely encounters academic discourse, candidly replied that she had never heard the term and that it was a strange expression that was "too broad and too vague." After I peppered her with several follow-up questions, I came to realize some interesting "facts" about the term *kenkyū* (though I don't know to what extent I can generalize my discovery).

Apparently for F, *kenkyū* (scholarly research) is a comically grandiose word. She explained that the term signifies something akin to "a scientific endeavor to uncover surprising truths about a highly unusual and mysterious object, organism, or phenomenon." It calls to mind the excavation of archaeological ruins or observations of cells, membranes, and microorganisms under the electron microscope. For this reason, when she heard the phrase *Nihon kenkyū*, the first thing that came to her mind was "What part of Japan would anyone collect for what purpose and how is that person going to analyze that specimen of Japan?" So I asked F what she thought of the term *Japan sutadiizu* (Japan Studies). To my surprise, this Japanized English phrase prompted her to utter, "Oh, I totally get *that*. That sounds like a serious academic field!" Clearly, *Japan sutadiizu* perfectly matched F's idea of *kenkyū*, that is, a serious scholarly endeavor to unearth intriguing truths about something very mysterious: Japan. Needless to say, in this case, those who undertake the endeavor must be Westerners.

Truth be told, the reason why *Nihon kenkyū* is an uncommon term is simple. In Japan, nearly all scholars in the humanities and social sciences are Japan specialists, whether they are art historians of *ukiyoe* or sociologists of *karōshi*. Therefore, the label *Nihon kenkyū* is "too broad and vague" and hence not functional in Japan's academia. Put another way, the reason why "Japan Studies" functions as a signifier outside Japan is that those who specialize in Japan are few and far between. That said, the vast majority of the nations in the world are typically studied as part of a region, such as the Middle East, the Caribbean, North Africa, Eastern Europe, and so on. Considering this, it is nothing short of a miracle, no matter what the reason may be, that there are universities around the world that grant doctorates in Japan-related disciplines, that there are academic associations and conferences of Japan Studies, and that there exist academic journals that specialize in Japan Studies.

It goes without saying that the interdisciplinary field of area studies, including Japan Studies, emerged against the historical backdrop of colonialism, the Cold War, and the West's maintenance of international security vis-à-vis its political adversaries. Due to the unsavory origin of the field, there have been many critiques of how the area paradigm shapes knowledge production. Nevertheless, it would be a mistake to abolish area studies. Instead, we must focus our efforts on reforming other more insidious assumptions that underlie our field. Our notions of the universal, the scholarly, and the rational are largely shaped by the subjectivity of heterosexual, able-bodied, well-educated, middle class, adult Caucasian males, whose native tongues are Indo-European languages, and who align themselves with Judeo-

Christian morality. By contrast, the subjectivities of women and minorities are rejected as being too particular, marginal, emotional, personal, unscholarly, and so on. Therefore, even if area studies, which occupies only a marginal part of academia, were abolished, the more serious contradictions and inequalities related to the creation of knowledge would not be resolved. It is more constructive for those involved in area studies to be fully aware of the imperfections and limitations of the field, and to engage in dialogue and collaboration with others to mitigate those drawbacks. Of course, Japan Studies scholars are no exception.

2. Why *Why Study Japan?*

This collection of bilingual essays is part of a Japan Studies project called "Springboard Japan," which I launched in 2021, when COVID-19 was still raging around the world. Indeed, the origin of this project has a lot to do with the racial tensions in American society that were uncovered during the lockdown.

In my adoptive home country of the United States, the COVID-19 pandemic not only caused countless deaths, illnesses, and job losses, it nearly put an end to democracy in America as we know it. The inauguration of the Trump presidency in 2017 had laid bare many schisms: the divisions between conservatives and progressives, racial/ethnic minorities and whites, the working class and the professional class, and urban vs. rural voters, to name but a few. The pandemic intensified these rifts, partly because the Trump regime fueled the "us vs. them" rhetoric to its political advantage. As a result, decisions regarding mask-wearing, vaccinations, and school-openings were often made based on the political identity of the individuals or the local political leaders. This deep-seated distrust that saturated the American society eventually led to the attempted coup and attack on the U.S. Capitol on January 2, 2021.

In the United States, where the right to bear arms is constitutionally guaranteed to citizens, handguns and machineguns sell like hotcakes whenever there is widespread political or economic unrest. According to a *New York Times* article (May 29, 2021), firearms sales skyrocketed during the pandemic and reached the highest level at the time of their report. With more firearms in circulation, many violent incidents took place, wherein unarmed Black citizens were killed or severely injured by the police or vigilantes. In response, Black Lives Matter (BLM) protests and demonstrations swept across the country, prompting, in turn, an angry backlash by armed anti-BLM groups. As such, the two years from the beginning of 2020 were such a dark and painful period for those who lived in the United States, since so many of us had to fear not only the threat of the virus but also the possibility of manmade disasters every day.

At the risk of sounding self-centered, I must confess that as an Asian woman living in the United States I felt real horror when I saw the sharp uptick in unprovoked assaults—some fatal—against Asian people. The most tragic example was the spree of violence dubbed the "Atlanta spa shootings" that happened in April 2021, resulting in the deaths of eight victims. It goes without saying that these anti-Asian hate crimes were triggered by the novel coronavirus that had emerged in Wuhan, China, but it is also true that the assailants were emboldened and legitimized by Trump's racist rhetoric. Whereas acts of police brutality against Black citizens have systemic causes in state-sponsored racial and socio-economic discrimination, hate crimes against Asian people were committed nonchalantly by ordinary citizens in broad daylight. Though I do not mean that Asian victims deserve more sympathy than Black victims, the assailants' ability to attack people who looked "weak" (i.e., women and the elderly) just because they were Asian was truly chilling. It points to the well-known fact that Asian Americans are seen as unassimilable and untrustworthy "perpetual foreigners" in the United States.

I became a naturalized citizen of the United States in 2000 and in 2025, my "career" as a U.S. citizen will surpass the number of years that I was a Japanese national. Yet, no matter how long I live in America, my Americanness will always fall short of that of a blond and blue-eyed Danish tourist who landed at John F. Kennedy Airport three hours ago. During the lockdown, the unspoken truth about Asians in America manifested itself in the most appalling and disgusting form. And this made me seriously interrogate my profession and my scholarly identity as someone from Japan researching and teaching about Japan in the United States.

Meanwhile, the time in lockdown allowed me to catch up with my fellow Japan Studies scholars in Japan and on the West Coast on Zoom. I named the project born out of these conversations "Springboard Japan" in the hopes that I could create something that helps others jump over the linguistic, cultural, methodological, and political barriers that stand between Japanese and American academia. Since its inception, the supporters of "Springboard Japan" and I have worked on translations of academic and semi-academic texts and made them freely available online (https://sites.dartmouth. edu/springboard-japan-demo/), held a symposium, and, voila, created this bilingual essay collection. Since "Springboard Japan" has so far been my unpaid side gig—fingers crossed for the success of this book—and I have been working little by little on it between my teaching, administrative work for my university, service work for my field, and my own research, the progress has been extremely slow. Yet I am very happy that I decided to do something to contribute to my field with the help from my colleagues, students, and friends I admire.

3. Contents and Structure of *Why Study Japan?*

I conceptualized this book as a bilingual anthology of nine responses by Japan specialists to the question of why we do what we do. When I was still forming the idea in my head, I had a vague image of an essay collection that would provide an opportunity for scholars in various fields to look back on their own "origin story" and somehow use it as a source of inspiration for post-Covid teaching and research. Nevertheless, the product we created turned out to be a highly eye-opening and thought-proving book that would likely appeal to people of all professions, age groups, life stages, and nationalities. *Why Study Japan?* is not an "educational" book per se, but it is actually educational; it is not a foreign language study book per se, but one can certainly use it for that purpose. Above all, this is a book that is jam-packed with a wide range of fascinating ideas and first-person perspectives that enrich the life of the reader.

The first half of this volume consists of nine Japanese-language essays (five originals and four translations). In the second half, you will see the same nine essays in English (four originals and five translations). Further, the nine pieces have been organized into four sections, the first of which is titled "**The Linguistic Barrier, the Methodological Gulf, and the Technologies to Bridge the Gaps.**" In this section are Takahiro Sasaki's "Why I Share Japanese Book Culture with the World," Yoshitaka Hibi's "How, of All Things, I Came to Use English in My Academic Work: Reasons and Methods," and Keiko Eguchi's "I Am not Strange: The Reason I Study Japan."

In this section, each author describes the utility of English in humanities research and provides tips for their fellow humanists to mitigate the language barrier. They also talk about how Anglophone scholarship and its Japanese-language counterpart in Philology (Sasaki's specialty) and Literary Studies (Hibi and Eguchi's specialty) differ in terms of methodological approach, even when the same exact text is being analyzed. Incidentally, all three essays note that digital translation technology and AI are helping bridge the gulf between the two academic worlds. Nevertheless, they contend that technology is not a substitute for dialogue or collaboration and that researchers should make use of those convenient tools without blindly elevating them above the human faculty.

Most of all, I must emphasize that the contents of Section 1 bear no resemblance to the millions of "how-to" books that reframe ordinary information as novel "hacks." These three essays are not what one consumes and extracts the information from but works to be appreciated for their form and content. Each essay will allow the reader to enjoy the personable voice of the author and their touching first-person account about their own journey as a scholar of Japan. Sasaki looks back on his adolescence as a boy who dreamt of becoming a novelist; Hibi on his time at UCLA as a visiting scholar, when he could not help but think of the young Natsume Sōseki in London (who was famously on the verge of a mental breakdown); and Eguchi on her time as a college student, when she decided to live unapologetically as who she was.

The second section, titled "**The Creation of Knowledge as Empowerment**," consists of essays by Mark Bookman ("My Life as a Disabled American in Japan: Intersectional Barriers and Inclusive Imaginaries") and by Setsu Shigematsu ("Whiteness and Japan Studies"). These two authors are not only scholars and teachers, but they are also activists in their respective fields. The compelling eloquence of Bookman and Shigematsu as scholar-activists shines a light on the fact that the humanities are built on the real lives of real people, unlike the common notion that the humanities lack "real-life utility." Bookman and Shigematsu's works are testaments to the fact that creation of knowledge can empower the socially vulnerable, reminding us that research and education should not merely be mental and verbal exercises.

The first essay included in Section 3 ("**Illuminating the Peripheries**") is Misaki Suematsu's "Connecting Classical Japanese Literature to the World: Tales Retold and Reinvented." Her essay makes it clear that Japanese classics, especially those beloved illustrated works from the medieval and early modern periods, such as the Ushiwaka-Benkei legend, have been continuously adapted, modified, and passed down for many centuries inside and outside Japan. And people in Japan today are consuming many of these motifs through modern media, including manga, anime, and video games.

In addition to the valuable, specialized information Suematsu offers in her essay, she also addresses the issue of college students' relative indifference toward Japan's cultural past. I, too, witness Japanese students' lack of interest in their country's history and their lack of remorse for their own ignorance. Part of the issue is that at my institution, which does not offer an English as a Foreign Language (EFL) program, all international students must be thoroughly proficient in academic English as incoming freshmen, which means that most, if not all, of the degree-seeking students from Japan attended English-medium schools that center on the International Baccalaureate Programme and curricula like it. Granted, it is nonsense to impose knowledge about Japan on young Japanese people for such absurd reasons as "because you are Japanese" or "because these facts are common sense." However, educators of Japanese language, history, and literature, myself included, ought to remind our students that the culture of pre-modern Japan is never separated from today's Japan and, as Suematsu has been already practicing herself, we need to find pedagogical tools and methods to spark genuine interest and curiosity among our students.

In his "Japanese Literature at the Intersection of Text and Narrative Content," Christopher Lowy, too, deals with a critical yet hitherto neglected issue that pertains to Japanese literature: visuality of the Japanese writing system. The Japanese writing system is characterized with extreme flexibilities not found in other contemporary systems. For instance, there are no definite, prescriptive rules to determine which one of the four scripts (hiragana, katakana, kanji, and romaji) should be employed to write out a given word, though there are non-binding orthographical conventions. Other flexibilities concern the textual direction and use of annotations via furigana. As Lowy points out, Western academia has long ignored the multilayered effects that the Japanese writing system has on Japanese-language literary texts. In the West— I will use the United States as an example—instructors of most undergraduate Japanese literature courses have no choice but to assign English translations of the primary texts. But for research, as well, many scholars whose native language is English understandably rely heavily on translations of the primary texts to save time. Given this, the visual rhetoric found in Japanese-language literary texts, which cannot be easily translated into English (or any other languages), was never a major concern in Anglophone academia. Yet Lowy is ensuring that we don't overlook critical questions. Now is the time for young, multi-talented researchers like him to innovate the methodology of analyzing Japanese-language literature even in Anglophone academia.

The fourth and last section of this volume, "**Between the Two Cultures, Societies, and Languages**," consists of my own essay, "Why Do I Study Classical Japanese Literature in the United States?" and Dylan McGee's "Neither Here nor There: Libraries of Knowledge, in English, in Japan." As described in the essays, we live in the country that our respective partner is originally from—Japan for him and the United States for me—and we navigate our professional and mundane realms via a language that is not our native tongue, studying and teaching Japanese literature while raising bicultural children. His essay and mine are mirror images of each other, capturing our liminal ontology of hovering between two cultures.

For these very personal reasons, I felt that I could really understand what McGee was conveying when I first read his essay. As I translated the piece, I decided to use the image of *nenashigusa* (rootless grass) as a throughline for his essay. *Nenashigusa* signifies the feeling of in-between-ness that I always sense in the United States; it is lonely and liberating at the same time. Among the nine essays compiled in this book, the most literary text is McGee's. It does not offer any "hacks," but the reader can take away a lot from his writing.

Part
1

The Linguistic Barrier,

the Methodological Gulf,

and the Technologies

to Bridge the Gaps

01

Why I Share
Japanese Book Culture
with the World

Takahiro Sasaki (Shidō Bunko, Keiō University)
Translated by Yuanhao Chen & Emma Cool

1. Why is English Necessary?

I spent my high school days reading novels, even during class. I dreamt about becoming a novelist and I managed to get into Keiō University's Faculty of Letters, where the students were divided into majors from the second year. Although I was torn between Japanese literature and Japanese history, the field of history seemed to me a bit too preoccupied with political ideologies, so I went on to major in Japanese literature, assuming it would be less politically charged.

Though I continued to love modern novels, I felt that they were not something I should study as a research subject, so I proceeded to take a seminar on medieval literature. My graduation thesis was on the 15th-century commentaries on the *Kokin wakashū* (Collection of Poems of Ancient and Modern Times), which was compiled at the order of the emperor in the early 10th century. Yet what I was most preoccupied with was not my graduation thesis, but my post-graduation career. After entering college, I could no longer write novels innocently like when I was in high school, and as a result, my dream of becoming a writer had withered away. That being said, there weren't any industries or occupations that interested me, either. Because I thought I wasn't suited to be a schoolteacher, I had not taken the courses required for a teaching certificate. Lacking a vision for my career path, I had painted myself into a corner.

One time, I went out for drinks with my thesis advisor and fellow advisees. At the bar, my advisor asked me point-blank about my post-graduation plan. Since I did not have one, I sort of half-jokingly answered, "I think I might as well become a *rakugo* storyteller." Although I sometimes did go to *yose* (theaters for *rakugo* performance), it was not as if there was a *rakugo* storyteller I wished to study under. Looking back, I am baffled by my own decision to blurt out such a strange answer to my professor's question.

An ordinary teacher would have urged me to get more serious about my future, but my professor's response was, "It's not unusual to see *rakugo* storytellers with a college education. But there hasn't been one who's got a postgraduate degree!" It never occurred to me that graduate school was an option, so I felt a vague glimpse of hope. I realized that if I went on to get a Master's degree, I could put off my career decision for two years.

What stood in my way was the fact that English—one of my weakest subjects since junior high school—was on the entrance examination for the MA program. I knew of an upperclassman who had given up on going to graduate school because he had flunked his English test, and I was afraid of following in his footsteps. I could justify the significance of studying English if I was researching modern Japanese literature because of the strong Western influences on such texts. However, I firmly believed that English would have no use for studying classical Japanese literature so I had put zero effort into learning English in college.

Fortunately, it turned out that all I had to do for the entrance exam was to translate long passages from English to Japanese using a dictionary. I thus got into graduate school! When I was wondering what courses to take, a senior graduate student asked me, "You're going to take the courses at Shidō Bunko (Shidō Library), right?" Today, I am a full-time faculty member at Shidō Bunko, but until I entered graduate school, I had no idea that Keiō University had a research institute with such a strange name.

Eventually, I learned that Shidō Bunko was an institute that supports research on premodern books produced in the Sinosphere (i.e., East Asia and Vietnam). As an undergraduate, I had been exposed to pre-1600 books and I did not think much about them. But when I seriously studied early16th-century manuscripts held at Shidō Bunko in my graduate seminar, I found myself completely besotted with them. I realized that I was a fan of old Japanese books. I did not consider specializing in old books as my research focus, however, as I could easily imagine that it would be a costly field in terms of both money and time.

At any rate, I couldn't decide my career path even during the two years I worked on my MA. Though I considered simply moving on to the doctoral program, the doctoral entrance exam, to my horror, required not one but two foreign languages! In addition to English, which I was not good at, I had to pass a French exam, a language I had only studied for one year. This seemed completely unreasonable to me. Indeed I failed the entrance exam the first time, though I want to believe that it wasn't because of the foreign language exams. Fortunately I managed to pass the following year. By this time, I had begun to hope that one day I could become a university faculty member and study classical Japanese literature for my career.

2. Encountering Japan Studies in the World

Near the end of the second year of my doctoral course, my mentor at Shidō Bunko asked me if I wanted to apply for a junior researcher position at the National Institute of Japanese Literature (NIJL). I had yet to think clearly about what to do after my doctorate, so I immediately jumped at the opportunity.

NIJL is a national research institution established in 1977 at the request of various Japanese literature associations. NIJL's main functions include archiving resources that pertain to Japanese literature, providing these resources to researchers, and promoting innovative collaborations among scholars. NIJL is currently located in Tachikawa, a suburb of western Tokyo, but back then, it was in Togoshi of Shinagawa Ward, a neighborhood full of the Edo-esque atmosphere.

Fortunately, after passing the initial screening and an interview, I received the position. The rule at the time was that a junior researcher could not get promoted to the rank of assistant professor, which means that I would have to eventually leave the post. Nonetheless, there was no term limit so I was able to make a living as a researcher of some sort for the time being. Since it was (and still is) not rare for one to have trouble finding a job even after completing a doctorate curriculum, I was deeply aware how lucky I was.

My job as junior researcher was to compile a bibliographical catalogue of scholarly articles in Japanese literary studies. Today NIJL's "Database of Research Thesis in Japanese Literature" is freely available online, but back then, we annually published physical copies of a catalogue. The division of NIJL I belonged to was in charge of recording the bibliographical information of each article in the scholarly journals sent to NIJL; organizing and archiving the data according to the time period, subfield, and so on; deciding on the order in which the categories are included in the catalogue; and submitting the manuscript to the publisher. My role was to check the content of the data, assign keywords, and decide the arrangement of the data.

At the time, there were over 500 articles a year on the *Tale of Genji* alone. It was a very difficult task to grasp the main points of all those papers and arrange them in a non-arbitrary order. I certainly learned a lot since I had to sort through studies outside of my specialty.

After all, I ended up staying at NIJL for six years in total. When I began pondering what to do next, my mentor at Shidō Bunko asked if I would be interested in becoming his successor, as he was reaching his retirement age. I did have some doubts about becoming a professional philologist, but I also knew I loved old books. Plus, there was no guarantee that I could get a faculty position at another university. I gladly accepted this offer, even though my status would remain that of a junior researcher.

Around the time that I was invited to return to Shidō Bunko, there was a movement to send young researchers abroad for a period. I, too, was invited to attend a university in Europe or North America for one year.

Although I found this idea fascinating, I had to decline the offer because of my lack of English skills and my new position at Shidō Bunko. In retrospect, I should have deferred my start date at Shidō Bunko by one year and gone ahead and studied abroad—but it never occurred to my younger self that such an option existed.

Thus, I went back to Shidō Bunko. But I was not the same me. I had spent six years at NIJL; this was a significant experience. In addition to conducting large-scale projects to survey the pre-1900 books scattered all over Japan and archive them in the form of microfilm, NIJL had been rigorously surveying pre-1900 books that existed outside Japan, as well. Furthermore, they had hosted Japan Studies specialists from foreign countries as visiting instructors. Even though I was not part of the division that managed these projects, I still learned a lot about Japan-related research happening outside Japan and the old Japanese texts that existed overseas.

My division at NIJL was exploring diverse ways to make use of digital technology in the field of Japanese Literary Studies, including the creation of various databases. As a result, I was given opportunities to visit Western countries. I first went on a trip to Europe and then the United States to study how Chinese characters were being used on digital platforms in the West. These trips were my first real encounters with Japan Studies in Europe and North America.

My first time in Europe was for the European Association for Japanese Studies (EAJS) Conference in Copenhagen, Denmark. This was such a huge event that the reception was hosted by the mayor himself and held at the city hall. From this opening until the day of the farewell party—for which a large restaurant next to Tivoli Gardens was rented out—I spent my time in Copenhagen in a state of shock and awe. What a difference between this and the academic conferences I attended in Japan! Numerous Japan Studies scholars from all over the world had gathered at the University of Copenhagen, located in the bustling center of the city (the university was founded in 1479). The scholars separated into their subfields and held lectures and research presentations for several days. I felt dizzy from watching people with various ethnic and national backgrounds enthusiastically discussing the classical literature, entertainment, art, and the like, of Japan in mixtures of English and Japanese. This felt so mismatched from the atmosphere of the Middle Age European style venue. I couldn't help but marvel at how people from other countries could be so passionate about Japan-related subject matters.

Expectedly, the presentations at the conference were mainly given in English; only the Japanese people gave presentations in Japanese. There were certainly some Japanese scholars who gave their presentations in English, and yes, they bedazzled me. I could hardly understand the content of the English presentations and I was making arbitrary speculations when Japanese proper nouns occasionally popped up. This is the time when I truly felt like I was paying the price for not studying English seriously when I was in school.

My first visit to the United States took place just before leaving NIJL to go back to Shidō Bunko. From New York to Washington D.C., Columbus, San Diego, and, finally, Los Angeles, I took to the skies to cross the American continent. At each stop, I visited the local libraries and museums and saw how Chinese characters were being used on their digital catalogues, beginning with the Online Computer Library Center (OCLC), headquartered in Dublin, Ohio. I also had chances to observe how Japanese classical books and artworks were stored and maintained at those facilities.

At the Metropolitan Museum of Art and the Sackler Gallery in the Smithsonian Museum Complex, I was not only overwhelmed by the quality and quantity of the Japanese art on display, but also shocked by the fact that each museum had its own facilities for large-scale restoration with specialists who had studied the techniques in Japan. The quality of the Japanese book collections at the Library of Congress was, of course, exceptional, but those at Columbia University and UCLA far exceeded my expectation, as well.

This business trip gave me a taste of something delightful. That is, there would always be people from Japan or advanced Japanese speakers staffed at the institutions with significant collections of Japanese books and other materials. As long as I showed up, the hosts would help out non-English speakers like myself. Since then, I have continued to rely on this truth. Even in the rare moments when nobody around me could speak Japanese, I somehow survived.

Back at Shidō Bunko, my main task was to survey collections of premodern Japanese books within the country. Thus, I got to see a variety of old books in numerous locations. Surveying books of various genres—including those beyond my specialties—helped me to better understand the overall characteristics of old Japanese books. I was very fortunate that both of my jobs at NIJL and Shidō Bunko required me to step outside of my comfort zone and broaden my horizon.

In addition, thanks to the connections I established at the NIJL, I became part of the research team that surveys the former Japanese book collection of the Japanese General Government of Korea Library (Chōsen Sōtokufu Toshokan), now belonging to the National Library of Korea. In total, I visited Seoul over 20 times. This collection also encompassed a wide range of fields, so the project was a highly enlightening experience. It gave me a new perspective that allowed me to see Japanese books in relation to those created in other societies.

Another opportunity that a personal connection I fostered at NIJL afforded me was to give a presentation of old Japanese books during a symposium hosted by the Institute of Advanced Japanese Studies at Collège de France. Further, this event prompted me to join international collaborative projects with Japan Studies scholars in France. I was blown away by my new French scholar-friends' depth of knowledge in old Japanese books.

Some of the research topics my French collaborators had chosen were of a type that I rarely encountered at universities or conferences in Japan. I realized that such studies were far-sighted, without being confined to typical curricula and programs of Japanese universities. They were truly getting at the essence of Japanese culture. I genuinely felt that we could no longer bank on the notion that Japan was the center of Japan Studies. I became increasingly certain that my hunch was correct as I started frequenting institutions in North America.

3. Disseminating Japanese Book Culture to the World

As I became used to overseas business trips, I encountered an increasing number of opportunities to go abroad. The typical way to conduct scholarly projects outside Japan is to obtain research funds from various organizations, including the Grants-in-Aid for Scientific Research (commonly known as *kakenhi*) offered by the Japan Society for the Promotion of Science. While one may apply individually, it is also possible to apply with collaborators for a multi-year project. More and more frequently, people began to invite me to join these overseas research projects on classic Japanese books.

Prof. Tōru Ishikawa, a well-known expert in illustrated manuscripts from the late-Muromachi period to the early-Edo period called *narae-bon*, is a professor at Keiō University's Faculty of Letters. *Narae-bon* are beautiful and fun to look at; many foreign visitors had purchased them and brought them home. Now a great number of them have been circulated and preserved around the world. As one of the foremost scholars who has been studying these texts, Prof. Ishikawa is also an expert in organizing international trips and executing research projects overseas.

I had the pleasure of participating in many of Prof. Ishikawa's projects and others organized by scholars who are not affiliated with Keiō. In this way, I have been able to make numerous international trips while accompanying my research collaborators, increase my knowledge of the location and the collections of Japanese classical books in Europe and America, and get to know many Japan Studies scholars. These invaluable experiences are my treasure—I would not trade them for the world.

Another big turning point came when I joined the "Laying the Foundation for International Comparative Research in Illustrated Books of the 15th–17th Centuries" project, funded by MEXT as part of the government's effort to support the formation of strategic research infrastructure at private universities in Japan. The project, led by Prof. Ishikawa, was carried out between 2009 and 2014. Experts from Keiō University—not only in Western,

Chinese, and Japanese books, but also in Japanese Christian history and Islamic history—joined the team, and my horizons naturally expanded through this research group. Seeing the medieval European manuscripts in the Normandy region of France and surveying the books in Portugal that the Jesuits had printed in Japan were valuable experiences that gave me a more comparative perspective for my work.

In addition, this project allowed its members to choose their own sub-projects freely. I developed my own sub-project plan, organized an international comparative symposium on divination books, and, for the first time, traveled to France and the United States alone. Though some may think this is nothing special, it actually requires quite a lot of courage for someone who is not fluent in English like me to travel abroad by himself. When I commuted to the Guimet Museum Library in Paris for a week, where the divination book symposium was held, I felt like I was a student on a study abroad program.

My visit to Princeton University was unforgettable. My acquaintance at the university invited me to survey premodern Japanese books in the library and the museum collections. With this opportunity, I decided to try out something new, in addition to surveying the collections, which is to offer a mini-seminar on old Japanese books for the interested students, faculty, and librarians at the university. This is because, despite the fact that I had participated in symposiums and workshops overseas and presented my own research to peers for years, I had never had a chance to teach the basics on premodern Japanese books outside Japan. Now that I was traveling all the way to the United States, I thought I might as well share the knowledge of Japanese books that could benefit the research and teaching of the people at Princeton University.

I would have given a seminar in English if I could, but this was not the case. So I asked my acquaintance at Princeton to gather the graduate students in Japan Studies. I talked for around three hours, letting the participants see, feel, and pass around the old books I had brought with me from Japan. For those who are not familiar with old books, touching, feeling, and seeing them in real life is the best way to learn how to appreciate them, and there is no better way to spark interest in old Japanese books than showing the beauty and intricacies of the real materials.

Some of the graduate students who participated in this mini-seminar are now working as curators at museums with premier Japanese art collections in the Unites States, or as members of the Japan Studies faculty at state universities. Although there is no causal relationship between my mini-seminar and their career successes, I am nonetheless deeply and personally touched by their achievements. Another unforgettable thing about this event is that the subject librarian who specializes in the Japanese-language books also took her time to participate in this seminar.

In North America and Europe, there are organizations of librarians and university faculty members formed for the purpose of publicizing and promoting the use of Japan-related materials. These organizations are the North American Coordinating Council on Japanese Library Resources (NCC) and the European Association of Japanese Resource Specialists (EAJRS). At spaces for the sharing of information and borderless cooperation, these groups provide excellent support for the field of Japan Studies in Europe and North America. The NCC also has a parent organization, the Council on East Asian Libraries (CEAL).

The aforementioned librarian at Princeton University was one of the core members of NCC and CEAL. Interested in what I had talked about, she asked if I was willing to give a lecture on premodern Japanese books during the upcoming workshop held in conjunction with CEAL's annual convention. This was certainly an opportunity to further promote my cause, so I excitedly accepted the invitation.

The following March, CEAL and NCC conventions were held in Chicago at the same time as the annual meeting of the Association for Asian Studies (AAS). We rented a room in the Japanese art section of the Art Institute of Chicago for the "CEAL Workshop on Japanese Rare Books in Chicago." The capacity was 20 people due to the size of the room, but the number of applicants exceeded 40. I realized that many people were in need of a greater knowledge in old Japanese books.

Some participants were from Canada and the UK, and in addition to librarians specializing in Japanese-language books, quite a few Japan Studies scholars were in attendance. Naturally, I talked about the old books I had brought from Japan and those in the collection at the Art Institute of Chicago. I could truly feel the deep enthusiasm among the participants—it was a blissful day for me.

What I simply tried out without much pre-planning at Princeton transformed into this event in Chicago; I felt like I was in a dream. Though I was very pleased with this outcome, it turned out that the lecture I gave in Chicago was just the beginning. After that, I was invited by those who were in the audience to give workshops and lectures at their institutions, including the University of British Columbia, the University of Hawai'i at Manoa, and the University of Southern California.

4. A Tailwind Called MOOC

The next big turning point came shortly after the Chicago workshop. Keiō University, to which I belong, joined FutureLearn, which is one of the platforms for Massive Open Online Courses (MOOCs), headquartered in London.

Since it was the first time a Japanese institution had joined FutureLearn, the organizers decided that the content of the inaugural course should be about Japan. Hence, Japan Studies scholars from various fields such as literature, history, and art were gathered from the university for a briefing session and I was one of them. After we were told about the history and current situation of MOOC, we started discussing who would be in charge of the first course; I raised my hand. Through my own experiences of giving workshops outside of Japan, I knew for a fact that there were plenty of people in the world who wanted to learn about old Japanese books, and that there was even room to spur interest among those who knew little about old books.

My self-nomination was approved and I became the lead educator for the course on old Japanese books. This was a three-week long course that would require the "students" three hours of studying per week. Since I could reuse some content from the workshops I had given, more than half of the content was already prepared. Unlike in-person workshops, however, the audience of the MOOC courses would not be able to touch the actual books. Therefore, I designed the course in ways that the audience would be able to see a maximum variety of books through high-quality, high-resolution videos and images. I wrote the lectures in Japanese and taught in Japanese, but I had to rely on someone to create and attach English subtitles to the images and pre-recorded videos. Fortunately, my acquaintance from Italy who had studied classical Japanese literature at a graduate school in the United States kindly agreed to help.

In July 2016, the inaugural "Japanese Culture Through Rare Books" course went live. In the promotional video, however, I was directed to introduce the content of this course in English. I could not believe someone who had avoided English all his life like me was calling upon the world in English for people to take the courses. On top of that, the video was uploaded to YouTube. When we were shooting this promotional video, I felt like I had been transported into a completely different world.

The biggest challenge I encountered during the online course was responding to the comments and questions that the audience had sent me through the chat box, which we made available to ensure that the participants would be able to interact with the instructor and other learners. However, most of the comments were, of course, written in English. The first time this course was published, it attracted nearly 9000 registrants from 140 countries and the comments exceeded 8000.

These comments were not only written in English, but many also required detailed explanations; this was something far beyond what I could manage. Thus, I asked a graduate student—a proficient English speaker who was also involved in developing the course—to pick out the questions that she thought were important and translate them into Japanese. I would then answer the questions in Japanese, she would translate my responses into English, and we posted them online.

This process was extremely laborious, but I learned a lot from these specific questions that came from people with different backgrounds and perspectives. I felt that teaching MOOC courses was such an educational opportunity not just for the learners but also for the instructors. I should note that I, of course, had been using a translation website from the beginning, but the quality was far from good, at least initially. However, as we re-published the course again and again, the AI of the translation website improved. Now I can rely almost solely on this service to respond to the comments and questions in English. Therefore, I have been helped not only by countless people, but also by the development of digital technology.

Luckily, the first MOOC course was well-received and some of my acquaintances in Europe and America told me that they had used it in their own teaching. Even after creating and publishing the online course, I continued to give in-person workshops at Yale University, Columbia University, the Freer and Sackler Galleries, Cambridge University in the UK, and the Guimet Museum Library and Strasbourg University in France. At these locations, more and more people would tell me that they had taken the online course. I felt that MOOCs and face-to-face meetings began to merge in a complementary way, signifying an important benchmark for our goals in a single, ideal form.

Just around that time, the global pandemic turned the world upside-down. On the FutureLearn platform, courses are normally offered intermittently, that is, they are open for three months, closed for three months, and are open again for another three months. However, during the Covid pandemic, the courses remained open. Though all the symposia and workshops I was scheduled to attend were indeterminately postponed, more and more people who were sheltering in place took the online course and I saw many comments that expressed gratitude for creating this and allowing them to spend their time at home meaningfully. Thus, around 25,000 people from about 140 countries have registered in my course so far and about 20,000 comments and questions have been submitted. Eventually, all the postponed workshops were held online. Though it was a pity that people were unable to touch and feel the books directly, there was definitely a silver lining. People across the world in great numbers joined us for these events, which would not have been possible if they had been in-person meetings.

5. From Now on

Upon the success of our first online course on FutureLearn, I was encouraged to create companion courses. Again, as the lead educator, I developed a new course focusing on traditional Japanese paper (*washi*) used for old books and released "The Art of *Washi* Paper in Japanese Rare Books" in July 2018. I am currently collaborating with the British Library to create a course that introduces and comparatively analyzes old books from Europe and Japan, but the production has been delayed due to Covid.

Today the comparative study of old books from different cultures is flourishing around the world, and online conferences and symposia centering on this type of research are commonplace. While people have invited me to speak at these events, most of them are conducted in English. So far, I have somehow managed to participate with the help of many people. That being said, it is still nearly impossible for me to join lively, spontaneous discussions and make contributions, due to the language barrier.

The more progress I make as a researcher, the more this massive language barrier stands in the way. It is easy to turn away from this obstacle and confine my scholarly activities within Japan. Nevertheless, I have convinced myself that it is my heavenly mandate to share the rich culture of old Japanese books with the world and to accomplish this goal, I am willing to do everything within my capacity. Doing so is my way of reciprocating the help that so many people have offered me thus far. I cannot help but think that the gods or spirits of old Japanese books are telling me to do this work in order to make up for all the years my younger self spent somewhat aimlessly.

Old Japanese books play a critical role in vitalizing Japan Studies around the world. Moreover, the vitality of Japan Studies in other countries is sure to energize research within Japan. I truly hope that I will be the last generation of Japan Studies scholars who is unable to speak English.

02

How, of All Things, I Came to Use English in My Academic Work:

Reasons and Methods

Yoshitaka Hibi (Nagoya University)

Translated by James Dorsey

1. Why I Began to Incorporate English into My Academic Work

Almost without realizing it, to date I've published three articles of various lengths in English, and I have two more coming out this year (2022). I find it surprising that a researcher of modern Japanese literature like me is now working in this mode.

I'm not about to begin boasting. My English is as unsophisticated as it has ever been; when I watch or read the news, I'm bombarded with unfamiliar vocabulary and when I listen to conference presentations or lectures, my brain shuts down as soon as things get complicated. At academic conferences I break out in a cold sweat when the Q & A time comes along, and all I can think about is how badly I'd like to escape. So, a self-congratulatory boast such as "Look at me! I'm publishing articles in English!" is not at all what this essay is about. On the contrary, my message is closer to this: "My English may be a mess, but I somehow muddle through. Why don't you give it a shot, too?" In other words, I would encourage people to give it a try—and starting with baby steps, as they say, is just fine.

Most of what I want to say here is related to *how* I have been able to incorporate English into my research agenda, but I would like to begin with the *why* of this development. So, why is it that, of all things, I've begun to use English in my academic work? The reasons are various and none of them is especially unique. Good research is distinguished by innovation, and one way to bring something new to the table is to step outside the established paradigms. For me, becoming acquainted with research taking place in languages other than Japanese is one way to learn what might exist outside those paradigms, one way to access an intellectual resource that feeds innovation. The academic work conducted in English is especially dynamic and theory evolves at a brisk pace. This is one of the reasons I began to use English in my research.

There is also the appeal of moving in broader research circles. If one's academic work is limited to the Japanese language, one generally operates in Japan alone, with but an occasional trip abroad. On the other hand, if one begins to incorporate English, the opportunities to present research outside of Japan increase exponentially. It's worth noting, too, that the potential destinations are not limited to North America; if one so desires, it's possible to find opportunities in Europe, Oceania, and the various regions of Asia as well. Being able to visit unfamiliar cities to spend a few days sharing research with people I would otherwise never have met is one of my major incentives.

Finally, I should not neglect to also mention how integrating English relates to the conditions under which universities in Japan currently operate. Many such institutions emphasize education in English and are keen to admit exchange students so, in certain cases, faculty may be expected to conduct their classes in English. I'm personally opposed to this popular bias favoring English, but that doesn't mean I would deny the value of incorporating that language into one's research.

Having outlined the *whys* of my incorporation of English into my work, I will now turn to the main concern of my essay: *how* I began to do academic work in English. The bulk of what I have to say is based primarily on what I remember of my personal experiences, but it is my hope that my experiences will provide some hints to both people wishing to begin conducting research in English or other non-Japanese language as well as to Japan Studies scholars who may have acquired the language later in life and may not feel particularly confident in their abilities to use it.

2. How I Began to Use English in My Academic Work

I first became aware of English language research on Japanese literature while I was a graduate student. My intentions at the time were to research the Japanese "I-novel" (*shishōsetsu*), the often autobiographical, first-person narratives of everyday life. The research group I belonged to, however, worked heavily with literary theory and comparative approaches, and the faculty were themselves, primarily, scholars of foreign literatures or comparativists. One of them once said to me, "Hibi-kun, there is some very sophisticated scholarship on Japanese literature being done in English. It's going to be increasingly important for you to be reading it."

I had entered graduate school in 1995, a time when literary theory and postmodern thinking was all the rage. In keeping with that, I often looked at the theory-heavy journals *Hihyō kūkan* (Critical Space) and *Gendai shisō* (Contemporary Thought) and I kept an eye out for the latest publications in critical theory and modern philosophy. This was all before the latest information on such things was available on the internet, so I was a regular visitor to the campus bookstore, which was run by Maruzen. Many of the volumes on literary theory and modern philosophy that were lined up on the shelves were translations from French or English. The white covers of the new releases from Misuzu Shobō and the Hōsei University Press glistened with an aura of intelligence. At the time it seemed to me that it was the works translated from Western languages that were at the cutting edge. So, when the professor told me to read pertinent materials in foreign languages, I took his advice to heart. As to how successful I was in acting on that advice, well, I'm rather loath to say. The fact is that I read but a meager smattering of the materials related to my doctoral dissertation.

I got serious about the matter after I completed my PhD and became a research associate at Tsukuba University. I thought I had better know just what Japan Studies in the United States was all about and how sophisticated the research there might be. On top of that, I had finished my dissertation and was looking for a new research topic to pursue. The Japanese Ministry of Education, Culture, Sports, Science and Technology was still offering its foreign research grants to scholars in those days. To applicants who passed their review, the grant supplied travel expenses and a living stipend, making possible up to a year of research at an academic research institution outside of Japan. I'll skip an explanation of the circuitous route required to obtain one of these grants in favor of telling you that, although I inconvenienced a few people along the way, in the end I was lucky enough to have my application approved. I decided to travel to the United States.

The Terasaki Center for Japanese Studies at the University of California, Los Angeles was the institution that hosted me. My grant application required the support of a researcher to serve as host, but at the time I did not know a single American scholar of Japanese literature. Following even the slenderest of leads brought me to "K," who had spoken of an acquaintance, "U," who was teaching in the United States. K introduced me to U, who kindly advised me, clueless as I was. In light of my particular research interests, she said, UCLA would be a good fit, and she offered to put me in touch with Michael Bourdaghs, who was then on the faculty there.

My proposed research topic was the Japanese language literature of Japanese-Americans. To be perfectly frank, it was not a research topic chosen after a great deal of thought. It was simply a matter of that topic sitting at the intersection of two motivations: a desire to explore something in the field of postcolonial studies and the need to work in an area that could be fruitfully pursued in the United States. It was only later that I realized just how fascinating this topic was.

After I had received approval from Bourdaghs and finalized the grant, New York suffered the terrorist attacks of 9.11. After dinner that day I was, as usual, about to watch the news on Japan's public broadcasting network, the NHK. When the broadcast began, the screen changed and, without a word of explanation, NHK aired footage of the skyscrapers emitting plumes of black smoke. I sat glued to the TV, watching deep into the night. In the days that followed many people asked me if I still really intended to go to the United States. I read of how dangerous it would be in Los Angeles, a logical city to target after New York, but I really had no way to determine just how great that danger might be. But of one thing I was certain—if I let this chance slip past me, there was no telling when another might come along. I decided I would go. My departure was set for May of the following year.

In preparation for my departure, I studied English. I bought favorably reviewed conversation textbooks and pored over them. This was rather helpful. I also employed an English tutor whose home I would visit for my lessons. To be honest, I cannot really say whether this was helpful to me or not.

3. Los Angeles, 2002

Los Angeles in May. The first things that made an impression on me were the American flags and the Los Angeles Lakers pennants. I had never really followed American professional basketball, so I was surprised to see so many cars flying the Lakers pennant as they rolled through town. The Lakers had made it into the playoffs that year for the third time in a row, and people had high hopes that they would bring home their third consecutive victory. Those Lakers pennants were ubiquitous, but so were the American flags. They flew from cars, windows, and rooftops. There was no mistaking it; I was in a country at war.

To cut right to the chase, my English did not get much better during the time I spent in L.A., a little under a year. It's not surprising. I spent most of my time shuttling between my apartment and the library, where I furiously read on microfilm the Japanese language newspapers published in San Francisco in the early 20th century. I did not make any real friends. And through a stroke of bad timing, both of the two faculty members specializing in modern Japanese literature, Michael Bourdaghs and Seiji Lippit, were not offering classes that year, being off on sabbaticals or something of the sort.

I had married while in graduate school and my wife, Chisa Amano (herself a specialist in modern Japanese literature), had accompanied me to L.A. She had sacrificed opportunities of her own in Japan to spend that time in the U.S. She proactively took advantage of the opportunities in Los Angeles, venturing out independently, but even so most of our time was spent together. Time together was a comfort to us both, but undoubtedly it was also one of the reasons we were rather insulated.

Natsume Kinnosuke, the author later known as Natsume Sōseki, wrote that during the two miserable years he spent studying in London, he felt like a shaggy mutt among the pack of wolves that were the English gentlemen around him. I'm not joking when I say that while in L.A. I would think about this and worry that, like Sōseki, I was close to having a nervous breakdown. The continually clear skies meant Los Angeles was bathed in sunlight and the students on campus all looked so cheerful, but I could not count myself among them. I couldn't understand what the announcers on CNN were talking about. The Fox news network was a little easier to understand, but the female reporters were too gaudy for my taste. Programming for children was the easiest to understand and I loved *Teletubbies*, who did not speak English—or, in fact, any human language at all.

My ability to understand written and spoken English improved at a snail's pace and my own writing ability not at all. Still, thinking back on it now, my extended stay in the United States was a very meaningful time for me. I gained valuable, lived experience of customs, mindsets, conventions, and some of the realities of American life. I learned how to navigate the libraries, how to do the shopping, and how to use public transportation. I now know to smile when you speak to a person you're meeting for the first time and to tip in restaurants and taxis. I realized that while not exactly ostracized, East Asians who struggle with English will be treated coldly. I came to understand that what we label "English" is actually comprised of a great variety of dialects tied to social class and ethnic origin. I found out that there are places and times of day that can be dangerous to an extent unthinkable in Japan. My attendance at lectures and my participation in seminars or conferences in America taught me things that would be useful in my future. The nature of conference rooms and proceedings, the format for Q & A sessions, and the strategies for small talk are all things I learned there and have put to good use at academic gatherings in other countries, as well.

I also gained a great deal from the experience of being a foreigner. Without being conscious of it, in Japan I had always been a member of the majority. During my stay in the United States, though, I learned what it means to not understand the language, not know the customs, not recognize the systems in place, not have a support network. I have experienced these things myself and I now know how inconvenient, unsettling, and stressful they are. I believe that my behavior and thinking have reflected those experiences even long after I returned to Japan.

I had one other stay, a short one, at an American university. Ted Mack invited me to the University of Washington as a visiting researcher in 2009. I had just moved to a new post at Nagoya University at the time and the circumstances there meant I could spend only a little less than a month in the U.S. Still, it was an experience for which I'm grateful. With Ted, I was able to collect data on Japanese immigrants. I was using Japanese most of the time, but as I had gotten much more used to speaking English, I was able to use it to expand the scope of my data collection.

4. Conference Presentations in English

I clearly remember the first time I gave a conference presentation in English. It was in Hong Kong in 2004. One of my former colleagues at Tsukuba University, Y, invited me to join him on a panel for the International Comparative Literature Association conference. I was terribly nervous. Though I had prepared the paper I was to read, I didn't think I would be able to participate in the Q & A session. The visit to Hong Kong, my first, had been fun, and I had enjoyed strolling around town in the crushing heat of August, but the thought of the Q & A session left me a nervous wreck. Much to my surprise, our panel had been assigned the largest auditorium available. As I prepared in my hotel room the day before my presentation,

I was overwhelmed by the delusion of an audience filling that auditorium and me, completely flustered, unable to utter a word once the Q & A session was underway. But, when the moment of truth arrived, the auditorium held no more than the panelists and a handful of others. The microphone echoed in that cavernous space and I found myself wishing that somebody—the custodians, even!—might join us to liven up the session.

In terms of my linguistic ability in academic English, the ten months I spent living in the U.S. did not advance me as much as the various conference preparations and presentations that came after that stay. Those occasions all put a concrete goal right before my eyes and I had a clear vision of the abilities and information that would be needed. What's more, the clock would be ticking. It was sheer terror that drove me to frantically prepare.

The easiest way to experience giving a conference presentation in English is, perhaps, to be invited to a panel. To propose an individual paper sets a high bar, since one must do all the preparatory work leading up to the event oneself. Presenting on a panel, in contrast, means the organizer will assume those responsibilities, including the advance planning, and as one of the presenters you can count on the other panelists to help you out and offer their advice. They'll also lend a hand during the Q & A session. If you, my fellow Japan scholars and monolingual Japanese speakers, meet scholars whose native languages are something other than Japanese and research interests are similar to your own, I recommend suggesting to them that someday you coordinate on a panel together.

Once one has gained a bit of experience, it becomes clear that the success of a conference presentation, including the Q & A session, really all hinges on what you have accumulated over the course of your usual research in the Japanese language. In the Q & A session, if you can manage to understand even just the crux of a question and somehow call to mind the vocabulary needed to express your opinion, then it's simply a matter of stringing the words together. Your answer may not be particularly clever, and the burden of making sense of it lies with the listener, but what you produce will serve as a response.

I'm ever more comfortable with the fact that I will never be fluent in English or get the pronunciation exactly right. But, after all, what's more important is genuinely engaging in the discussion and bringing to the table some pertinent information and opinions. My point should be clear if we compare it to alternatives. Imagine a researcher speaking eloquent Japanese, but whose pronouncements are trite. Then compare that person to a non-Japanese researcher who requires our linguistic support to communicate but has something worthwhile to say. Without a doubt, I'd rather collaborate with the latter, and I would hope to be counted in that category myself.

5. Writing in English and the Matter of Machine Translation

The improvements in machine translation over the past few years have deeply impacted the work I do in English. It now quite accurately translates for me when I'm reading or writing. Still, when it comes to reading specialized materials, I feel I get a more accurate sense of a text when I read it in the original language myself. That being said, I cannot match the speed made possible with machine translation so, when an understanding of the basic gist is all that I need or I'm pressed for time, I work with machine translation.

In my case, when I'm writing in English, the benefits of machine translation are even more dramatic. I used Google Translate in the middle of the second decade of the 21st century, but essentially only for a comparison with the English I had come up with myself. That changed immediately upon the release of MiraiTranslate in 2019. I feel my own English writing abilities will never match the natural English generated by this application. DeepL Translator came next, and for academic uses it represented another major step forward. From that point onward I found that I began to play a different role— I was no longer needed to produce English from scratch, but rather required to check that the machine translation did indeed match my intentions. These days I consider my applied English ability to be a composite of me and machine translation.

Even with all the technological advances, human ability combined with machine translation still comes up short. For conference presentations or article writing, I use machine translation and then consult a professional English editor. I complete my manuscript in Japanese, run it through machine translation, and then edit the English that has been generated. Once those steps are completed, I send the manuscript to a professional rewriter, who sends it back a few days later. I then do another round of edits myself. It seems that for a short oral presentation at an academic conference, this process produces acceptable results. One should remember, though, that machine translation works better with certain kinds of Japanese language usage; keeping that in mind improves the outcome. I make sure that the subject of the sentences is clear and I keep the sentence structure simple.

Is this process, then, all that one needs? Regrettably, I would have to answer in the negative. The language used for manuscripts and oral presentations differs, to be sure. However, in both cases, the expression of very sophisticated research findings requires a finely nuanced use of language. That fact may be one distinguishing characteristic of the humanities. In the written medium, eloquence generates a rhetorical power that both attests to the researcher's prowess and adds to the overall appeal. Whether English or Japanese, truly refined discourse is premised on an astounding amount of specialized knowledge that is teased out in language where the finest nuances are carefully controlled. This is especially true in the close reading of texts and when delving into topics requiring delicate interventions.

Written texts demand a higher level of erudition than oral presentations. The bar for refined language is raised even higher when writing for release from a publishing company. One English manuscript I recently submitted had been proofed and corrected by a professional editor whose native language is English, but all the same it was heavily edited once again by the researcher responsible for the volume. That specialist had a preference for a different set of vocabulary and expressions. I suppose my vocabulary and word usage were at about the level of a native speaker high school student while the volume editor was looking for language at the level of a humanities scholar. That level of linguistic prowess is beyond me, beyond machine translation, beyond a professional rewriter. I have no choice but to recognize that fact.

I'm resigned to this state of affairs and believe there is really no way to change it. The day my own English reaches that level will not come in this lifetime. Still, in that being reborn and starting all over again is not an option, what I *can* do is, first of all, polish the manuscripts as I compose them in Japanese. After that, I do what I can. Should my English writing still be clumsy, there are those who will lend a hand. And that is enough.

6. Singularity in Japanese Literary Studies

What does the future of research hold as the quality of machine translation continues to improve? Here, to close my essay, I'd like to speculate a bit on the changes that the digital environment will bring to scholarship.

Not long ago the concept of "singularity" was all the rage. The word comes from the future predictions of Ray Kurzweil, who used it to designate the time when artificial intelligence surpasses that of humans. Working on a smaller scale than Kurzweil's, I would like to speculate on issues that may well be in our not-so-distant future. I would like to provisionally label these speculations "singularity in Japanese literary studies."

As artificial intelligence will not drive researchers out of the field of Japanese literature any time soon, my use of the word "singularity" here refers to the moment when developments in technology bring revolutionary and irreversible changes to our current research paradigms. What might these developments be?

- Machine translation that is, for all intents and purposes, serviceable will be developed, making it possible to read Japan Studies scholarship from around the world in one's native language via a fluid translation. Additionally, research published in one's own language will be translated into other languages, each version sounding natural to native speakers of those languages.
- Databases of academic publications from all countries and in all

languages will be aggregated, making it possible to search across them.
- Literary works and related publications, including journals, both past and present, will be completely searchable.

Might not all of this be possible in the next ten or twenty years? How will our research and teaching change when this sort of "singularity in Japanese literary studies" becomes a reality? Certainly, our very conception of our research field will radically change. The amount of research we will need to account for will dramatically increase, which is a daunting prospect, but it will also mean that we will be able to read the newest, most pertinent articles almost as soon as they are published anywhere in the world. The challenges in presenting one's research orally in languages other than one's own will also be diminished. Think of academic conferences with simultaneous interpreters. Those interpreters will be replaced by smartphones. Both those presenting and those asking questions will be able to do so in their native tongues. Trepidation due to the linguistic challenges of Q & A sessions will be diminished.

One of the major advantages of this development is that sharing the fruits of one's research can be done through one's native language. At present, Japanese literary studies are conducted in communities nestled within certain nations and geographic regions spread across the globe. Though some coordination of efforts is sustained on an ad hoc basis, most of these communities are essentially evolving independently. These communities might be compared to island universes, distinct galaxies spread out across boundless space, and between which some travel takes place. If a time came when all inhabitants conducted research in English or, for that matter, Japanese, the diversity of these island universes that comprise the world of Japan Studies would evaporate. Machine translation might play an integral role in preventing such homogenization and in prolonging the lives of these island universes.

The scenario, however, is not entirely a rosy one. The presence of mediators in the form of simultaneous interpreters, talented as they may be, would diminish the intimacy that comes from direct dialogue. During the current pandemic we have all been made keenly aware of the way distances between people have influenced their feelings of intimacy and estrangement. We have confirmed our knowledge that interpersonal connections come from dialogue between people sharing space and time, they come from breaking bread together. In order to maintain and strengthen such connections, we must not rely too heavily on either interpreters or interpretation devices; we must commit ourselves to the study of languages and cultures other than our own.

The paradigm suggested by sustaining island universes, too, is not without its drawbacks. Japanese literary studies as they are conducted in Japan, North America, Europe, China, Korea, Taiwan, ASEAN, and South America each operate under their own unique conditions and have their own distinct national flavor. The standards for judging what sorts of research are interesting or cutting-edge, too, differ. The positionality of Japanese literary studies is also varied, as it may be considered a part of area studies (East Asian Studies) or treated as another of the many foreign language literatures. In some regions, such as those connected to Japan through colonization or with a history of students sent to study in Japan, it makes sense to treat Japanese literary studies as part of a country's own modern literary history. In places with Japanese immigrant communities, Japanese literature may function as a touchstone for ethnic identity. Depending on the way Japanese literature is positioned, the expectations for research in the field change and the research is targeted to different audiences. With the advent of "singularity in Japanese literary studies" such divisions between research communities are unlikely to continue to parallel the divisions between nations. As the island universes come into contact with each other and mergers arise, forces will begin to eradicate those differences. The direction those forces might take will be a matter of debate and possibly lead to conflict and collusion as players joust to determine which influences win out. Real world issues such as population, language, distance, and geopolitics will be factors determining the degree of influence wielded by each of those players in our shared realm of Japanese literary studies.

My third dimension of "singularity" is now right before our eyes. The digitization project conducted by Japan's National Diet Library is moving forward, with an ever-increasing number of texts now totally searchable. As I write this essay in March 2022, the "Next Digital Library" service makes it possible to search through the entirety of texts no longer protected by copyright (approximately 280,000 texts). Although copyright restrictions will continue to be a factor, the number of texts available through this service is likely to rapidly increase. All of us, but especially those researching modern literature, must adjust our approaches to research accordingly. It's likely that there will be fewer cases in which scholars enjoy an advantage due strictly to their easy physical access to large libraries holding copious amounts of secondary sources. Relatedly, more of us will be faced with the question of how to evaluate, how to prioritize, and how to use the massive tranche of materials we will find. There will be a renewed interrogation, too, of how we're to analyze the vast amount of material that we acquire, and computer-mediated reading will surely be part of our answer to this question. I eagerly look forward to the types of research that will be made possible.

Our current age may also be one in which we address the issue of translation between the "languages" used in the field of information sciences. The essay I will be charged with writing ten years from now may very well be titled "How, of All Things, I Came to Use Computers in My Academic Work: Reasons and Methods."

I Am not Strange:

The Reason I Study Japan

Keiko Eguchi (National Institute of Technology, Toyota College)
Translated by Rhiannon Liou & Sachi Schmidt-Hori

For better or for worse, I know that I was not the most typical of children. I was a rather high maintenance child growing up and my mother often had to work hard to make sure I was doing OK. Around middle school, my friends' comments about my quirkiness started to sting a little. Every time I did or said something that did not match everyone's (the majority's) expectations, I was told I was different. Looking back now, during my formative years, I had zero doubt that I belonged to the majority, and I tried to gain some sense of security by telling myself that I was one of them. I feel that my strong desire to validate who I am—someone who often questions what others regard as "the norm" and says or does things that diverge from "the norm"—has always propelled my research in Japan Studies.

1. When Did BL Begin?

I must admit that my goal in high school was to fit in. I didn't need to distance myself from the things I liked, but I made myself at least pretend to enjoy what everyone else enjoyed, making sure not to deviate too much from their norms. I wonder if I actually managed to do that. At the time, I thought I'd done a decent enough job, but in hindsight, I don't think I was very successful. Still, I tried. And when I was about to graduate from high school, I had an acute realization: I just wasted the past three years trying so hard to fit in! Ever since then, I started acting without caring about what others thought, although stopped caring does not mean that I accepted the idea that I was any different from others. Therefore, when I entered college, I began "rebelling" against the world (what I imagined the world to be, not how it really was), which took the form of searching for proof that I wasn't a weirdo. Of course, this was just for my own self-satisfaction and to reassure myself, because I felt that without that reassurance, life might be a bit difficult. So, what did I do as a college freshman on a mission? I took two courses of action. One was having exchanges with international students. Even though we are all humans sharing time on this earth, different nationalities have different notions of what "normal" is. While I may have been strange in Japan, from a global standpoint, I may not. The second way was through pursuing Japan Studies. I entered the School of Letters at Nagoya University in order to study what I'd always been interested in: history and literature. When you study the classics and history, you realize that although the Japan of the past is spatially contiguous to the Japan of today, it holds vastly different notions of what normal is. I was going back in time to search for people like me to prove that though I might be strange in modern Japan, I may not from a historical perspective.

As it turned out, this strategy was a tremendous success for me. I learned much through my interactions with international students, such as how, for instance, some cultures may not be pleased with Japan's constant encouragement to do everything five minutes ahead of schedule. When you visit a friend's house, it may be just as polite to arrive exactly on time as it is to arrive late, depending on what country you're in. I came to realize the apparent truth that the norms of "here and now" are not universally applicable, be it the way human relationships are formed or how affections are expressed; the list goes on. This revelation brought me great relief.

During my freshman year of college when I enrolled in one of those first-year seminars to learn the fundamentals of academic study, I met my mentor, who would go on to help me for many years and eventually become my PhD advisor. That seminar, whose course description on the syllabus simply read "We will learn about books," was an extremely nerdy class for freshmen, where we began with questioning what a "book" is in the first place. One of the group projects was to give a presentation about finding "a first book." What was that, exactly? Could we get by with presenting something written in hieroglyphs or cuneiform? Our group decided that everyone else had those ideas fully covered, so we decided to search for the first book about a particular topic.

This was the end of the 20th century, 1999 to be precise. After a back and forth of ideas, we ended up on the topic of "boys love" (BL), a genre featuring stories about male-male love. We discussed things like how those BL books that we girls used to consume somewhat clandestinely had recently (i.e., in the late-1990s) begun to become really mainstream and ubiquitous in bookstores. That led us to wonder when BL books were first published. In addition, by sheer coincidence, there was an international student from Korea in my group who shared that the first gay-oriented magazine had been published in Korea that very year. That was when our group decided to make our presentation about "Japan's very first BL book."

Now, dear reader, just how long ago do you think that such a book was written (note that the BL I am referring to here is simply love stories between two men)? Because my classmates and I were looking for the answer to this question back when information was still mainly sourced through books rather than the internet, we all headed to the library. There, we found the *Tanbi shōsetsu/gay bungaku bukku gaido* (An encyclopedia of aesthetic novels and gay literature, Kakinuma & Kurihara, eds., 1993). Allow me to clarify that the male-male love genre first started being referred to as BL around 1994 and this nomenclature finally caught on after 1996; before then, the term "aesthetic novels" (*tanbi shōsetsu*) was often used. This resource was a gold mine for us students in our search for Japan's first BL, and it was in that book that I learned of a story called *Aki no yo no nagamonogatari* (A long tale of an autumn night; hereafter *Aki no yo*).

Aki no yo was written in the Muromachi period (1333–1600) and tells the tragic love story of the monk Keikai from Mt. Hiei and *chigo* Umekawa from Miidera. *Chigo*, or Buddhist acolytes, were adolescent boys who served the high-ranking priests at major Buddhist temples and were sometimes objects of the monks' romantic affections. Works mainly from the medieval period that feature romance between a monk and a *chigo* are called *chigo monogatari*. Of course, these stories cannot be treated the same way as modern BL. Yet the fact that literary works on male-male love were commonplace enough to become the genre of *chigo monogatari* (though the genre name was not coined until the early modern period), was shocking to my freshman self. My group presented *Aki no yo* as the first BL book. I was a touch nervous as to whether or not our professor would end up accepting this topic.

As it turned out, my nervousness was proven to be completely unfounded. Far from it. I was pleasantly shocked by the professor's feedback, which was actually a piece of information about an upcoming seminar for sophomores and above and the students in that class would read the entire *Aki no yo* together. Above all, what surprised me most was that the BL genre I read for fun could actually be a subject of academic study. At the time, I never imagined that things people consumed for entertainment could be researched at a university; at least, that is what I thought was the norm. Even though I had suffered under the world's definition of "normal," I, too, was uncritically accepting a "normal" that had no basis in reality. The dispelling of this notion is what inspired me to become a scholar.

2. Lovable Outcasts of the Muromachi Period

I wrote my graduation thesis on *Kaze ni momiji* (Maple leaves in the wind), a tale in which tragedy strikes a nobleman who falls for a youth dressed as a woman. Now, a new fated encounter awaited me in graduate school. It was brought to me by my mentor: *Shin kurōdo* (The new chamberlain), an illustrated scroll featuring a young woman dressed in man's clothes as the protagonist. While *Kaze ni momiji* was a work of pure text, *Shin kurōdo* featured illustrations along with narration, in addition to "in-picture dialogue" (*gachūshi*) embedded in the pictures. Further, this work's simple, monochromic drawings gave off an impression of a manga.

In this tale, three daughters of a mid-ranked aristocratic family take center stage. When the parents ask their daughters about their plans for the future, the oldest says she will enter the nunhood, and the middle one says she will enter the imperial court and live a life of glamour. However, the youngest declares that she wishes to "run around as a man." She indeed begins to work as a male chamberlain at the imperial court. As her older brother also holds this post, she is referred to as the "new chamberlain," which is the origin of the work's title.

Later, the emperor learns of the new chamberlain's true identity and she earns his affections while still clad in male attire. She eventually gives birth to his child, a baby boy, but as the emperor already has many princes, her own child cannot hope to ascend to the throne. Though the emperor's affections for the new chamberlain surpassed that for her middle sister, who was already in the imperial service, his love for the protagonist gradually wanes, as she begins to take on a haughty attitude. After this, she heads to her oldest sister's convent, takes the tonsure, and becomes a nun. In the end, the two sisters attain enlightenment, while the rebirth into the Western Paradise for their parents and middle sister are suggested, as well.

Though modern media such as manga and dramas that center on women dressing as men have been popular, the oldest instance of this trope can be traced back to the late-Heian era tale of *Torikaebaya* ("I wish I could switch my kids!"). On the one hand, *Shin kurōdo* follows in the footsteps of these tales of cross-dressing ladies, while on the other hand it deliberately manages to part from earlier conventions established in works like *Torikaebaya* and *Ariake no wakare* (Partings at dawn). The most apparent divergence is the use of the protagonist's motivation behind dressing as a man. In *Torikaebaya* and *Ariake no wakare*, while the protagonists do choose to dress as men, it is because external circumstances, such as the curse of a goblin or family succession issues, force them to make that choice. In *Shin kurōdo*, however, this choice is driven almost entirely by the heroine's own volution. For a typical daughter of an aristocrat like her to voice her desires and actually follow through on them means she was almost certainly an outcast, even in the Muromachi period. After reading this story, I became obsessed with this outcast character; she was the exact ally I had been searching for.

During the late-Muromachi period when the *Shin kurōdo* scroll was created, the imperial family and aristocracy were financially struggling and the court could not afford to install imperial consorts. Therefore, all the ladies entering the rear court remained as non-royals. In *Shin kurōdo*, too, the middle sister of the new chamberlain enters the imperial service under the moniker Harima no Naishi and bears the emperor a princess and a prince (actually the new chamberlain's son), which is a realistic representation of a mid-ranking aristocratic lady's dream come true. To put it another way, when the emperor could not take a formal wife but was allowed to have many concubines, every court lady had a non-zero chance to become an "imperial mother" (mother of the sovereign) so long as she earned royal favor and was able to birth a baby boy. In this environment, the art of courtly etiquette became critically important for these women. Winning the emperor's love without inciting jealousy among her colleagues and maintaining a façade of poise and flair were matters of utmost concern to the ladies of the court.

It was against this backdrop that a genre of literature known as *jokunsho* (instructions for maidens) became popular. The earliest iteration is found in the Kamakura period (1192–1332), namely, with *Menoto no fumi* (A letter from the nurse) by the nun Abutsu-ni, in which she instructs her own daughter, Ki no Naishi, on how to become a successful lady-in-waiting. When comparing the teachings detailed in *Menoto no fumi* as model behavior for aristocratic women of the medieval times and the actions of the protagonist in *Shin kurōdo*, it becomes apparent that the latter was being presented as an example of someone who completely departs from the norms.

Take the unveiling of the family's plans for their children's education at the beginning of *Shin kurōdo*, for instance. In the first section, we find the father's remark, "Regardless of what may come in life, please live with your heart as your guide. To go against parental guidance is part of human nature. In the end, one must trust what their heart dictates." In contrast, the

Menoto no fumi teaches the exact opposite, as section thirteen reads: "To first and foremost exist in the world while living a sheltered life and obeying the parental guidance will enable one to easily avoid many criticisms." And section two teaches that "doing as the heart desires will do naught but invite wickedness," cautioning children against following their own hearts.

It is curious that the daughters in *Shin kurōdo* do in fact follow their hearts, with the youngest daughter, the new chamberlain, being the most extreme example. At that time, daughters of mid- to lower-ranking aristocrats had to choose one of the three paths available to them: to serve royals or upper nobles as a lady-in-waiting; become the wife of a man of equal status; or become a Buddhist nun. The middle daughter chooses the first path and the oldest the third. The youngest, however, opts out of all three options and selects the radical notion of entering government service as a man. I cannot help but think that the female readers of the time with limited life opportunities must have admired this unusual protagonist who lives her life according to a line in section five, "conducting myself just as well as any man, woman though I may be."

What I find most interesting about this work is that the conclusion does not include a heteronormative happily ever after. For many tales with female protagonists, a happy ending normally consists of marriage, motherhood, and prosperity for generations to come. Yet in *Shin kurōdo*, the main character becomes a nun. If she had been a man, this would have been an example of *shukke tonsei-tan*, or romantic tragedy of a man who renounces the world and becomes a monk upon the death of his lover. In this story, though, it doesn't simply end with the heroine's entering the nunhood—she achieves enlightenment as a woman, as a result of religious devotion. Do you realize how incredible this is?

There existed a belief in the medieval era positing that women were born with "five hindrances" that made it difficult for them to attain posthumous enlightenment. As this term, originating from the *Lotus Sutra*, was continuously re-interpreted in Japan, it came to imply that women were sinful by nature. So, how is a woman supposed to achieve enlightenment?

The solution is once again found in the *Lotus Sutra*. Through the process of *henjō nanshi*, a woman is believed to be able to transform into a man and thus acquires a chance to become enlightened. Out of several ways to achieve *henjō nanshi*, the method of choice in *Shin kurōdo* appears to be reciting the Mantra of Light. As such, in the scroll's final image, figure 1, the third daughter (formerly known as the new chamberlain) and the oldest daughter are shown devoting themselves to Buddhist practices.

At first glance, they seem to be succeeding with their training, but reading the in-picture dialogue shows that this is not the case. Since the third daughter has a masculine face, she is mistaken for a man and the public spreads a rumor that a monk is living at the convent. This is where the oldest daughter asks her younger sister to cover her head with a habit so that she appears more nun-like. The third daughter's response to this is remarkable: "People talk about being reborn a man, yet I feel as though I have to live to be reborn a woman!" In other words, the protagonist is complaining that being instructed to act feminine in spite of her goal to be reborn as a man makes her feel like there is such a thing as *henjō joshi* or "transforming into a woman" as a Buddhist goal. All of this drama notwithstanding, she achieves enlightenment and the whole family realizes a Buddhist-style happy ending. Could there be any other female protagonists as defiant as this one? Without a doubt, *Shin kurōdo* is an incredible critique of the established social order.

What I want to draw attention to here is the purported authorship of *Shin kurōdo* (2 vols.). The Suntory Museum of Art owns a copy of the first volume only and a copy of both volumes belong to the Osaka City Museum of Fine Arts. While these are the sole surviving copies, only the set in Osaka bears the name of the supposed author: Go-Kashiwabara-in Kyō no Naishi (1483–1543). That is, according to an appraisal from the Edo period (1603–1867), a woman is credited as the author. Go-Kashiwabara-in Kyō no Naishi was a lady-in-waiting and talented calligrapher who served Emperor Go-Kashiwabara. The possibility that this incredibly provocative work, which defies the gender norm of the time, has been attributed to the brush of a woman who likely composed it for the pleasure of her fellow women inspires me to no end.

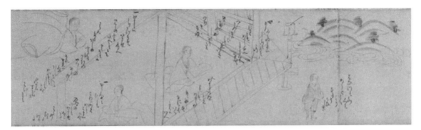

Fig 1: *Shin kurōdo emaki*, section 16, Osaka City Museum of Fine Arts

3. Encounters with Japan Research Overseas

For personal circumstances, I ended up working as a high school teacher after finishing my master's degree, but my adviser ensured that my connection to research would continue uninterrupted. After completing the research project on *Shin kurōdo* with my fellow advisees, we internally published the results as part of the university's annual research report and I set about beginning a new reading circle with another work at its heart. This next piece was *Chigo imamairi* (*Chigo* the rookie), another multi-media tale comprised of text, illustrations, and *gachūshi*, just like *Shin kurōdo*. This story tells of a *chigo* from Mt. Hiei who transforms himself as a lady-in-waiting in order to get close to the noblewoman he's fallen in love with. Whereas the previously mentioned *Aki no yo no nagamonogatari* featured a *chigo* who is discovered by and pursued by a monk from a rival temple, in this tale, it is the *chigo* who discovers and pursues the young lady. Yet still, *Aki no yo*'s substantial influence on *Chigo imamairi* is discernable, including the plot where the *chigo* is kidnapped by a *tengu*.

It bears stating that the stories I have mentioned before this section— *Aki no yo, Kaze ni momiji, Shin kurōdo*—are largely unknown to the general public and research into these works, even in the Japanese language, is extremely limited. *Chigo imamairi* is no different in this regard. This is why I was incredibly surprised to learn that it has been studied overseas. In 2009, Professor Sachi Schmidt-Hori of Dartmouth College (though she was a graduate student back then) published a critical introduction and English translation of *Chigo imamairi*, and in 2012 Professor Melissa McCormick of Harvard University published a research article on the same work, as well. I had never even imagined that there were fellow researchers interested in and studying these writings, let alone outside Japan. I'm embarrassed to admit this, but I'd never thought there was a need to study abroad or to learn the English language in order to conduct research on Japanese literature. Nevertheless, I saw with my own eyes that there was actually research into and academic papers written about this work outside Japan, even though it had been largely ignored in Japanese circles. I thus realized the error in my thinking: research about Japan could not be done in Japan alone.

Through translating Prof. McCormick's research article into Japanese with my fellow members of the *Chigo imamairi* reading circle, I repeatedly felt the differences between Japanese-language and English-language scholarships on Japanese literature. In Japan, focus is placed on textual analysis and thereby discovering new truths. However, not only was Prof. McCormicks' study grounded in a close reading of the text, but it also focused more on the structural analysis and theorization of the narrative. Although it is to be expected that methodological differences between us exist, given that Prof. McCormick's field is art history and ours is literary studies, as I grew increasingly more familiar with Anglophone studies on Japanese literature, I came to realize that there are indeed differences between Japanese- and English-language research methods, which I found incredibly refreshing. While studying literature within the bounds of Japan, I never realized that I had unwittingly stuck to "normal" Japanese research methods. Encountering Japan-related studies done overseas allowed me to take an objective look at how Japan Studies within Japan works for the first time.

In March 2015, members of the *Shin kurōdo* reading group including myself were invited to the Association for Asian Studies' (AAS) annual convention in Chicago. The AAS is the world's largest international conference on Asian Studies. Professor McCormick, whose work enabled me to have this cultural exchange through *Chigo imamairi*, served as chair, and we held a panel discussion on the themes of *Shin kurōdo*. This was my first time at an international academic conference. I was blown away by the gigantic scale of the AAS conference and the immense difference in atmosphere. Sheraton Hotel and Towers had been rented out for the event, with three hundred and twenty-two panels scheduled over four days. I was free to listen to the presentations in any panel that interested me. No handouts or papers were distributed. More priority was given to discussions than presentations. The entire conference had a consistently cheerful atmosphere similar to that of a festival. As such, I experienced firsthand that Japanese academic conferences were not the universal standard.

Through familiarizing myself with Anglophone research on Japan and participating in this international conference, I came to know the merits of both Japanese and Western methods. Not only did this fuel my desire to continue pursuing my research agenda, but it made me realize that it is indispensable for Japan Studies scholars in Japan and their counterparts overseas to interact and exchange ideas. To have two sides stimulating one another as they conduct their research will certainly enhance the progression of Japan Studies. Though the language barrier may very well be a factor in the lack of collaborations and interactions, this is something Professor Schmidt-Hori's approach can assist with.

In 2020 and 2021, I participated in an online workshop organized by Professor Schmidt-Hori, the main feature being the dual usage of English and Japanese. Presentations were given in the individual's preferred language, with questions and answers allowed in both Japanese and English. Further, to elevate the quality of the Q and As, all the papers were pre-circulated among all participants with instructions to look them over before the event. In fact, each presentation was a brief summary of the pre-circulated paper and the speaker was not allowed to read the paper verbatim. For me, being able to read the English-language papers in advance and in their entireties (rather than just the abstracts) was a tremendous help.

Unexpectedly, it was the coronavirus pandemic that normalized and accelerated the use of digital archives and e-books as well as the implementation of scholarly events via Zoom. As a result, we now live in an era where almost anyone can conduct research from almost anywhere in the world by accessing digital archives to freely look up articles from all over the globe in furtherance of their research, with a small caveat of language barrier. Therefore, I feel that the time is coming where it will be possible for scholars to hold large-scale collaborative studies that allow for mutual critique and correction.

4. Conclusion

I stated in the beginning that the motivation behind my research was to prove that I am not strange, that the "normal" of the here and now are not absolute. Through my studies, however, I realized that I, too, held many preconceived notions of what is "normal." To bring to light my own presumptions and analyze them through exchange and research with those from other cultures is absolutely essential for me. From the start, studying premodern Japanese literature was a means for me to relativize the "now." What's "normal" is not universal. Furthermore, there have always been individuals who defied what was considered "normal" throughout history. Through affirming and reaffirming this fact, it has become easier for me to live this life.

I spent thirteen years working at a high school, during which time I returned to graduate school and obtained my PhD. Now, I'm employed at a technical college. Even though the environment has shifted slightly from high school to technical college, I still get to interact with young people as an instructor. It was during my time as a high school teacher that I made the decision: I would become a mediator for other youths who struggled with navigating life as I did. Everything I learned and lived through gave me a sense of security, and now I want to give that back to society. In the grand scheme of time and space, the "normal" of the here and now is a trivial matter; that's what I want to teach the young people in my classes. Furthermore, it is my sincere hope that I will be able to use my research to convey this to many others.

Part
2

The Creation of
Knowledge as
Empowerment

My Life as a Disabled American in Japan:

Intersectional Barriers and Inclusive Imaginaries

Mark Bookman (Tokyo University)

Accessibility means, and has meant, different things to different groups of people in Japan. I have come to appreciate this reality as an American wheelchair user living and working in Tokyo. When I permanently moved to the archipelago in 2018, I went online to search for apartments. Out of 240,000 available, nine hundred were listed as "barrier-free." Each was accessible to someone, but none were accessible to me. The reasons varied: a raised entryway; a narrow bathroom door; an expensive renovation cost; and so forth. Eventually, I found a place to live, but I still had to rely on members of the public to assist me in negotiating environmental barriers when I went outside. Indeed, I recall many occasions when well-intentioned citizens tried (and failed) to carry my 300kg wheelchair upstairs as if it were a smaller Japanese device, endangering me and themselves in the process. While I would normally ask professional caregivers to assist me in overcoming such obstacles in the United States, Japan's rapidly ageing population, declining birthrate, and shrinking workforce had contributed to a significant labor shortage that made it hard for me to locate personal attendants. In fact, local government officials decided to reduce my legally mandated disability service hours from twenty-four each day to five, explaining that my fiancée (an exchange student) must provide for my cooking, bathing, and other needs "because she is family and they could not find caregivers." I was excluded from different sectors of society, at least in part because of my international identity. And I was not alone in that regard—many disabled persons raised in Japan faced similar challenges due to their "intersectional" identities figured in terms like age, class, and gender (Crenshaw 1989).

Scholars of disability in Japanese and global contexts have frequently used autobiographic writing as a tool to highlight otherwise overlooked accessibility problems and brainstorm solutions. In this essay, I build on their work by reflecting on my own experiences as an American wheelchair user traveling back and forth between Japan and the United States from 2008 until the present day. To begin, I discuss how my physical impairments and status as an immunocompromised individual led me to discover Japanese anime at a young age and develop a fascination with Japanese culture. I then recount how encounters with barriers to education, employment, and other sectors of society in Japan helped me to recognize my identity as a disabled person and inspired my research agenda. By unpacking the ways that my understanding of the relationship between Japan Studies and Disability Studies has informed my pedagogy and praxis as both a professor and policy consultant, I provide a model for future investigations of accessibility issues as well as efforts to resolve them. Ultimately, I argue that each member of the public plays a part in erecting and dismantling barriers for disabled people and invite my readers to consider their role in creating a more inclusive society.

1. Discovering Japan through Disability

For all intents and purposes, this essay never should have been written—at least by me. I was born sixteen weeks ahead of schedule and many parts of my body had yet to finish developing. The doctors told my parents that I would likely not live beyond thirty days, let alone thirty years. And yet, despite the fact that my eyes were not fully formed, my lungs weakened, and my body so small and frail that my father's wedding band could easily fit around my thigh, I somehow survived. For the first few years of my life, it seemed as if the symptoms of my prematurity would eventually fade, and I would "catch up" to the other kids around me in terms of physical and cognitive capacity. By the time I turned four, however, it was clear that my muscles were headed in the wrong direction. Rather than meeting age-appropriate milestones for strength and agility, I fell further behind other children. And by the age of eight, my doctors started to suspect that something else may be at play. I underwent several tests and was eventually diagnosed with a rare variant of a neurodegenerative condition called Glycogen Storage Disease Type IV, which affects around six people on the planet. Characterized by progressive muscle weakness, that condition later led to reduced cardiac function and my hospitalization at age ten, when I received a heart transplant after several months of waiting. As part of my post-transplant regimen, I was required to take immunosuppressive medications and accordingly lost my freedom to venture outside and spend time with my peers at local playgrounds. It was my isolation, in part, that inspired me to explore philosophy and encounter Japanese culture.

I remember distinctly the struggle of watching my friends through a schoolhouse window and wondering why I alone was not able to join them. What made my body so different from theirs? Was there a reason that I was subjected to frequent medical examinations and they were exempted? As I pondered these questions and others like them, I began to read a lot of books on existentialism. After all, where else was I, an angsty and rebellious preteen, to find my voice but through Nietzsche? The answer, it turns out, was Japanese animation, which I had plenty of time to watch on television. During the early 2000s, as I gradually adjusted to my indoor lifestyle and my interest in philosophy started to pique, Japanese animation was experiencing a renaissance moment in the United States. Media products developed after the "bubble crash" of the 1990s during the so-called "internet boom" era were full of dystopian tales about troubled cyborgs that I simply could not consume fast enough. Indeed, I empathized significantly with the technologically-infused protagonists of properties such as *Ghost in the Shell: Stand Alone Complex*

(2002–2005) and *Full Metal Alchemist* (2003–2004), whose modified bodies allowed them to achieve feats of strength but left them with social anxieties. By watching the fictional adventures of characters including Motoko Kusanagi and Edward Elric, I gained insight into my own experiences and what it meant to live with disability in the real world. But the lessons I learned through Japanese animation were not limited to anecdotes about disability. I also discovered facts, figures, and stories about a far-away land known as "Japan."

While Japanese animation had offered me several depictions of the island nation, I decided by the time that I was sixteen that I would travel there myself one day and make my own judgments. Thankfully, I did not have to wait too long, as I received a Japan-U.S. Youth Exchange Scholarship to study at Waseda University in the Summer of 2008, just a month after my seventeenth birthday. At that time, I was still able to walk (albeit with a slight limp), so my cultural exchange experience was not so different from others who traveled to Japan through the government-sponsored program. I stayed with a host family, studied language at school, practiced kendo, and sang at karaoke booths while forging new friendships and deepening my interest in and understanding of Japanese society. In fact, I had such a good time during my two-month excursion that I resolved myself to return to Japan for a second time after I enrolled in a university in the United States during the fall of 2009. Unfortunately, it would take me several years to find my way back as I had coursework to complete and grappled with other challenges, not the least of which was my transition to using a wheelchair. Although I did not fully recognize it at the time, my gradual loss of ambulation profoundly affected my mental health and I temporarily lost interest in my studies as I fought to "save" my failing body. My battle against my body continued for the better part of three years until my friends and family finally staged an intervention and I came to terms with my physical decline in the Spring of 2012. Soon thereafter, I decided that I was ready to spend another semester in Tokyo at Sophia University.

My four-month stint at Sophia University was coordinated by the Council on International Educational Exchange (CIEE), a non-profit study abroad organization based in the United States. As a U.S. based institution, CIEE was intimately familiar with the rules and regulations regarding reasonable accommodations for disabled students outlined by the Americans with Disabilities Act. For that reason, I trusted that they would help to ensure my experience was accessible and inclusive. I was right, for the most part; CIEE did an excellent job securing my wheelchair-accessible housing, mapping out easy-to-follow transit routes, and arranging in-class accommodations like notetaking. In retrospect, their success at setting up readily useable facilities and services for a disabled student like myself is particularly striking, as such efforts were not mandated under Japanese law until the enactment of the Law for Elimination of Discrimination Against Persons with Disabilities in 2016. Despite CIEE's best attempts to create an individualized and seamless study abroad experience for me, however, there were ultimately some aspects of my daily routine that they could not anticipate. When my travels and nights of debauchery with friends took me off the beaten path and away from my circumscribed "academic bubble," I inevitably encountered barriers in the built environment. A single step outside the entrance of a bar or restaurant was enough to keep me out of such spaces and inconvenience my companions, who had little choice but to join me in seeking out new venues. Still, such obstacles were a relatively minor annoyance given that CIEE had already arranged most of my services, and I completed my curriculum on Japanese Buddhist philosophy with few issues.

After traveling back to the United States and graduating from Villanova University in 2014, I was afforded a chance to continue my research on Buddhist Studies in Japan as a Fulbright Fellow. Excited to have been awarded such a prestigious fellowship, I eagerly accepted without thinking about my access needs. After all, I had already made things work in Japan on two separate occasions. My ignorance proved to be disastrous (or fortuitous, depending on your outlook) as my third study abroad excursion was characterized by serious challenges that set it apart from my previous trips. For the first time, I was asked to find my own university affiliation and faced the difficulty of being rejected by more than ten schools that were unprepared to support a disabled student such as myself. I suppose I should not have been too surprised. Even today, only 1% of university students in Japan identify as disabled, and administrators lack experience supporting them with tasks (JASSO 2021). Even so, I was taken aback, especially when an official from the Japanese Ministry of Education told me that they could not help me as I was the first wheelchair user ever to study abroad in Japan. Despite a lack of guidance, I eventually secured an affiliation with Tōyō University in Tokyo, only to encounter a new set of barriers related to finding accessible housing and inclusive transportation. For months, I jumped from hotel room to hotel room trying to create a workable living environment while juggling my Buddhist Studies research (of course, most field sites were also filled with stairs). Around half-way through my year-long program, I started to ask myself: "Do I actually care what Buddhist monks think if I cannot get inside their temples? Maybe I should study disability instead?"

2. Discovering Disability through Japan

As I gradually transitioned from Buddhist Studies to Disability Studies, I began to analyze the origins of barriers to accessibility in my life by keeping a record of my daily activities in Tokyo. Each day, I woke up and had a caregiver help me sit up in bed before transferring to my wheelchair, which an engineer built. I then drove my wheelchair across my "barrier-free" apartment, which an architect designed, and got into my modified shower, which a medical equipment specialist set up. After getting dressed, I left my apartment and followed tactile pavement installed by a city planner to reach a nearby train station, where I used my government-issued disability pass to buy a ticket. An attendant helped me onboard by preparing a ramp and I finally arrived at my destination, only to rely on many other people to assist me in overcoming any additional obstacles that I encountered. My life was like a puzzle, with hundreds of individuals whom I had never met trying to solve it. Furthermore, the pieces did not always fit together as such "access-makers" were sometimes absent, or their activities not coordinated in such a fashion as to support a disabled foreigner like myself. Accordingly, I found myself unable to leave home, pursue an education, and achieve employment. My exclusion led me to ask a series of interrelated questions: Why do barriers to accessibility exist? For whom are they an issue? What kinds of barriers are there? And how can barriers be dismantled? To unpack these questions, I enrolled in a PhD Program at the University of Pennsylvania in 2015.

At Penn, I explored how diverse stakeholders have constructed notions of accessibility in Japan by pursuing projects in history, anthropology, sociology, political science, and media studies. First, I researched the laws that governed accessibility in Japan, only to discover that those laws promoted "idealized standards" of access that rarely aligned with "lived realities" of disabled people. To better understand how diverse demographics of disabled individuals experienced accessibility within Japan's legal frameworks, I began to read ethnographic studies and qualitative data analyses. However, such scholarship often focused on relatively narrow populations of disabled people and did not fully explain why members of the public approached accessibility in the ways that they did. To unearth the origins of public perceptions regarding accessibility in Japan, I started to investigate representations of disability in artifacts of popular culture such as anime, manga, fiction, and film. While the "younger me" was particularly excited to return to the roots of my fascination with Japan by examining those representations, I also recognized that they were products of specific contexts. As such, I resolved myself to write my doctoral dissertation on the history of accessibility in Japan. Thankfully, I did not have to start from scratch, because other scholars had already highlighted how certain individuals and institutions played important roles in shaping that history at different points in time. Building on their work to help make sense of my own encounters with barriers, I put together a project I called "Politics and Prosthetics: 150 Years of Disability in Japan" (Bookman 2021).

In "Politics and Prosthetics," I argued that efforts to improve accessibility for disabled people in Japan between 1868 and 2021 have excluded as many impaired individuals as they empowered. To identify which populations of disabled people have been privileged with accessibility and why, I analyzed government records, news media reports, and documents from advocacy organizations. My evidence suggested that economic pressures tied to macrosocial processes like industrialization, urbanization, militarization, democratization, and ageing have played a critical role in shaping the politics of accessibility in modern Japan as they have led architects, engineers, educators, and other stakeholders to focus on the needs of persons with diverse impairments at different points in time. Equally influential have been international flows of information, materials, and people working in the disability welfare sphere, which have inspired Japanese politicians to pursue domestic reforms.

My dissertation project illustrated why scholars of Japan must explore technologies created by and for disabled people to fully grasp numerous aspects of the country's culture, ranging from military actions and modes of governance to marketplace and material innovations. It also explained why academics interested in social justice issues in places like the United States and Europe must investigate the history and politics of disability in Japan. I argued that Japan mattered because it has the world's third largest economy and fastest ageing population. Interested parties have exported the nation's assistive technologies overseas, and its access-making activities have served, and most likely will continue to serve, as successful models to emulate and cautionary tales to avoid for other countries.

While "Politics and Prosthetics" was primarily a descriptive project, it also offered numerous prescriptive takeaways for activists and local officials. For example, the project demonstrated how access-making activities can have a variety of intended and unintended consequences for disabled and nondisabled individuals. It also revealed how access-making activities always involve a large cast of actors including architects, engineers, educators, policy makers, disabled stakeholders, and members of the public, whose daily efforts must be coordinated if their outcomes are to be desirable. Indeed, my study of accessibility in Japan showed that coordination of access-making activities must take place across multiple and interlocking scales of analysis: local, regional, national, international, transnational, and otherwise.

To facilitate such coordination, I argued that "identification of barriers to communication about barriers" was a necessary first step. My project helped to achieve that objective by inviting reflection on barriers to communication in Japan's present and uncovering their origins in the nation's past through rigorous historical inquiry. Although the project was limited in many respects and subject to numerous constraints, it advanced a conversation about how we might create more equitable policies at local and global levels. Using accessibility in Japan as a case study, it helped illuminate the path towards a more inclusive future. And yet, as a disabled individual living and working in Japan who continued to encounter barriers to accessibility each day, I was not content to simply highlight that path for others to follow. I felt compelled to try to fix issues that affected me by pursuing a career as a professor and consultant.

3. Putting Pedagogy into Practice

My transition into the world of teaching and consulting began when I was a student at Penn. From the Fall of 2016 to the Spring of 2018, I worked as a Teaching Assistant in the Department of East Asian Languages and Civilizations for courses such as "Japanese History and Civilization" and "Japanese Popular Culture," which asked students to critically examine the borders of "Japan." As I was given relatively free reign to develop my own course modules and pedagogical methods, I designed a curriculum focused on voices missing from prevailing narratives about the archipelago. By asking my students to consider how various social, political, economic, and cultural processes have created hardships for vulnerable demographics of women, children, old, and disabled people in Japan at different moments, I helped them to cultivate awareness of their historical positionality. I also started conversations about how my students could use such awareness to enact social change, not only in the context of Japan but also within their local communities through outreach initiatives. Drawing on my own experiences as a disabled individual in Japan, I put together one such initiative that profoundly influenced my professional trajectory: the Accessibility

Mapping Project (AMP). Launched during my final semester of coursework as a graduate student on Penn's campus in 2018, the AMP is a digital crowdsourcing platform for identifying and resolving barriers to accessibility. Given the AMP's significance in shaping my approach to subsequent disability inclusion projects, I believe it prudent to briefly discuss its conception, development, implementation, and constraints.

The AMP began as an attempt to build a more inclusive accessibility map for my university. While Penn had a collection of campus maps that outlined the location of some barrier-free features like ramps and elevators, they were often out of date and failed to account for users' specific needs. For example, the maps had icons to indicate "accessible entrances" to buildings but did not provide details about the kinds of disabilities and mobility devices that those entrances could accommodate. If my experiences in Japan had taught me anything, it was that such information was necessary to ensure that as many people as possible could use the facilities and services set up by my university, and that I could not identify problems without soliciting feedback from members of the community. Working alongside students, faculty, and staff from many different departments, I created a mobile app that allowed users to share their intimate experiences of accessibility (positive and negative) by uploading video, audio, pictures, and text to a shared online database that anybody could view. Further, to raise awareness about the AMP, I organized a series of "Map-A-Thon" events in which disabled and nondisabled users traveled around campus together and explored issues that needed to be fixed. Collectively, the participants of such Map-A-Thons helped each other recognize how accessibility takes many forms, from push-button doors and braille signage to lactation spaces and prayer rooms. After witnessing their exchanges, I came to view the AMP not only as a map-making tool, but also a pedagogical program for facilitating dialogues about otherwise "hidden" barriers to accessibility. And I resolved myself to develop similar programs in Japan as soon as I had the chance to do so.

In August of 2018, I traveled to Japan for the fourth time to carry out research towards the completion of my doctoral dissertation as a Japan

Foundation Fellow at the University of Tokyo. Using the connections that I had cultivated with members of Japan's disabled communities during my previous trips, I quickly found adequate accommodations and started my work on accessibility. Not a month after I arrived, in service of the preparations for the Tokyo 2020 Paralympic Games, I received a flurry of requests to mobilize my personal and professional expertise in Disability Studies, including my research as a historian and ongoing initiatives with the Accessibility Mapping Project. Perhaps the most public of my early outreach initiatives was a TEDx talk that I delivered in March of 2019, which I called, "Paralympics as Possibility: The Past, Present, and Future of Accessibility." In that talk, I discussed how my experiences traveling back and forth between Japan and the United States had alerted me to the existence of "intersectional barriers" to accessibility for disabled people in both countries, figured in terms like age, race, class, gender, sexuality, and religious affiliation. I also highlighted how the Tokyo 2020 Paralympic Games offered a chance to identify and resolve those barriers by gathering data from visitors through apps like the Accessibility Mapping Project. Not long after my talk, I started to receive messages from government officials looking for advice about how they might use the Games to create accessibility for different groups of disabled people.

One of my first forays into disability policy consulting was participating on an investigative committee tasked with creating new accessibility guidelines for hotels and taxis before the Games. I recall distinctly the discomfort I felt being the only foreigner at the table when it came to decision-making, especially when I was asked generalizing questions such as "Do you think disabled people from abroad would prefer Japanese or Western-style hotel rooms when they come for the Games?" I could not possibly speak about other American wheelchair users' preferences, let alone account for differences in opinion across countries, cultures, impairment types, and other factors of identity. Still, I needed to offer some kind of concrete suggestion to inform the actions of local stakeholders. My recommendation to the committee was that stakeholders should try to preempt user diversity by setting up a range of customizable options based on Japanese and Western models. To determine what accessibility features were necessary, the committee might deploy crowdsourcing technologies like the AMP and poll visitors prior to arrival. I was pleased that the committee responded favorably to my recommendation and augmented their activities by soliciting additional perspectives about accessibility from other disabled individuals. Unfortunately, their efforts to develop inclusive feedback mechanisms were constrained by a lack of time and resources for implementation ahead of the Paralympics. Still, the fact that my suggestion had helped to diversify access-making activities for the 2020 Games to some extent was personally rewarding and motivated me to expand my consulting efforts.

Over time, I gradually began to engage a wide array of public and private entities in Japan and the United States in conversations about "intersectional barriers" and the "puzzle of life" as I had come to experience it. The goal, of course, was to promote collaboration among stakeholders in different parts of society. Consider a series of blog posts that I wrote for a disability-focused tourism organization, Accessible Japan, which investigated the inclusivity of sightseeing spaces for guests with diverse bodies and minds. In those blog posts, I offered my personal perspective about how easy (or hard) it was as a wheelchair user to navigate locations ranging from mountains in Kamakura to maid cafes in Akihabara and I invited other disabled travelers and members of the general public to contribute their opinions. By swapping photos and stories in the comments section, readers of my blog posts identified many barriers that I had not considered: lighting conditions; the availability of diaper changing stations; the overpowering scent of coffee or cleaning chemicals for people with sensory issues; and others. Their insights broadened my horizons when it came to thinking about accessibility and shaped my recommendations to partners like the Asia Society, Chambers of Commerce, and United Nations, whom I worked with on projects related to education, transportation, and disaster risk management.

In June of 2021, I began my current job as a Postdoctoral Fellow at the University of Tokyo, which has afforded me a platform to continue my research, teaching, and social inclusion projects. By organizing classes and workshops about "intersectional barriers" to accessibility in Japan's past and possibilities of empowering disabled people in the present through crowdsourcing tools, I have carved out a space for academics and practitioners in different fields to design an equitable future. For example, consider a course that I taught in the Spring of 2022, "Towards an Inclusive Society," in which I brought together students of architecture, engineering, education, medicine, and related disciplines to investigate problems faced by disabled people today and brainstorm solutions. By participating in group mapping exercises, my students helped each other recognize the limits of their perspectives about accessibility and how they might learn from their disabled counterparts. Further, my students came to understand that such lessons were immediately relevant to them, because after all, they (or their loved ones) may also become disabled due to old age, injury, accidents, or illness. Discussing accessibility inside the classroom allowed my students to reimagine the outside world, as evidenced by their reports about barriers in their own communities like stairs and other obstacles. I can only hope that my students will continue to use their knowledge about "intersectional barriers" to innovate their disciplines and improve accessibility for individuals in diverse cultural contexts. Maybe then, other disabled people will not have to struggle as I did when I first relocated to Japan.

4. Concluding Remarks

In this brief autobiographical essay, I have reflected on my experiences as a disabled person traveling back and forth between Japan and the United States over the last thirteen years to reveal how the study of the archipelago can serve as a gateway to creating more inclusive global societies. Using my body as a research object, I have explained how Japan Studies and Disability Studies can be meaningfully brought into conversation through the investigation of "intersectional barriers" to accessibility, which sit at the heart of my pedagogy and praxis as a professor and policy consultant. My analysis has highlighted how disability helped to facilitate my initial encounter with Japan and emphasized how numerous obstacles in Japan led me to "discover" my identity as a disabled person. In fact, "disability" is only one of many identities that I have "discovered" through my life in Japan. I could easily rewrite this essay to focus on challenges that I have faced (or opportunities obtained) in Japan due to my age, race, class, gender, sexuality, religious affiliation, or other identity factors. Thinking about how such factors have shaped my access to education, employment, entertainment, and other sectors of society would allow me to start dialogues about inequalities that could benefit many potential stakeholders, including affinity groups inside and outside Japan.

My personal priorities govern the decisions that I make about the identities that I examine. With that said, I want to conclude by asking you, dear reader, about your potential contributions. If you have ever broken your leg, become pregnant, pushed a bike, or had an ageing family member, you likely have realized that accessibility helps everyone. How might your own experiences of obstacles and "intersectional barriers" to accessibility in Japan contribute to local and global conversations about the creation of equitable and inclusive societies? Maybe if you shared stories about times when you had trouble finding housing, using public transit, or succeeding in school with people around you, you could come up with solutions that help others. Tell one person about a barrier that you faced, or how you overcame it, and they might tell another. Before long, entire communities might take up the barriers that you raised and implement solutions. In this essay, I have shared my story with you as a model for this sort of collective problem solving. I now invite you to share your story and join me in making a more accessible society for everyone.

Whiteness and Japan Studies

Setsu Shigematsu (University of California, Riverside)

What characterizes postwar Japanese academic discourse is the absolute silence about issues of racism, either East or West. ~Naoki Sakai

A rupture — a break in the façade — is erupting from intersecting pandemics, each reflecting intersecting systems of domination and extraction. ~ Cheryl Harris

◆ Part I: Whiteness and Its Function in Japan Studies

On June 15, 2020, a petition was submitted to the Association for Asian Studies (AAS) with 1410 signatories. The petition called for the Association to "acknowledge publicly that anti-Black racism is an endemic issue in Asian Studies" (McLaughlin & Wang). This petition co-authored by Associate Professor Jolyon Baraka Thomas and Harvard University Ph.D. candidate Kimberlee Sanders was put forward after the police murders of George Floyd, Breonna Taylor, and other Black Americans, that catalyzed protests across the United States and around the world. The following day, the

Board of the AAS released a statement affirming its commitment to building "diversity and equity" without acknowledging the specificity and significance of anti-Black racism or its relationship to whiteness and white supremacy as endemic to Asian Studies. As one step toward addressing, analyzing, and dismantling anti-Black racism in Japan Studies, I offer this essay as a means to examine how whiteness and white supremacy function in the field of Japan Studies.

Whiteness Studies has become an academic subfield across the disciplines and fields of History, Literature, Sociology, Geography, Architecture, Arts, Film, and Legal Studies since the 1980s–1990s. Over the last two decades, Whiteness Studies has emerged within Japan Studies to examine how whiteness operates within Japanese culture (Bonnett 2002, Fujikawa 2007, Russell 2017). That said, whiteness has yet to be adequately examined *as constitutive of Japan Studies, as an epistemic problem in its structuring logic and methodologies*, and an unspoken value encoded into the established rules of the academic game.

Cheryl Harris' seminal work on whiteness as property provided a basis to understand whiteness not only as a racial category or identity (represented by phenotypic or physical characteristics), but as metaphysical and conceptualized as rights and entitlement to economic benefit protected by law and by institutions. In "Whiteness as Property," legal scholar Harris argues:

> the valorization of whiteness as treasured property in a society structured on racial caste [whereby]... the set of assumptions, privileges, and benefits that accompany the status of being white have become a valuable asset that whites sought to protect and that those who passed sought to attain— by fraud if necessary (1713).

Whiteness is a historical sociocultural construct of modernity, a discursive formation and conceptual-material assemblage that functions as a source of systemic racism and relative dehumanization of non-whites (Du Bois). While whiteness has a historical correlation to white people, it extends well beyond persons considered white. Whiteness is not merely epidermal, requiring possession of the taxonomy of white racial features; whiteness refers to a spectrum of codes, behaviors, signifiers, symbols, and signs—it is a complex and shifting semiotic system. Within colonial-modernity's racialized spectrum of white supremacy and antiBlackness, whiteness has become hegemonically constituted by and affiliated with the logics, systems and structures of power-freedom-sovereignty-domination.

Some possess the privilege of whiteness by virtue of their racial identity, and others possess and achieve relative degrees of whiteness due to their wealth, class, education, profession, linguistic ability, national affiliation, religion (Judeo-Christianity), and so forth. Hence, this essay is not narrowly about or limited to the white identity of scholars in Japan Studies, but addresses how whiteness operates as a logic, as racial capital, as a signifier of privilege, that is socio-economic, cultural, linguistic, and as a marker of hierarchized geopolitical, spatial, and institutionalized power. Moreover, Anti-Black racism and antiBlackness are not the same, as elucidated by João Costa Vargas in *The Denial of AntiBlackness* (2018; Vargas 2021).

While Harris' analysis of whiteness as property refers to U.S. society, considering the historical relationship between the U.S. and Japan—prior to, during, and after the inter-imperialist Pacific War, commonly known as WWII, followed by the U.S. Occupation from 1945–1952—the formative role of the U.S. government in shaping postwar Japanese society and the establishment of Japan Studies cannot be easily overstated. The relations between the U.S. and Japan have been continually managed and (re)narrated through the field of Japan Studies. As historian Takashi Fujitani has written:

Based upon these wartime foundations, the U.S. postwar order would operate through the active inclusion of Japan (along with its imperial system) as a junior partner, *which Japanese studies would produce knowledge complicit in establishing and maintaining this relationship*...this field of area studies was tainted by racial thinking during its incubation period in the war years...most of its practitioners in the immediate postwar decades were white except for a number of Japanese American scholars who, more often than not, were forced to occupy a kind of native informant status... (Fujitani 2001:391 emphasis added).

Following what Fujitani has pointed out, what is notable is that for more than half a century, white scholars have remained dominant and have arguably worked to maintain this racial hierarchy, which is representative of this geopolitical racial-gendered history. Little has changed in terms of the racial and gender identities of the experts or their methodologies. For example, the *Journal of Japanese Studies*, known as the flagship journal in the U.S., has an editorial board and advisory board sans Japanese scholars (at the time of this writing); the contributors and reviewers of books are overwhelmingly non-Japanese, as are their suggested reading lists. The non-Japanese scholar-experts are presumed to demonstrate mastery and expertise over their field and objects of study. It remains a tacit or unspoken fact that this racialized-gendered structure not only exists but persists. Given the proclivity of scholars toward critique, why is it that most (white) scholars do not believe that this racial-gendered power structure is problematic?

This essay critiques how whiteness also functions as a form of neo-colonial entitlement that is presumed and practiced among scholars with white privilege and has remained largely unchallenged by Japanese who see themselves as white adjacent. White entitlement to speak about the Japanese and Japanese matters often without appropriate or adequate concern about the discursive and material effects of their knowledge production has been normalized rather than problematized. This common sensibility that operates as neoliberal white entitlement to extract and represent the other continues into the twenty-first century, but perhaps it is time to examine its implications.

1. Whiteness and the (Non)West Japan

Stuart Hall's oft-cited phrase "the West and the rest" must be complicated to address the status of Japan due to its history as an imperial and colonizing power. Since Japan's modernizing process was predicated on its importation of western institutions, legal frameworks, and technologies to "catch up with the West," this process created a hybridized modernity for Japan. In the late nineteenth and first half of the twentieth century, Japanese leaders (re)produced a racial hierarchy through their imperial-national ideology and the expansion of the Japanese Empire, repeating and constructing what Stefan Tanaka has described as Japan's orient (Tanaka 1995). Rather than destroying white supremacy—a global racial structure that historian Gerald Horne (and others) have detailed and documented—Japanese instead reproduced a historical pattern of racialized-gendered colonial domination (Horne 2004). Given how Japan became part of the Axis powers alongside Italy and Germany, during its alliance with the Nazi regime, some officials argued that the Japanese should receive preferential treatment over other colored peoples (Gerhard 2015). Japanese orientalizing and colonizing of Asia is also indicative of this mimetic economy of identification with white western powers. Through the expansion of imperial-colonial forms of racialized-gendered relationality, the Japanese sought to gain recognition of Japan's national status and the treatment of its citizen's abroad from white imperialists.

While the term West still has important politico-cultural significance in the 21st century, this essay focuses on whiteness since it has become a globally recognized signifier of power, property, and human value (Wynter 2003). In the postwar period, due to Japan's relative economic power, in Apartheid South Africa the Japanese were granted the status of "honorary whites" despite being East Asian (Osada 2002). The fact that Japanese have in such contexts achieved proxy or honorary white status recalls Fanon's pithy formulation: "The cause is effect: You are rich because you are white, you are white because you are rich" (Fanon 2007:5). This racialization through colonial territorialization has expanded to become the world order. Whiteness indexes divisions and distinctions that are not reducible to the West/East binary construct.

Although forms of whiteness and whitening practices can be located in premodern Japan and are affiliated with class, caste, and aristocratic privilege, the meaning of whiteness in the premodern context does not have the same function as modern whiteness. While discourses, aesthetics, and representations of whiteness can be traced to values, standards of beauty in premodern Japan, Mikiko Ashikari has noted that contemporary values of Japanese white skin beauty are linked to modern constructions and concepts of a Japanese race (Ashikari 2015:88–89). Although modern whiteness does not function in the same manner as premodern aesthetic values, such alignments can reinforce and legitimize the valorization of whiteness as arising from native Japanese values. While the relationship between the premodern aesthetic value of whiteness and modern whiteness requires careful study, such an inquiry is not the point of this chapter. Rather, my focus is on how *whiteness operates in Japan Studies* among its practitioners as part of the conditions of institutionalized privilege and the geo-politics of knowledge production.

2. The Formation of Japan Studies

In *positions: east asia cultures critique*, Naoki Sakai and Harry Harutoonian discuss the cold war formation of Japan Studies and its colonial structure. In their dialogue, they describe the "structure of area studies" as a "kind of colonial structure" of instrumentalist knowledge that is "realized in the formation of Japanese studies in the States" (Harutoonian and Sakai 1999:595–598). Harutoonian describes the instrumentalist knowledge and assumptions of area studies:

Once that system of studying an area was put into place, establishing an arrangement of studying a particular area to serve the state and its interests, there was never any need to further question the grounds on which this was being done...Japan was always seen as a field, as if it was filled only with raw, unmediated data, occupied by natives, waiting to be observed and studied...We'd come from the outside and bring our Western gaze to look at the natives and make sense of their habitat...Once the language was grasped, then you would be able to understand Japan as a coherent and unified totality, as a unified culture...we still study Japan as a kind of junior partner to the United States (597–599).

Harutoonian and Sakai laid out foundational analyses of the cold war colonial formation of Japan Studies underscoring how the purpose of area studies is to serve state interests. While there has been substantial criticism of how cold war politics shaped the founding of Japan Studies, there has been comparatively less analysis of its *racial-gendered* formation. I build on Harutoonian and Sakai's foundational critique as it is arguable that the impact of their analysis has not sufficiently unsettled the dominant structures, methods, assumptions, and patterns of the field. Many scholars in the field do not acknowledge that this neo-colonial structure and its attendant racial-gendered pattern is problematic.

Moreover, there is also a need to point out the unaddressed or under-addressed gendered economies in the aforementioned criticism. In terms of the racial-gendered formation of the field, the historical dominance of cis-white male scholars, followed by cis-white women scholars, has been taken for granted as normal and thus not openly discussed, much less critiqued as problematic. There has been a widely known pattern for the cis-white male researcher to be married to a Japanese wife or have access to Japanese women and/or Japanese men, and reliant upon native informants. Some white cis-women scholars have also been coupled with Japanese men and/or rely on and extract knowledge from their native informants. This pattern epitomizes a racial-gendered and sexualized relationality indicative of longer historical patterns but largely relegated to a private matter. This is not an indictment of individuals but a means to reckon with gendered forms of racial power as it relates to geopolitical knowledge production.

Even when white scholars are not married to or partnered with Japanese, many white scholars may have turned to Japan to get away from their own whiteness and/or a more manifestly white-dominated society oftentimes not coming to terms with how their whiteness constitutes the conditions of possibility of their scholarship on Japan. While it is understandable that some white people desire to get away from their white-dominant worlds, they are likely, albeit even unintentionally, to reproduce various forms of white hegemony in their respective fields of area studies.

3. Linguistic Skills as Entitlement to Extract

When non-Japanese scholars obtain language skills—which function as racialized academic-capital—this linguistic aptitude is presumed to grant non-Japanese access to and entitlement to extract knowledge of Japanese matters. Non-Japanese are rewarded and lauded for their Japanese language abilities, especially those who are white (as a compound effect of their whiteness since they are rewarded by institutions designed for them). The acquisition of linguistic skills—typically based on class privilege—is then presumed as the *right to* access primary sources as authentic knowledge. Obtaining the natives' permission is not required, but as I argue below, typically welcomed by Japanese. Non-Japanese scholars' relative breadth of cultural knowledge and familiarity with the cognate literature of the field is often not as thorough as that of native Japanese trained in the same field and non-Japanese scholars remain reliant upon (but not beholden or accountable to) the native informant. This extractionist neo-colonial model remains firmly in place as the normalized modus operandi whereby the scholar's relative linguistic abilities enables access-extraction which then translates into an *entitlement* to interpret the significance, value and meaning of Japanese matters. There is professional-economic reward for Japanophilic curiosity and desire which in turn fuels greater levels of consumption and knowledge accumulation.

Bilingual, bicultural Japanese-descended and mixed heritage scholars also participate in and can also replicate this structure to gain recognition from and within the established hierarchies of white dominated institutions. On the one hand, the presence of bicultural, bilingual, and mixed-race Japanese scholars could threaten to change the racial composition of the field, possessing the potential power (linguistically) to make concerted efforts to transform the academic rules of the game, but, on the other hand, this would require rejecting our own access to relative whiteness and being intentional about transforming the field in anti-racist and anti-colonial ways.

The fact that white scholars are committed to and invested in Japan Studies mistakenly assumes that they are not reproducing white privilege and presupposes that they cannot be racist toward the Japanese they are studying. But racism is not primarily about individual discrimination, personal bias or preference. Throughout modernity, whiteness—as an ontology and epistemic position—has been passing as objective and neutral and thus hitherto unproblematized for those with power. As George Lipsitz writes, whiteness "never has to speak its name, never has to acknowledge its roles as an organizing principle in social and cultural relations" (Lipsitz 1995:369). Whiteness has functioned as the standard of what has been deemed objective, human, unbiased, ungendered, apolitical, and thus rarely challenged in academic fields such as Japan Studies. It has been effective in asserting universality so much so that other perspectives are deemed particular and not universal, tainted, or colored by a political agenda and hence not objective, but reactive (Wynter 2003). Founded on cis-normativity, whiteness demands exclusive possession of its putative neutrality and objectivity and balks defensively at attempts that point to a lack of self-criticism, authoritative othering, and calls for accountability for racialized privilege. The historical and institutional establishment of the field has (re)produced white dominance and privilege by not marking its specificity.

4. White Interpretation and Compulsory Citation

With some exceptions, the dominant method of knowledge production in Japan Studies is to utilize non-Japanese theory and interpretive frameworks to interpret the native Japanese object. Citing proper white male sources of authority is understood as the standard to demonstrate one's belonging and training in academia: Marx, Weber, Hegel, Kant, Heidegger, Freud, Benjamin, Foucault, Derrida, Deleuze, Zizek, Agamben, Schmitt, and on and on. These are some of the white male philosophers who were foundational to my training during undergraduate and graduate school and comprise part of the white male canon of theory. Despite their rationalizations of and complicities in various systems of colonial, racialized-gendered state violence(s), they signify established authority and serve as the sources of white legitimacy. Citing white male sources as signifiers of power and authority demonstrates one's allegiance in a politics of recognition. Those who readily demonstrate that they abide by these established standards of white-centered authority are deemed proper and serious scholars respectful to the established order. Scholars following this protocol are rewarded with jobs, fellowships, grants, promotions, and recognition within a circuit of white privilege. Those who do not replicate this pattern can be marginalized from the field as outliers.

While required readings certainly incorporate texts by authors of color, such works risk being treated as tokenized "minority inclusion" if we do not question the dominance of the white male canon and its ongoing effects. This relatively established and closed circuit of knowledge production ensures the continuation of this racial-gendered hierarchy that needs to be criticized and challenged. This compulsory pattern of citation entails and reproduces the white-ificaiton of legitimate knowledge, perpetually guaranteeing that white authority is properly recognized and maintained.

◆Part II: Japanese as White-Adjacent in This Dynamic of Complicity

There is a dynamic of complicity that involves scholars with varying degrees of white privilege and Japanese who benefit from and wish to maintain their white-adjacent privilege. In this structure, Japanese seek recognition of their value from white scholars who bestow on Japanese attention through their interpretation, criticisms, and study. Due to Japanese identification with Japanese objects of study, *the desire for recognition by white scholars* can matter more than the accuracy or validity of the interpretations of those objects. Being worthy of study and the possibility of representation in academia is considered positive and good; being represented in the western-white world via analysis and interpretation demonstrates Japanese value to the world. Japanese culture has been a world-wide source of inspiration, emulation, and imitation in the arts, theater, film, architecture, design, fashion, food, technology, martial arts, etc. But when whites and westerners emulate the Japanese this recognition matters greatly, if not the most, because white (imperial) powers are widely considered to be the gatekeepers and ultimate brokers of the standards of modern civilization. Being deemed by westerners as "uncivilized" has served as justification for conquest and genocide.

5. *Akogare* for Whiteness as Racist Love & Anti-Black Racism

Japanese deference to and *akogare* for whiteness can be understood as an outcome of the above-described process of modernization that was permeated with racialized-gendered power dynamics. Based on his study from the mid-1990s to 2016, John Russell writes that representations of whiteness in Japan provide "a template of whiteness toward which many Japanese believe they should aspire" (Russell 2017). From aspiration to admiration to *akogare* (longing or yearning for) this complex relationship to whiteness is certainly not without ambivalence, contradiction and periodic resentment, bitterness, and even hostility, which is common to relations of unequal power. While it is understandable that Japanese respect for whiteness is largely as result of a Eurocentric modernization process, the extent to which Japanese love of whiteness reproduces, elicits, and solicits Japanophilia from persons identified as white constitutes a circuit of (imperial) racial white love and white-adjacent recognition and mutuality that needs to be explicated and critiqued for the ways it replicates a global framework of white racial capital and white supremacy.

The fact that many Japanese scholars are also married to or partnered with whites signals to other whites (and lets non-whites know), don't worry, we love (your) whiteness, intimately. I was previously married to a cis-white-male and recognize the importance of self-critique and how discomforting it can be. Such forms of "consensual intimacy" can also function to legitimize structures of gendered-racial power. We need to question how such racial-gendered patterns signify investment in whiteness and consider how such critique may impact white-adjacent privilege. Japanese who are aware of their white-adjacent privilege comply with the greater privilege of those who epitomize whiteness because dismantling white supremacy would mean losing our status as white-adjacent in a global hierarchy of race.

Japanese are often not only in denial of their deference to and *akogare* for whiteness but have not adequately considered how their love of whiteness reproduces antiBlackness historically and globally (Jung and Costa Vargas 2021). If whiteness has been constitutive of Japan Studies, scholars need to consider how whiteness is constituted by and predicated on antiBlackness, antiBrownness, antiAsianness and antiIndigenousness as a spectrum of hierarchized racial value. For Japanese to confront their love of whiteness would also entail confronting (our) anti-Black, anti-Brown, anti-Asian and anti-Indigenous racism. This confrontation with systemic racism would then point to a recognition of the historical and colonial structure of racism in Japan toward Okinawans, Ainu, Koreans, Chinese, Taiwanese, Filipinos, South Indians, Thai, and othered Brown migrant workers, the list goes on (Koshiro 1999; Lie 2009; Hirano 2022). Japanese deflection of our anti-Black, anti-Brown, anti-Asian, anti-Indigenous perspective and values maintains the pervasive structure of Japanese white supremacy. Insofar as this pattern contributes to a global structure of white supremacy and avoids and deflects confronting one's complicity in systemic racism, the depth, scale, force, and effects of white racism and Japanese racism need to be interrogated, studied, and addressed (Shigematsu 2021).

This silent pact between persons identified as white and Japanese constitutes a politics of recognition and comprises a circuit of white racial capital that reproduces a complex spectrum of whiteness. Drawing from Glen Coulthard's critique of the politics of recognition which calls for a rejection of this investment in recognition from dominant white society, I ask readers to reflect on how practitioners in Japan Studies may be complicit in the reproduction of the racial capital of whiteness through the established academic modalities and methods which are fleshed out in the next section (Coulthard 2014). A possessive investment in whiteness—by white scholars and white adjacent Japanese scholars—remains under-acknowledged due to the discomforting potential that such exposure and interrogation could cause some to lose their relative privilege and entitlement. As for scholars who believe that they have transcended their whiteness, this essay asks readers to consider the following.

6. Methodologies of Whiteness: Rules (of) the Academic Game

Here, I address the methodologies of whiteness understood as the rules of the academic game. Scholars are trained to internalize and abide by the following rules and demonstrate their belonging to academia. These rules of the game have been established by predominantly cis-white males and cis-white females relying on a circuit of recognition and citational practice whereby non-white scholars can belong as long as they play by the established protocols. While there are other rules, let us begin with the following.

1. Do not question, critique, or challenge the racial economy of subject-object relationality whereby the white-scholar-expert speaks for and about the non-white other object of study. This structure of neo-colonial knowledge production in Japan Studies operates through a racial economy that presumes an epistemic structure and division in which the Japanese object-other is to be studied and the subject-scholar with greater white privilege interprets and evaluates. Japanese objects of study include not only literature, film, art, philosophy, religion, history, and culture, but Japanese behavior, thought, psychology, and sexuality.

2. Do not question the interpretive paradigm—theory originates in and belongs to the West and reinforces whiteness. Japan Studies experts utilize Euro-

American, Eurocentric, continental theory as the authoritative references for interpretation described above. Westerners and those with white privilege provide the theory to analyze Japanese objects and phenomena. In this paradigm of racial epistemic privilege, the white producer of knowledge determines the significance of Japanese matters, perpetuating white knowledge-power privilege through a citational practice that predominantly references English or European language scholarship by other white scholars. Some Japanese scholars may be cited, but do not typically compose the essential theorists to recognize. The racial economy that governs this fundamental methodological division reproduces white-epistemic perspective in a global geo-political knowledge-power formation.

3. Do not question the racial-gendered history and composition of Japan Studies that has been dominated by cis-white males, followed by cis-white females who largely reproduce the methodologies of cis-white males. Even though there are some Japanese scholars, mixed-heritage, people of color, and a small number of Black scholars in Japan Studies, they are expected to play by the same rules that are designed to reproduce this racialized-gendered hierarchy.

4. Do not question the legitimacy of the nation-state or challenge state interests beyond a liberal humanist reformist critique. Scholars are expected to reproduce knowledge that aligns with and maintains the cis-heteropatriarchal setter-colonial nation-state and recognize governmental-militarized policing of national borders as legitimate and thereby normalize ongoing settler-colonial conditions.

5. Do not question the extractionist model which involves taking and making knowledge from the field and its others with little to no accountability to the people or those communities. Academic protocols in place to conduct research on human subjects aims to prevent direct harm done to subjects during the research process but does not guard against the (discursive)

effects of the research outcomes. The other is meant to be grateful for the fact that they are represented and recognized in the English language domain. Work on or about the other, rather than *with, alongside of*, or *in support of* the other, is the proper academic objective disposition.

6. Do not question individualistic intellectual property (IP) commodification. Even though the process of study is reliant on a series of people, ultimately the product of study takes the form of a book, journal article, book chapter and becomes an individual's IP, copyrighted by either the individual scholar or by a university press or publisher, as part of a capitalist circuit of commodity production.

7. Do not question the linguistic economy whereby English language publication from prestigious university presses located in the West have the highest value; to be represented in English means you have greater value due to your proximity with the language of imperial white-human-life.

◆ Part III: What Is to Be Done?

Although some white and white-adjacent scholars will not admit their white privilege and how their adherence to these established academic rules reproduces white racial capital, *other scholars with white privilege can use their racial-gendered privilege to work to dismantle structures and practices of white supremacy*. While many Japan Studies scholars do not openly support white supremacy and antiBlackness, many may be unwilling to face how an analysis of their own possessive investment in whiteness constituted through the methodologies described above contribute to systemic and institutionalized white supremacy. While most Euro-American area studies scholars have not overcome this racialized framework inherent to orientalism, this framework cannot be individually or fully overcome without changing the material conditions upon which this neo-colonial extractionist modality and methodology of knowledge production has been historically formed. This analysis does not refute the impressive amounts of knowledge accumulation and production that white and white-adjacent scholars have achieved, but is a call to reckon with and address the racialized-gendered conditions that enabled such accomplishments.

Many may critique, find fault or reject all or parts of this analysis, and I am certainly not asserting that my argument is unassailable or without limits, problems, and contradictions. My intent is to encourage and facilitate dialogue and to discuss the dynamics of whiteness and anti-Black racism, anticipating that we will have significant differences, divergences, and conflict. Unless we address our various complicities in forms of institutionalized white supremacy, we will continue to perpetuate contemporary forms of reformist multicultural white supremacy as the more acceptable side of an anti-Black global system (Rodriguez 2021:35–58). Accountability for white privilege begins with collective dialogue and action rather than individualistic forms of white guilt that shut down rather than clarify complicity in systemic and institutionalized anti-Black racism that manifests in a spectrum of quotidian and brutal forms.

As a starting point for discussion and potential action, I offer some suggestions for those willing to confront the systemic whiteness of the field. Here are some practices and principles that scholars and students of Japan Studies can consider in order to transform the field.

1. **Acknowledge the Problem**: Stop assuming that your scholarship is apolitical, objective, neutral and therefore respectable. Academia functions as field of power relations that has material effects and unacknowledged harms.

2. **Change from within**: Use your racial-gendered power for systemic and institutional transformation. Publicly address the racial-gendered dominance of knowledge production in writing and action and change policies and practices of your programs to address it (See Matsumura 2022).

3. **Knowledge as Political**: Expose and hold accountable those who work for the state as consultants and informants and function as ***embedded academics***. Like embedded journalists, embedded academics curry favor by complying with rather than challenging (state) power.

4. **Politics of Citation**: Practice a deliberate politics of citation that rejects reproducing the canon of cis-white knowledge-makers. Sara Ahmed has articulated this politics of citation clearly (Ahmed 2016:17).

5. **Politics of Translation**: Actively and continually commit to and invest labor and resources to projects of translations of people of color anti-racist and anti-colonial theorists, philosophers, thinkers, writers, as paradigms and interpretive frameworks.

6. **Designate Funding**: Allocate a percentage of programing funds and personal income to invest in translation and anti-racist work.

7. **Individualism to Collectivism**: Forge practices that critique and change standardized systems of neo-liberal individualistic knowledge production. Co-author and co-create in ways that center marginalized voices and perspectives.

7. Conclusion

This critique of whiteness calls for a collective reckoning in Japan Studies and further acknowledgement of its effects of anti-Black racism. Practitioners can minimize, deflect, and silence these unsettling issues and challenges by not addressing these racial-gendered historical conditions of dominance. I raise these points as a call for reflection, dialogue, and action. It is my hope that Japan Studies scholars will dialogue about and collectively take action to address these racial-gendered structures and work to transform these conditions. Otherwise, whiteness will remain supreme and unquestioned, and we will be complicit in perpetuating its unacknowledged anti-Black institutional, economic, psychological, symbolic, material, and bodily harms.

Part
3

Illuminating
the Peripheries

06

Connecting Classical Japanese Literature to the World:
Tales Retold and Reinvented

Misaki Suematsu (Nagoya Gakuin University)

Translated by Brian Bergstrom

1. The Image of "Classical Japanese Literature"

Most people, when hearing the term "classical Japanese literature," tend to associate it with words like "ancient" and "remote." Even people who were born and raised in Japan likely think of it as something entirely irrelevant to their everyday lives, while the term may remind junior and high school students of frantically cramming grammar and vocabulary for exams. For university students, too, it is an area they hardly study unless they are literature majors. Once they enter the workforce, most people do not ever think of Japanese classics—if pressed, they may say something like "Oh, I faintly remember learning about *that* in school."

I am currently teaching classical Japanese literature as an elective course for university students not specializing in Japanese literature. I have only taught this for a year and a half so I am still new to the endeavor, exploring through trial and error the most effective strategies for teaching it. The majority of the students in the course seem to be taking it just to earn the credits they need to graduate (though this may be true of most university students who are taking any courses). In fact, to my amusement, some students show no qualms about sharing in their course evaluations things like "I signed up despite having no interest in Japanese literature, because I needed the credits" or "I enrolled in this class because it perfectly fit my schedule."

These are the students I ask on the first day of class, "What comes to your mind when you hear the term 'classical Japanese literature'?" Many answer with the names of tales taught in secondary school, be it the *Tale of the Bamboo Cutter*, the *Tale of Genji*, the *Pillow Book*, or the *Tales of the Heike*. Some students remember struggling to understand classical language in junior high and high school, while others remember engaging teachers who instilled a healthy interest in the classics. Whatever the case, though, I have learned that the images most students have of classical Japanese literature are formed during their secondary education.

When I teach literary texts from premodern times (ca. 8th–18th century), I do so because it is my area of specialty, of course. But there is another motivation—I want to change the preconceptions these students, who will probably never engage with classical Japanese literature again after my class, have of what Japanese classics might be. Even though more and more young people have recently been inspired to take an interest in history and the classics due to pop cultural treatments of those subjects, the image of classical literature has remained fixed. Few people seem to think of it as something relevant to their lives in any immediate way.

So this essay is an attempt to share with my imagined audience— the students who admit to having no interest in Japanese classical literature— what I have learned during my short career in teaching students like them. I would like to show this audience that classical Japanese literature is far more accessible and exciting than they might imagine and that it is a literature with the potential to connect to both the contemporary moment and the wider world.

2. Tales Retold and Reinvented

First, though, I would like to briefly describe what my research entails. My main subjects of inquiry center on vernacular tales dating from the 14th through the 17th century and I am primarily concerned with the creation and reception of *otogi-zōshi*, the genre that includes well-loved stories like

"Urashima Tarō" (Urashima the Fisherman) and "Issun-bōshi" (Little One Inch). Above all, what interests me most is examining the people's desire and motivation to "reinvent" pre-existing narratives, either by producing alternative versions of the same stories or producing "spin-offs."

There are over four hundred known *otogi-zōshi* tales and most accompany visual elements as in illustrated scrolls and picture books. Just as people today enjoy manga and anime, people in premodern times also enjoyed immersing themselves in worlds woven from both prose and images. Unlike a lengthy work like the *Tale of Genji* (ca. 1008), which stretches across fifty-four chapters, *otogi-zōshi* are usually short and contained within one to three volumes.

Besides being illustrated short tales, another distinctive feature of the *otogi-zōshi* corpus is the sheer variety of its subject matters, themes, and styles. Some portray courtship among the nobility, others the exploits of the warrior class; some expound upon Buddhist virtue, others the upward mobility of ordinary folks; and many feature personified animals and even plants. This diversity in genre reflects a readership that went beyond the Kyoto aristocracy, including provincial samurai and commoners. Despite the heterogeneity in content, however, *otogi-zōshi* tales are also extremely formulaic in terms of the pattern of storytelling. As a form of illustrated storytelling that is both diverse in some ways and homogeneous in others, it might be useful to compare *otogi-zōshi* to the manga and "light novels" (fiction targeting adolescent readers) of today.

One reason why the *otogi-zōshi* tales are both generically diverse yet textually uniform is that they are mostly written retellings of prior works, being influenced by and even directly alluding to pre-existing court literature, military epics, *setsuwa* anecdotes, and so on. There is a tendency these days to dismiss stories that resemble preceding works as "rip-offs," but these tales were composed at times when there was no concept of copyright and the connection between narrative and author was tenuous, not to mention that most premodern prose texts were composed anonymously. As such, stories were freely altered and extended over time, resulting in *otogi-zōshi* versions that differ greatly in their presentation, settings, characters, narrative developments, and even endings of the earlier/source texts.

Of course, such reinvention is not confined to just *otogi-zōshi*. Whereas the rapid canonization of the *Tale of Genji* led to its narrative content remaining relatively fixed, many courtly tales written in a later period frequently imitated the *Genji*, extended its narrative, and/or filled in gaps of the original story with invented side stories. *Otogi-zōshi* tales and noh plays frequently borrowed characters from the *Tale of Genji*—or even its author, Murasaki Shikibu, herself—to create brand-new stories within their respective genres. This type of writing practice might be compared to the creation of fan fiction in the present.

This cycle of retelling and reinventing classical literature continues even today. Not unlike how contemporary culture and technology are built upon a foundation of historical precedent, literary works do not exist in a vacuum. They are not confined to the periods in which they were written; rather, they transcend their time and continue to acquire new readership and generate fresh responses long after they were first composed. It is no rare thing even today for a classic tale to be reborn as a new piece of media. To give an example, for many people today, including myself, their first encounter with the complete story of the *Tale of Genji* is through Yamato Waki's manga adaptation, *Asaki yume mishi* (Not dreaming a fleeting dream). Year 2013 saw the release of *The Tale of the Princess Kaguya*, Isao Takahata's anime adaptation of *Taketori monogatari* (Tale of the bamboo cutter, ca. 10th century), and this winter will see the much-anticipated anime version of Hideo Furukawa's modern translation of the *Tales of the Heike* (ca. 14th century). These works are far more than simple representations of the original works; they incorporate the creators' interpretations and introduce new themes into the retelling, which makes them more properly understood as reinventions. Modern culture is filled with such extensions of the legacy of classical literature.

3. Classical Literature as Inherited Memory

There are also certain iconic images derived from classical literature that firmly take root within modern culture through repetition—something I may call "classics as inherited memory." For instance, let us consider the manga *One Piece*, the series that has been recognized by Guinness World Records with the most copies published and sold by a single manga creator in 2014 and again in 2022. *One Piece* takes place in an alternate world with main characters who are pirates and is thus a work with a strong fantastical element. One of the story arcs is set in "Wano Country," a place depicted using a plethora of references to Japanese folk tales and classical literary works. In "Wano Country," there exists a villain Gyūkimaru, a fighting monk on a mission to "collect" swords by force. At first glance, one can see that Gyūkimaru is modeled after the famous warrior monk Benkei, the vassal of Minamoto no Yoshitsune (1159–1189). Furthermore, in the fighting scene, a railing is visible in the background, indicating that this battle is occurring on a bridge, just like the noh play *Benkei on the Bridge*.

The episode of Yoshitsune's first encounter with his eventual retainer Benkei is probably the best-known one even among the numerous vignettes featuring Yoshitsune. Originally found in the *Gikeiki* (A chronicle of Yoshitsune, 15th century), the story goes like this: "Benkei, who made a vow to collect a thousand swords, attempts to complete his mission by taking his one thousandth sword from Ushiwaka-maru (Yoshitsune's childhood name). Upon total defeat, he instead becomes Yoshitsune's loyal retainer." In these retellings, Yoshitsune is stereotypically portrayed as a youth whose androgenous beauty contrasts with Benkei's great size and hypermasculine demeanor. Even among my students, many were already familiar with the image of the "beautiful boy Yoshitsune" and the "monstrous Benkei" from picture books they read as children or from portrayals in modern media such as video games and manga. This striking visuality of the dyad does not appear in earlier accounts like the *Tales of the Heike*. Rather, such an image emerged a few centuries later, spreading via the *Gikeiki* and other Muromachi-era tales. In *Gikeiki*, the young Yoshitsune, then called Shanaō in his capacity as

Buddhist acolyte (*chigo*), is mistaken for a woman whose splendor rivals that of Yang Guifei, Lady Li, and other legendary beauties.

Another transformation concerns the location of the fateful encounter. Whereas the *Gikeiki* portrays the fight between Yoshitsune and Benkei as taking place at Kiyomizu Temple and Gojō Tenjin, in the *otogi-zōshi* and noh play renditions, it takes place on the Great Gojō Bridge. Over time, the latter was chosen for this iconic scene, perhaps because the liminal nature of the Great Gojō Bridge renders it symbolically rich as a site for their battle. As such, the fixed composition of Yoshitsune and Benkei on the bridge was passed down in this particular form, not only in illustrated scrolls and picture books, but also on votive tablets and as the subject of ukiyo-e prints. The remarkable stability of this specific tableau was made possible by its being passed along not only as a story but also as an image. Consuming Yoshitsune and Benkei in this way is still commonplace today, as observable in children's picture books, novels, television dramas, video games, and manga.

Further, there are works that, rather than borrowing the image of Yoshitsune and Benkei directly, reinvent them to create a brand-new story. The girls' manga called *Ryō* by Rinko Ueda, serialized in *Margaret* from 1995 to 1999, transforms Yoshitsune and Benkei entirely. This retelling proposes a version of Yoshitsune that is female—a present-day high school student named Ryō. Benkei appears in the story having traveled in time from the Genpei War (1180–1185) and he takes Ryō back to the Heian period with him (I should note that, even in this version, the initial meeting between Benkei and "Yoshitsune" takes place atop the Great Gojō Bridge). Benkei, while still tall and brawny, is also depicted as a dashing and handsome man, and Yoshitsune/ Ryō gradually falls in love with him. Despite all the reinvented elements, *Ryō* maintains the gendered image of the androgynous Yoshitsune and his hypermasculine vassal Benkei, who devotes himself to serve his beloved lord. Of course, it has been observed that "gender-bending" motifs are common within girls' manga (Fujimoto 2010) and are hardly confined to works dealing with Yoshitsune. Nevertheless, it bears emphasizing that it is unusual to see the sex/gender of historical figures changed even in a fictional narrative. It seems safe to interpret the transformation of Yoshitsune into a teenage girl in *Ryō* as stemming from his femininely beautiful image from the *Gikeiki*, which has been passed down through history. The manga's female author probably took this pre-existing notion as an impetus to reimagine the tale of Yoshitsune as a woman's story.

As such, what I call "classics as inherited memory" has been passed down over generations, and in this process, authors at times tweak and spin the shared "memory" to tell the stories in novel ways. These new stories are not intended to be faithful transmissions of the original in the manner of modern Japanese translations done by scholars or manga adaptations of the classics as an educational tool. And for this very reason authors can freely and creatively tell stories that people can find both familiar and fresh at the same time; perhaps, such adaptations can be dubbed "classics living in the present." Indeed, we live surrounded by narratives from earlier times retold and reinvented.

As evident from the fact that the statue of Yoshitsune and Benkei stands right by Kyoto's Great Gojō Bridge today, the tale of "Benkei on the Bridge" has always been tied to the old capital (though the present site of the bridge differs from its location when the "Benkei on the Bridge" tale was being popularized). However, as eras passed and the iconic image spread beyond the geographic boundary of Kyoto through a variety of media, the pair of Yoshitsune and Benkei became a part of the classics as memory and it has been shared, reproduced, and inherited by those who belong a larger community we call "Japan." In today's globalizing world, though, is this cycle of retelling and reinventing Japanese classics something confined only to Japan? In closing, I would like to consider Japanese classical literature from the perspective of geographical boundaries.

4. Classical Japanese Literature in International Society

It is clear that Japanese literature is not something whose impact is limited to the boundaries of Japan—we can see this, for example, in the excellent reputation of masterworks like Murasaki Shikibu's *Tale of Genji* overseas. During the Meiji period (1868–1912), the *Genji* was translated into English, German, and French to start and now there are translations available in thirty-two different languages. Further, from March through June of 2019, the Metropolitan Museum of Art in New York City held a large-scale exhibit called "The Tale of Genji: A Japanese Classic Illuminated," featuring illustrated scrolls, screen paintings, clothings, among other artworks, inspired by the *Genji*. This also attests to the continuous interest in the *Genji* outside of Japan.

The *Pillow Book*, composed by Murasaki Shikibu's contemporary Sei Shōnagon, is another extremely beloved classical text and was also translated into an abridged English version by Arthur Waley as early as the 1930s. Speaking of the *Pillow Book*, in August of 2021, the Japanese translation of Finnish author Mia Kankimäki's book *Things that Make One's Heart Beat Faster* gained much attention in the media. The book portrays the author attempting to understand Sei Shōnagon, to whom Kankimäki lovingly refers as "Sei," as deeply as possible, in spite of the vast differences in time and culture they lived. Interestingly, this book became very popular in its native Finland, and it was translated into Estonian, German, and Italian, before it was published in Japanese.

In this way, the works written by the women of the Heian period are well-regarded outside Japan and appear frequently in translation. Nevertheless, translation is not the sole means by which Japanese classics are introduced to foreign countries; Japanese classical manuscripts have been collected overseas, not so much as texts to be read, but as artifacts to be appreciated. Directory of Overseas Collections of Old and Rare Japanese Books, Other Print Materials, and Manuscripts, a database maintained by the National Institute of Japanese Literature, provides information on where Japanese classics in their various versions are held outside Japan. Even only looking at recent information, it appears that 165 institutions around the world have such holdings.

It is especially common for foreign collections of old Japanese books and scrolls to include illustrated texts. When I use images from such materials in my class, students often respond by saying, "I didn't know there were so many Japanese scrolls held outside Japan" or "Why are foreigners so interested in reading Japanese classics?" Most of these holdings in the United States, France, Germany, and other Western nations, were originally gathered by foreign collectors in the modern era and exported out of Japan; because illustrated manuscripts can be enjoyed even by those who cannot read the text, the demand was great. Sorimachi Shigeo, a well-known antiquarian bookseller of the Showa period, talks about the frequent orders he received from Europe and America, including from the Spencer Collection at the New York Public Library and from individual collectors interested in those colorful *narae* books, in his *Ichi koshoshi no omoide* (Memoirs of an antiquarian bookseller, 1992), a clear account of how illustrated scrolls and books ended up leaving Japan at that time. Though some of these pieces have since been catalogued as part of private or institutional collections, there will certainly be more discoveries of extant manuscripts in the future, further expanding the known number of foreign-held classical Japanese literary works. These sorts of overseas collections of old Japanese texts are repositories of materials useful for learning about Japanese literature and culture, not only for academics but for the local communities where the collections exist. In sum, Japanese texts and artifacts that are preserved outside Japan can help spark interests in Japanese history and culture among the general public and perhaps exchanges of culture and understanding between that country and Japan.

Another curious aspect of this phenomenon of "exporting old books abroad" pertains to the fact that the transmission of Japanese scrolls and manuscripts may have helped shape literatures outside Japan. Professor Tōru Ishikawa of Keiō University has pointed out that Jonathan Swift's *Gulliver's Travels* was likely inspired at least in part by *otogi-zōshi* like "Onzōshi shimawatari" (Yoshitsune's voyages among the islands), "Hōraisan" (Mount Penglai), among others (Ishikawa 2019). "Onzōshi shimawatari" tells the story of Yoshitsune visiting various fanciful islands as he hunts for a legendary treatise on military arts, including an island populated by men whose upper bodies are horses, an island populated only by women, and an island inhabited by little people. The obvious parallels between this and *Gulliver's Travels* have been pointed out by many, but recently, it has been discovered that Swift likely had direct contact with illustrated Japanese manuscripts containing "Onzōshi shimawatari," which means that the influence of this story on *Gulliver's Travels* may be even greater than previously thought. In other words, even though a great number of the Japanese materials held overseas today were collected during the modern period, examples like this suggest that Japanese classics may have had an impact outside Japan long before the dawn of modernity.

Returning to the manga *One Piece*, this work, too, contains scenes drawn from *Gulliver's Travels*. Thus, we can see the fascinating transformations of a narrative: "Onzōshi shimawatari" likely inspired *Gulliver's Travels*, which in turn was incorporated back into a contemporary Japanese manga narrative. Yet this type of retellings of stories across national, cultural, and linguistic borders is nothing new. For instance, the 16th-century Chinese masterwork, *Journey to the West*, was shared across Japan and the Korean Peninsula against the background of the intra-Asian cultural network since early times and it has been reinvented repeatedly up through the contemporary moment. This cycle of reinvention of literature is only expected to spread faster and further than ever before, thanks to the advancement of digital technologies, much as Japan experienced a robust expansion of readership during the early modern times driven by the advent of woodblock printing technology.

Perhaps there will come a day when these works cease to be "Japanese" classics at all. Professor Haruo Shirane of Columbia University has said that works that have been translated, placed among the literatures of other countries and regions, earned readership from people all over the world, and have influenced the literature and culture of regions and countries outside Japan should be regarded as "world literature," and that works like the *Tale of Genji* and those by Haruki Murakami already number among them (Shirane 2012). In the present age, when information from all over the world can be shared more rapidly and easily than ever, any sort of classical literature can become part of a shared intellectual heritage, out of which what we may call a world culture will likely emerge and flourish.

5. Conclusion—Connecting Japanese Classical Literature to the World

In this essay, I have examined the spread of works of Japanese classical literature from the perspective of their retelling and reinvention throughout the centuries. Looking at it this way, Japanese classics do not exist in a vacuum or in isolation. Rather, they are connected to the present moment and larger cultural and geographical contexts. Classical literature provides us with fertile ground for the creation of new culture and the possibility of international exchange.

Perhaps I should clarify by pointing out that the term "world" in my title "Connecting Japanese Classical Literature to the World" is not merely referring to the internationalized society of today. A literary work contains a world of its own and it also facilitates as a portal through which the reader can enter different worlds. If it's a work from a different time period than the reader's own, the text bridges the temporal gaps between the worlds, too.

Equally important as the literary tradition that has persisted over centuries, however, is what has been filtered out in the process of retelling and reinventing stories. For instance, if one reads earlier versions of well-known children's stories like "Princess Kaguya" and "Urashima the Fisherman," one will be struck by the stark differences in the characters, plot, style, and so on. This is because texts cannot help but transform according to the demands of the time, the people, politics, and the like. However, the elements that are absent in the modern renditions and the unsettling feelings we may experience when encountering older versions of the same stories are the things that teach us about the culture and values of the past. It is important to embrace the discomfort and ask ourselves why such changes occurred and why we feel strange about the closer-to-the-original versions. In so doing, we will learn not only about the culture and think of the past but also about those of our own time, which we tend to take for granted. Through relativizing our own truth while using the past as our mirror, we will be able to better understand others from different times as well as our contemporaries who share different cultural, religious, political, and ethnic backgrounds.

Classical Japanese literature is the body of literary works that links the world within the text, the world that produced it, modern Japan, international society, and other diverse worlds. And it invites us readers to travel to new, fascinating worlds.

Japanese Literature at the Intersection of Text and Narrative Content

Christopher Lowy (Carnegie Mellon University)

There's no way around it: the Japanese writing system is strange. Not only are there three different character sets (Sinographs and two different kana sets) that constantly and regularly mix, but there is also incredible freedom on the part of an author to represent words or sentences in ways that challenge well-established orthographic conventions. Another notable feature of the Japanese writing system is the ability to annotate a single character or character string in a line of text. Quite a mouthful, I know. And it should come as no surprise that some authors take these tools, all of which have a long history intimately linked to the development of writing in Japan, and they use them as vehicles for visual representation meant to complement a larger narrative context. Sometimes the effect is so subtle there is little to comment on; sometimes the effect is so large that one cannot discuss a text without considering the role written language plays in furthering the narrative. As you might imagine, fiction that falls into the latter type of text is visually striking. In such a piece the reader might encounter unfamiliar forms of familiar vocabulary, little annotations telling them to read a Sinograph in an unfamiliar way, or diacritics used in novel (and thus alienating) ways. This sort of fiction is overflowing with what I call textual visuality. It is also no coincidence that literature meaning to foreground non-standard Japanese—and, implicitly, challenge the hegemony of modern standard Japanese—is often swimming in textual visuality. The result of this textual visuality is two-fold. First, it aids the reader in making their way through unfamiliar literary terrain, especially in the case of literature making extensive use of non-standard Japanese. Second, it makes explicit the distance between a reader and the text before them. After all, if the reader was truly intimate with the text, they would not need annotations to help them read it. But why does written Japanese have these tools and where did they come from?

1. All Roads Lead to —?

My interest in writing systems developed before my interest in Japan. As a young boy I was drawn to the unreadable—books and scripts and languages that I knew meant something to someone but were beyond my comprehension. My obsession with unreadable scribbles was well-known to my friends and family. In fact, for my birthday one year my parents gifted me two books that would change my life: Edward Maunde Thompson's *An Introduction to Greek and Latin Paleography* and Peter Daniels and William Bright's *The World's Writing Systems*. I don't know why my parents chose these two books—someone at a bookstore must have convinced them—but I spent countless hours poring over them. It would be many, many years before I could understand what I was reading (and I still can't read Greek or Latin, let alone their handwritten forms). Nevertheless, my fascination with written language only intensified. It was within this period of intensification that I developed an interest in the most complicated major writing system in use today: modern written Japanese. I was delighted to learn that many authors were conscious of the script they used and that it often played an important role in their literature. Reading Akutagawa's *Cogwheels* and Tanizaki's *The Key*, for example, was eye-opening for me. Little did I know that the Japanese writing system I was studying was just the tip of a much larger iceberg...

My interests led me to begin formally studying Japanese as a college freshman and studying abroad as a junior. After a short summer stint at Waseda University I moved to the Tohoku region to begin a year-long program in Miyagi Prefecture. This was just a few years before the earthquake and tsunami that would cast the world's attention upon northern Japan. The goal of my year abroad was to study the *language* but my heart was in *literature*. Even if I couldn't understand anything, I was determined to audit courses in modern and contemporary Japanese literature. One night, though, my friend half-jokingly suggested I try something harder: *kanbun*, the classical Chinese language as it is read and written in Japanese. I was sold. I still remember the sense of awe I felt sitting in a classroom in Sendai learning a dead language vis-à-vis a language I barely understood. This was my first encounter with classical Chinese, which I will refer to as literary Sinitic (Saitō 2021). Since I was studying abroad at a university specializing in training future primary and secondary school educators, my first encounter with literary Sinitic was, strictly speaking, in the context of *how to teach* it to middle and high schoolers in Japan (the subject is mandatory, to the chagrin of many). That made no difference to me, however, since I, as someone who had studied Japanese only for two years, understood virtually nothing of what was being said about the Tang poetry we were examining nor how to explain it to students.

Nevertheless, I managed to understand two things. The first thing was that it is possible to utilize a fixed set of markings to annotate a text written in literary Sinitic, thus transforming the grammar and syntax into comprehensible, if somewhat stilted, classical Japanese. The expansion of this annotated text into a form of classical Japanese is called *kakikudashi-bun*, which one scholar calls a "written-out-text" (Crawcour 1989). This written-out-text contains a mixture of Sinographs (Saitō 2021) and *kana*, and somewhat resembles the way modern standard Japanese appears on the page. The second thing I learned was that this is often a subjective practice that can result in multiple acceptable renditions into classical Japanese of the same literary Sinitic source text. In other words, it is not unusual for two people to produce two different (but acceptable) versions of a classical Japanese text despite having started from the same source text. There are various reasons why this might happen, with perhaps the most common one being a preference on the part of the annotator (or author) for either readings based in a Japanese vocabulary (*kun'yomi*) or readings based on the Chinese pronunciation (*on'yomi*) of a Sinograph.

This means that, for example, annotations to the poem "Moonlit Night" (月夜) by Du Fu 杜甫 could direct readers to read (that is, verbalize) the opening line "The moon tonight in Fuzhou / she alone watches from her chamber" (Owen 2015) 今夜鄜州月 / 閨中只獨看 as *kon'ya Fushū no tsuki / keichū tada hitori miru naran* (Suzuki 1928) or *koyoi naru Fushū o / keichū nitewa hitoe ni hitori miru naramu* (Yoshikawa 1952). Notice how different these opening lines sound when they are read aloud; it is hard to believe they are the same poem! Nevertheless, it is significant to stress that these are not different translations of the source poem. In fact, the English translation by Stephen Owen cited above, based on the Chinese original, would be a fine translation of either of these two Japanese readings cited above. That is, these two different annotations are not competing translations of Du Fu's poem. Instead, they are an intermediary step between source text and translation that provides each commentator with space to assign desired readings to the same source text with the aim of clarifying pronunciation. This practice of annotating a text is very old, of course, and there are historical reasons a commentator would prefer one style of annotation over another. But for me, sitting in that classroom in Sendai, I could only think about the creative potentiality afforded to authors utilizing the Japanese script.

Fast forward a few years. I'm in Tokyo, hungry, and looking over the seasonal menu at a long-gone branch of a mildly famous noodle shop. However, instead of the food, my attention was on a particular string of characters strewn across a poster hanging just behind the counter I was seated at: 旬を！《^^》！しむ。 ♥温まる (*shun o tanoshimu. kokoro atatamaru*), meaning something like "relish the seasonal foods and warm your heart." What surprised me was the use of *hiragana*, one of three character sets used in modern Japanese, to annotate the character strings ！《^^》！ and ♥ . This irregular usage of script, namely, the annotation of emoji-like characters with *hiragana*, was something I had never seen before. And yet, at the same time, it seemed somehow related to the annotations of literary Sinitic I first encountered in Sendai years earlier. What were the mechanisms that made these annotations possible? Did authors make use of this potential for annotation? Were they just a contemporary phenomenon? The seeds were planted for my first major research project.

2. Literature or Linguistics, Neither or Both?

I knew from the get-go I would study the role of script in literature written in Japanese. *How* I would do that, however, was a completely different matter. It quickly became obvious to me that my area of interest sat squarely on the border between two fields that tend to talk over each other: literature and linguistics. Both fields do share one thing in common, though, which is a general tendency to ignore written or printed language. For the most part, the study of literature concerns itself more with the content of a text and less with the way a text conveys that information to a reader. There are obvious benefits to such an approach. When we talk about Natsume Sōseki's *Kokoro*, for example, we are generally talking about the abstract concept of *Kokoro* (the words and ideas expressed therein) removed from a specific text sitting in front of us. This unchaining and abstraction allow us to talk about the original newspaper serialization, subsequent reprintings and variant editions, and the freely accessible Aozora Bunko document all in a seamless fashion. Talking about *Kokoro* in this way also allows us to think about and comment on the text in English, Japanese, or any language of our choosing. One problem stemming from this translingual and transmedia approach is a necessary flattening of what we can call *the particular*. The particular can be anything from the way the text looks on the page, the medium we are engaging with, or the language we are reading it in.

Similarly, most linguists ignore written language because it is at best an imprecise tool for recording spoken language, the target of their analysis. While most linguists today don't actively disparage written language, they still tend to think of written language as an entity that provides little insight into the way spoken language exists "in the wild." My sense is that the current ubiquity of audio recording technologies has exacerbated this sentiment.

Though literary scholars and linguists certainly do not view written language as an "enemy," they nonetheless view it with an indifference that results in the privileging of other things. Perhaps one reason for such posturing is because the two fields were, until relatively recently, grouped under a larger discipline called philology. The story of philology is an interesting one, and one that has a long tradition in the Sinographosphere. The takeaway for us is that, in the most general sense, philology is the study of literary texts to better understand oral and written language(s) and both literature and linguistics were subsumed by the larger philological tradition. For this reason, when I began to undertake my research on the role that written language plays in the creation of literary texts, it turned out that there wasn't a set vocabulary for describing the phenomena I set out to describe. I myself needed to identify the various characteristics of the Japanese writing system and describe them. The result of this analysis led to what I call the "architecture of the Japanese script."

3. The Architecture of Script

Before getting into the architecture of the Japanese script, it is important to understand the parameters of the term script in isolation. At its broadest, script refers to a generally codified and complete set of characters, numerals, and markings used to represent language that may or may not be tied to a single language. English, of course, is generally written in the Latin script. And while the relationship between English and the Latin script is stable, this is not always the case. For example, the script used to write the Hebrew *language*, which belongs to the Semitic family, is the Hebrew *script*. The Hebrew script, in turn, is used to write a variety of languages, including non-Semitic ones, such as Ladino (a Romance language), Yiddish (a Germanic language), and Judeo-Persian (an Iranian language). The grammar and vocabulary of these non-Semitic languages are far closer to Spanish,

German, and Persian, respectively, than to Hebrew.

The point here is that the relationship between the Hebrew script and the Hebrew language is not an inevitable one. That is, the Hebrew script can easily be used to write a Romance language. For this reason, we ought to think of a script as an entity distinct from a particular language. While it is true that some scripts can represent a language more easily (or intuitively) than others, it is also true that novel combinations of script and language can lead to new features in a script. The Chinese script, for example, is well suited to represent modern standard Chinese. Conversely, when the Chinese script came into contact with languages from different family trees such as Vietnamese, Japanese, or Korean, it was necessary to modify the script to represent unfamiliar grammar, vocabulary, and sounds. Japanese, for example, is a highly inflected language and this means that if Sinographs were going to indicate a myriad of inflexions, it makes sense to distinguish Sinographs used as semantic markers from those to indicate pronunciation. And Sinographs did change; the various processes of cursivization and abbreviation resulted in the creation of *hiragana* and *katakana* (Frellesvig 2010).

The idea that a language's structural features influence the way a script develops can be called the typological model (Handel 2019). This insight goes a long way to explaining how and why the use of Sinographs changed across the various linguistic environments they were exposed to. Such insight, however, does not help us understand the relationship between script and literature as it exists today because authors, for the most part, use script removed from its historical context. Put another way, the historical conditions that gave rise to a script is one history while the application of that resultant script is another. To examine the latter, we must understand the limits of the script, or the line between intelligibility and unintelligibility. The contours of these limits can be understood as an "architecture," a set of rules and conventions those writing in each script must adhere to so as to ensure intelligibility. If script broadly refers to the various components of a codified set of markings used to represent language, then an "architecture of script" refers to the rules and conventions that govern the particular way(s) a script functions together with a particular language. One architectural feature of the Hebrew script, for example, is that it is written from right to left. That is why when Judeo-Spanish is written in the Hebrew script texts are written from right-to-left but left-to-right when written in the Latin script. The architectural structure of the script is what determines a text's directionality.

4. The Architecture of the Japanese Script

Understanding the architecture of written Japanese puts us in a position to analyze how the Japanese script functions in a literary text relative to narrative content. There are at least eight features worth noting.

1. Three primary character sets: Sinographs, *hiragana*, and *katakana*
2. Typographic markers
3. Bidirectionality
4. Predictable space distribution
5. Interlinear glosses
6. The existence of a base text
7. Interchangeability
8. An expansive or "open" set of Sinographs

Three of these are especially important when thinking about the relationship between literature and script: the three primary character sets (no. 1), interlinear glosses (no. 5), and the base text (no. 6).

The "three primary character sets" refer to Sinographs, *hiragana*, and *katakana*. Two sets of 47 base characters (5 vowels, 40 consonant/ vowel combinations, and the singular consonant /N/ sound) are derived from Sinographs but function independently from them and from each other. Sinographs refer simply to the set of Chinese characters that are used in Japan today. *Hiragana* is generally used to write grammatical inflections, words of Japanese origin, and Sino-Japanese vocabulary too difficult to read if written in sinographs. *Katakana*, on the other hand, is generally used to write words of foreign origin, scientific names of plants, animals, etc., and onomatopoeia.

"Interlinear glosses" are annotations that appear to the right side of a Sinograph in the body of the text in right-to-left/vertically oriented writings and above text in left-to-right/horizontally oriented ones. The most important type of interlinear glosses are called *furigana*. The primary function of *furigana* is to make a desired reading explicit to the reader (this is what makes possible the multiple readings of that Du Fu poem cited earlier). Readings, however, can vary significantly from one author to another and from one example to another even within a single text (Konno 2009). As one scholar has demonstrated, and I will discuss later, a single text can serve as witness to as many as eight different usages of *furigana* (Shindō 1982). It's from this flexibility that the expressive potential of the Japanese script becomes apparent within the realm of literary fiction.

Finally, the "base text" is the main body of text that remains when all interlinear glosses are removed. In many contexts, the base text is all that is needed for the successful communication of ideas in literature, and it is what is modified by *furigana* and other glosses. The relationship between interlinear glosses and the base text is a hierarchical one, as the base text must always be present in any text written in Japanese, whereas interlinear glosses are not necessary elements of a text.

Confusing, right? But understanding the architecture of written Japanese is critical for understanding how the following examples from a variety of literary texts are possible. Imagine what your reading experience would be like were the *furigana* to suddenly disappear. Most likely, you would not be able to read aloud the text accurately or understand the meaning of each line and term.

	Japanese Text	English Translation
1	吉里吉里人と非吉里吉里人ば識別するんでがすと。(Inoue 1981)	Discerning the people of Kirikiri from people who are not, you say?
2	厚い茶封筒は、膝の上に置かれたままだった。茶封筒を見つめ、指先でその上をなぞった。 ウ・リ・ナ・ラ 우・리・나・라 (母国) 小さく声を出しながら、茶封筒の上に四文字のハングルを書いた。(Lee 1988)	The brown envelope was still on her lap. She stared at it and traced the top of it with her fingers. —Saying *u li na la* ("our country") in a small voice she traced four hangul characters onto the envelope.

| 3 | だからあんた、なーんにも心痛ミする
ことじゃないんだよ。(Sakiyama 2006) | So, there's absolutely nothing for you to anguish over. |
| 4 | 「像てきたね」/「なにが？」/「側脸が你
のお爸さんに」/「はあ？像てねえよ」
(Yokoyama 2014) | "You're starting to look alike." / "What is?" / "You look just like your father from the side." / "Umm, we don't look anything alike..." |

Each of these texts make use of *furigana* to render non-standard Japanese comprehensible to mainstream readers (no. 1 and no. 3) and to incorporate non-Japanese text into a narrative (no. 2 and no. 4). In other words, each of the five authors cited above use the same architectural features of the Japanese script, the base text and interlinear glosses, with different intentions and, critically, in ways that extend far beyond simply showing pronunciations.

5. Script as Resistance: Inoue Hisashi and *Kirikirijin*

Though it is easy to dismiss the sort of literature that makes heavy use of written language as either ludic or exceptional, such an attitude is actually devastating to the field of Japan Studies. A continued disinterest in the printed text has resulted in a lack of serious scholarly consideration of how these texts can, as just one example, use printed text as a space of resistance against the hegemony of modern standard Japanese and the Japanese nation-state. One potential reason behind the lack of engagement is that these texts can be tough to read and even tougher to translate. Another is that some researchers are hesitant to pay attention to the uncommon features of the Japanese script, for it can be interpreted as an affirmation of the "uniqueness" of the Japanese language and, more egregiously, the Japanese people. This is not true, and we should not let misguided approaches prevent us from considering the function of script in literature. In fact, neglecting this aspect of the Japanese language results in the silencing of voices that need to be heard the most, as it is often marginalized voices that most effectively mobilize the architectural features of the script in ways that challenge the notion of a Japanese (language) identity. Ignoring the tools of their resistance deflates the efforts of authors to resist the narrative of Japanese homogeneity. Let's examine in a bit more detail the way two authors use the architecture of Japanese within their literature.

Inoue Hisashi, fondly remembered as one of modern Japan's most popular dramatists, was also a prolific author. Using his work to critique the pervasive elitism around him, he often took aim at bureaucrats who equated the *culture of Tokyo* with the *culture of Japan*. One primary concern of Inoue's, whether on stage or on paper, was the topic of language and regionalism, and the way they relate to questions of identity (Rimer et al. 2014). Inoue's interest in the language and culture of the Tohoku region, where he was born and raised, plays an outsized role in his works. One unfortunate consequence of this regionalism has been a lack of engagement in English-language scholarship with much of his oeuvre. His works can be difficult to understand for those accustomed to reading modern standard Japanese, that is, Tokyo Japanese. And while not impossible to translate, Inoue's penchant for dialect-heavy dialogue limits the potential reach of his literature. A prime example of this is Inoue's well-known and voluminous *Kirikirijin* (The People of Kirikiri). The text describes the impoverished people of Kirikiri, a fictional village located in the north somewhere near the border between Miyagi and Iwate Prefecture, and their declaration of independence from Japan. The text is largely about the periphery (Kirikiri) striking back against the center (Japan) and how they utilize the tools of the center to create and maintain power: bureaucracy, education, public works and, of course, language.

The representation of language in *Kirikirijin* is striking. Inoue inundates the reader with non-standard language through a heavy dose of *furigana*, with the visual impact of those glosses serving as a reminder of the space between the center (Tokyo) and periphery (Tohoku). It would not be an overstatement to say the text is largely unreadable when *furigana* are removed. Striking, too, is the versatility with which Inoue employs *furigana*. As mentioned earlier, the linguist Shindō Sakiko describes no fewer than eight distinct uses of glosses in the text. Significantly, she demonstrates how Inoue's seemingly frenetic use of *furigana* is more measured than it initially appears (Shindō 1982).

6. Yokoyama Yūta and a Biscriptal Identity

If Inoue Hisashi uses *furigana* to highlight the gulf between the center and the periphery, then Yokoyama Yūta uses script to highlight the complex identities and the relationship(s) between them that exist within a single person. Specifically, *furigana* is a tool for Yokoyama to visualize the shifting psychological state of an individual torn between the Japanese and Chinese languages and, significantly, the Japanese and Chinese writing systems. This condition, what might be called a "biscriptal crisis of identity," manifests itself in the actual Sinographs Yokoyama uses in his *Wagahai wa neko ni naru* (I Will Be a Cat), published in 2014.

The text describes a young man, Kakeru, struggling with an identity torn between Japan and China. Kakeru lives with his mother, who is Chinese, and lives in China, but must travel to Japan, where his father is from, to renew his visa. Kakeru has attachments to both countries and both languages. To represent the bilingual and biscriptal nature of Kakeru's psyche, Yokoyama combines familiar readings of Singographs with unfamiliar Sinograph combinations that take both familiar and unfamiliar forms. Specifically, he utilizes the vocabulary and Sinographs used in China today in sentences composed in Japanese grammar. The base text, in turn, is made intelligible by *furigana*. The result is a script practice rooted in a transnational identity that challenges the national and linguistic borders between two nation states. It also creates a literary conundrum: just what language is the text written in and how would it sound read aloud? Imagine seeing Narita Airport—usually written 成田空港 in Japanese—appearing as 成田机场 !

While the first two characters for Narita are the same, the final two are clearly different and the differences are two-fold: 空港 (lit. "airport"), read *kūkō* in Japanese, and 机场 (lit. "[air]craft field"). First, the actual Sinographs Yokoyama used to convey "airport" are taken from the simplified character set used in mainland China and the same compound in the Japanese character set would appear as 機場 . Second, the reading of *kūkō* assigned to the two characters 机场 / 機場 is incongruous with how the characters would be read, namely, *kijō*. Because 机场 is meaningless to most readers of Japanese, the reading of *kūkō*, supplied by *furigana*, is necessary to create meaning. Throughout the text, Yokoyama achieves two things. First, he establishes a script practice reflecting Kakeru's shifting psychological state, and second, the author has the reader internalize his otherwise strange combinations of Sinographs and readings. In other words, by the end of *Wagahai wa neko ni naru*, the reader will have obtained literacy in a new set of Sinographs and various associated readings. As such, both Inoue and Yokoyama exploit the same architectural features of the Japanese writing system to create innovative and eye-opening literary spaces.

7. Conclusion

These are exciting times for Japan Studies as the field continues to widen its scope to include topics that have been overlooked or underrepresented. It is within this context that we can consider the role of script in literary fiction, especially given its ability to raise the voice of authors from the periphery that have been excluded from or are otherwise absent in consideration of canonical authors. It also gives us the opportunity to consider familiar authors in a new light and question the role of digital technology on literature. Not all authors use script as a vehicle for expression, but for those who do, we ought to have the vocabulary to describe this technique and understand how it interacts with narrative content. These texts are often unique, self-conscious experimental narratives at representation, but even these extreme experiments adhere to an architecture of script. Next time you glance at ads on the subway, are killing time with manga, or re-read your favorite novel, pay attention to the ways the various functions of the Japanese script are tweaked for literary effect. Then, ask yourself if that text could exist as what it is without these curious features.

Part
4

Between the Two Cultures, Societies, and Languages

Why Do I Study Classical Japanese Literature in the United States?

Sachi Schmidt-Hori (Dartmouth College)

1. Introduction

As the editor of this book, I asked eight colleagues to contribute an essay by answering the question: "Why study Japan?" This piece is my own partial answer to this same question, wherein I will reflect on why I teach and study classical Japanese literature and do so in the United States, of all places. Yes, I have spent more half of my lifetime in America, my adoptive home country, published research only in English, and taught Japan-related courses at multiple universities to students who know little about Japan.

Unsurprisingly, it is rare for someone who grew up in Japan to decide to study Japanese literature at a graduate school outside Japan. There are a limited number of people who do so to begin with, and most of them return to Japan after completing their MA's or PhD's. I did receive my graduate education in the U.S., but I did not move here for this purpose, as I will explain below. So when people ask me why I came all the way to America to study Japanese literature, I don't know what to say. To be honest, when people ask me why I chose *premodern* Japanese literature to study, I don't know what to say, either. I started graduate school in 2000, intending to pursue a career in teaching Japanese as a foreign language, and I did receive my MA in Japanese linguistics. Nevertheless, under certain extenuating circumstances that I will not detail here, I decided to switch my track from Japanese linguistics to Japanese literature for my PhD and I chose to focus on premodern texts mostly because I was interested in historical linguistics.

One thing that's crystal clear to me is that I would not have become a scholar, let alone a Japan specialist, had I not suffered from depression when I first moved to America and worked for a cosmetic-testing lab for several months (as an English-to-Japanese translator of the testing protocols and reports). It's not easy to explain how this chain of events unfolded, but it went something like this: in 1997, I crossed the Pacific Ocean and immigrated into this country to be with my fiancé. Unfortunately, my younger, naïve self had mistaken American society for a little paradise inhabited by perpetually jolly people and I jumped into this Wild West with no reservation. My life then turned into episodes of Squid Game. One day, I was badly injured (metaphorically) while playing the survival game, fell flat on my face (again, metaphorically), and I was unable to get up for more than a year. I could not eat much, laugh, smile, enjoy my newly-wed life, answer the phone or the door, or leave the apartment. I hated myself and I wished I could have disappeared. Yes, I was DEPRESSED. Still some more time passed before I finally decided that I needed to do *something*. I chose studying for the GRE so I would be able to apply to graduate schools in several months. Memorizing unfamiliar vocabulary and practicing math problems helped me redirect my focus away from myself and I gradually recovered from my depression.

Why did I become depressed to begin with? I think it's because I was completely blindsided and traumatized by the giant gulf between the Story of America that I had bought into and the cold reality I found myself in. It never occurred to me that mainstream America would be hostile to an Americanophile like my younger self. Yes, I regret that I was so ignorant about the country I was moving to permanently, but I would have better prepared myself mentally and emotionally if those glowing representations of America had not permeated so much of the planet via Hollywood movies and other forms of media. The familiar message that America loves diversity comes with many caveats, I must say.

Then, why did I decide to go to graduate school while battling depression? I think it's because I needed to convince myself and others that I was more than an Asian face. Though race, gender, and cultural background can't be altered, many universities in the United States allow you to pursue a post-graduate education for free and they even pay you through a teaching assistantship, research assistantship, or scholarship. I was able to gain lots of experiences in teaching and research while in graduate school, which helped me to land a tenure-track position as an ABD ("all but dissertation"). In short, I was able to become the teacher-scholar that I am today thanks to the harsh dog-eat-dog environment I had unwittingly stumbled into a quarter century ago. If I had never met my husband and never left the comfort of my home country, I would never have known what it feels like to be a racial-ethnic-cultural minority and non-native speaker of the dominant language, nor would I have thought deeply about who I am, why I exist, and how I may be able to benefit others.

2. My Motivation for Teaching and Research

Despite having no long-term career plans when I first arrived in this country, I now have the best job in the world. I wake up every morning and pinch myself. This brings me to consider the motivation behind my teaching and research. To put it in simplest terms, what drives my teaching and studying of Japanese classics is a desire to make people in this country slightly "happier" through my work. Before deciding I must be a delusional Pollyanna, hear me out. The humanities—as opposed to divinity—exist for the purpose of exploring the most fundamental humanistic questions, such as "Who are we?" and "What is life for?" I believe that we, the students and scholars in the humanities fields, explore these questions, not for the sake of exploration per se, but as a means to an end: to enrich our lives and thus attain something we may call peace of mind.

My desire to use research and teaching to help others feel "happier," or more precisely, "slightly less tense, irritable, judgmental, and self-righteous" does not originate from a sense of condescension or pity for them, of course. But for the past 25 years I have observed people in America, the wealthiest and most economically and militarily powerful nation in the history of mankind, and I am constantly reminded of the simple fact that a country's superpower status does not necessarily make its people content or empathetic. That said, I am not crazy enough to believe that Japanese classics can help the most abused and deprived peoples in our society. Rather, the ones I try to speak to through my work are my super smart students, many of whom will join the most privileged socioeconomic class of this country, as well as my fellow U.S.-educated Japan specialists, especially those who are interested in feminist readings of premodern Japanese literature.

Based on my personal observations and social science research (Haidt 2013, Henrich 2020), American society tends to value consistency and unambiguity when it comes to moral judgement. As for the United States, which has been dubbed (or proclaimed itself to be) "the world's police," being "right" seems to occupy an integral part of their collective national identity, if you will. This is discernible if you listen to one of the State of the Union Addresses or watch almost any big-budget Hollywood action movie. I would also argue that "the world's police" identity of America has spilled over into academia, a domain where intellectual discourses originating in the U.S. are disproportionally predominant. When I hear my students' reactions to Japanese classics (albeit in English translations) or read English-language research articles and books on courtly tales from ancient or medieval Japan, I cannot help but notice their strong conviction to tell right from wrong. Granted, having a moral compass is a great thing. The problem, however, is that, when my students and the feminist scholars in my field analyze premodern Japanese narratives, they tend to say or write things that are, in my opinion, futile at best. They seem unable to accept that premodern non-Western tales do not quite reflect the modern American standards of gender-sexuality ideals, including the abstract notion of "gender equity," subversions of gender stereotypes, modern American legal concepts such as sexual encounters between adults and minors or between two parties without explicit consent as sexual exploitation or assaults, and so on. Let's mull over how weird this phenomenon is.

You may say literary interpretations are subjective and one should feel free to read literature as one sees fit. Yes, there is a grain of truth to such an idea. But there are clearly pointless ways of reading literary texts, too. Imagine a Japanese tourist traveling all the way to the Gobi Desert, Machu Picchu, or the Great Wall. He (or she) then erects a tent, enters it, busts out his phone, watches a travel documentary about Kyoto temples as he eats rice balls wrapped in seaweed that he had brought from home, goes back to Japan, and tells his friends, "Oh, Kyoto is the best!" True, it is his choice to waste his money, time, and energy this way but won't most of us wonder why he does that? Similarly, when my students read classical Japanese literature as if they were watching an American Netflix drama and give "negative reviews" because they do not approve of some characters' behaviors, trust me, I will not pat their backs saying, "Literary interpretations are subjective. Y'all get As."

Just to give you one example, consider the *Tale of Ochikubo* (10th c.), a relatively light-hearted, romantic courtly tale with a "happily ever after" ending. The heroine, Lady Ochikubo, is a beautiful and sweet young lady who has since early childhood been locked up in a dungeon-like space of the mansion by her wicked stepmother. But her life changes for the better when the hero of this tale, a young, attractive, up-and-coming nobleman named Michiyori, falls in love with the Lady, marries her (while she is still in confinement), and rescues her from the horrific condition that she has endured since the death of her birthmother. In any case, as a rule of the premodern Japanese courtly tale, an idealized female character is almost always sexually naïve, which means that, when the romantic hero enters his love interest's bed chamber to consummate their relationship, the narrator ought to describe how surprised, upset, and horrified the lady is. We will not see the heroine happily burning incense, changing into her favorite lingerie, and pouring red wine into two glasses. The point of illustrating her dread is not to portray the man as a predatory criminal but rather to emphasize her propriety, noble upbringing, and sweet nature. In the case of *Ochikubo*, the narrator even explicitly states that the Lady was embarrassed about her plain white undergarment (she was deprived of material luxury by her stepmother) and that's why she was sobbing. Alas, such a fine point, however, flies out the window, because for my students, it is not okay for a man to enter into a woman's bedchamber (or a dungeon) without permission, let alone to have sex with her. *I agree*. If we are talking about a real-life situation in today's society, that is.

Needless to say, I never scold my students for reading literature like a Rotten Tomatoes reviewer, because I trust that they are willing to learn something new, especially if it's counter-intuitive and eye-opening. So, for the duration of the term, I bring up and reiterate a few core ideas about a thousand times: "I see your point! But you could have said that without taking this class. Could you incorporate what we have discussed so far and try again?"; "Is that comment about the text or about you/us/America? What can we extrapolate from the text?"; "What is your evidence? I can give you 300 pieces of counterevidence. How should we reconcile the contradiction?"; "Let's not say 'cheating' because we are talking about a polygynous society. If you had been born a Heian aristocratic lady, your father, brothers, grandfathers, half-brothers, uncles, male cousins, and nephews would have had multiple wives and you would not have thought anything of it."; "Let's not confuse a female character's resentment of being neglected by her man with a feminist manifesto calling for abolishing polygyny"; "As a rule, medieval courtly tales do not depict the consensual and mutually monogamous sex of two individuals, because, well, it's a bit boring, and this genre is concerned with the characters' social, psychological, and religious conflicts as they are entangled in romantic/sexual relationships," and so on.

Another thing I try to drive home through teaching is that these classical tales are not intended for Anglophone university students living in the 21st century. This certainly does not mean we should not read these texts, but it does mean that we are not good at comprehending them, just like we are not ideal readers of a random stranger's personal note written for another stranger. If two siblings exchange text messages, making fun of their mother whom they both love dearly and a hacker leaks this thread to the world, people may think they are the most ungrateful, unfilial, spoiled children. A transcript of an ethnic joke during a stand-up comedy bit can mean a whole range of things, depending on who the comedian is and what kind of rapport the comedian and the audience share. Context and intended audience matter.

These pointers usually help my students grow into more skillful readers of the Japanese classics, and after a couple of weeks, most get the hang of using contextualization and introspection to unpack narratives. One of my favorite scenes from the *Kagerō Diary* (10th c.) is when the narrator/ diarist, the Mother of Michitsuna, receives from her sick husband a letter in which he asks her to come over and comfort him (back then, married couples normally lived separately). She wants to rush out and see him but her ladies-in-waiting urge her not to do so. This is because in Heian society "who goes to see whom" is socially prescribed according to class and gender and a woman of fine upbringing should not get up and go see her husband (unless he is emperor). Doing so would relegate the Mother of Michitsuna to the rank of a lowly mistress. My students and I have animated conversations about this booty call, analyzing what an aristocratic lady stands to gain and lose in either situation. In the *Kagerō Diary*, the narrator ignores her attendants' disapprovals and spends a steamy night at her husband's home, which makes her very relatable to us.

Things are far more complex when it comes to the trend of research in my field, because, obviously, I am not the one in charge. I am worried about the fact that classical Japanese tales have been routinely analyzed through the lens of contemporary liberal Western standards and the ideals of gender and sexuality in English-language scholarship. Within the corpus of studies on the *Tale of Genji* (ca. 1008) alone, there are several works that center on the questions of (mostly) male characters' morality and (mostly) female characters' agency (e.g., Field 1987, Bargen 1997, Childs 2010, Sarra 2020, Jackson 2021) but not enough other types of gender-sexuality analyses regarding this massive piece of literature. Though the scholars who show concern for the well-being of the fictional characters probably mean well, it is unnecessary for them to take up the role of the medieval Japanese literary world's police officers who figuratively jail the bad actors or become "protectors," "advocates," and "spokespersons" for the "victims." Isn't this mode of reading painful? Or is the pain the point? Above all, not only does denouncing the behaviors of fictional characters of tales created in medieval Japan do nothing to improve the lives of the most marginalized people in our society, but it can also make us worse-off; this type of research could give us a false sense of accomplishment done for having something to help solving those contemporary issues.

3. For Whom Does "Feminism" Exist?

Many mistakenly assume that the U.S. is the birthplace of feminism and as a result the term "feminism" is commonly equated with so-called "Anglo-American Feminism" (AAF). This is a critical point because using the unqualified label "feminism" obfuscates the fact that this is *not* a universally applicable ideal. There is a great chance that many authors of Anglophone feminist criticism—that is, literary critiques largely based on the ideologies related to AAF—are oblivious to how contemporary academia endows them with a "leg up" in the form of linguistic, national, ethnic, institutional, and other privileges; it never occurs to them to question the validity of AAF as an analytical framework of premodern and/or non-Western literature. The prominence of AAF among the intellectual, cosmopolitan class may not be about pure merit; it may have a lot to do with its association with the economic, political, and military behemoth: the United States of America.

If the primary goal of my field is to improve our collective understanding of premodern Japanese literary texts and tradition, we need to refrain from reading the primary texts as if they were modern novels or fieldnotes taken by anthropologists and confusing our moral outrage at the figures, motifs, and plots for literary critique. Feminist readings of non-Western texts based on the "truths" and "justice" that are inherent to AAF are, again, reminiscent of "the world's police" identity of the United States as well as the hierarchical dyad of the West and the East, where the enlightened subject-self (i.e., the Anglophone scholar) evaluates, criticizes, patronizes, edifies, and rescues the object-other (i.e., the fictional character in the tale) who inhabits the mysterious Orient. Imagine the reversal of this phenomenon: an Asian scholar tries to publish an English-language study of a Shakespearean play, in which he or she criticizes the plot, characters, and/or the playwright for not conforming to the Buddhist ideal of detachment or the Five Confucian Virtues (benevolence, righteousness, propriety, wisdom, and fidelity). Would academia acknowledge the intellectual merit of such an article? Our collective field—or perhaps academia at large—will benefit if scholars can free themselves from their self-appointed positions as the world's opinion leaders, preachers, judges, saviors, and role models vis-à-vis the culture or population they research.

Furthermore, it bears mentioning that the feminist ideal of "gender equity," whose meaning we tend to assume is self-evident, is actually an abstract notion and a moving target that has no precedence or concrete shape (if it did, all of us would know them). Not only is the concept of "gender" a modern construct, but what "gender" and "equity" each signify also changes over time and differs between contemporary individuals, including specialists. Therefore, no one can describe what "gender equity" looks like in absolute terms; no one can prescribe it to anyone or anything. That being said, if there were a concrete, universal form of gender equity, should scholars prescribe it to premodern narratives retroactively (or even contemporary novels, films, dramas, song lyrics)? Should art be always morally just and pristine? Will moral art make our society moral? Or will it make us even more intolerant of anything less than "perfect"?

4. Gender-Sexuality Standards in American Society

Question: why do most people in both Japan and the United States seem to believe that the United States is more progressive than Japan when it comes to gender and sexuality? *Duh*, you may say, but what is our evidence? Have we checked to see if there is not a mound of counterevidence? What do we mean by "progressive" anyways?

I have noticed that my students, including those who know almost nothing about Japan, have picked up and thoroughly internalized the notion of "America: Japan = progressive: conservative = equities between the sexes: inequalities between the sexes" and apply this "truth" to their reading of Japanese literature with zero hesitation. Obviously, these binaries are not meant to be simple parallels but are organized as hierarchical dyads. Nevertheless, they are not recognized as hierarchical as a result of a deep analysis. Rather, the students have learned the heuristic (i.e., the hierarchical relation between the two locales) and they are simply applying this formula to whatever aspects of the American and Japanese cultures they want to contrast. This is easy to do and we are experts at this game, since almost any characteristic can be spun positively or negatively, just as we can describe the same person as either "innocent" or "gullible," "proud" or "snobbish," "modest" or "passive," "outspoken" or "brash," and so on, depending on our feelings.

What's interesting to me is that my students tend to equate the gender-sexuality norms of the U.S. with those of liberal urban centers such as San Francisco and New York City, even though the vast majority of them are from places other than these two cities. This reminds me of the rosy media representations of America I had completely absorbed and embraced prior to moving to this country. It goes without saying that there are plenty of ultraconservative, ruby red states in the United States, not to mention that San Francisco and New York aren't exactly prejudice-free utopias. But such nuanced knowledge tends to be pushed into the back of our brains; just like how knowing that the Ebbinghaus illusion is an optical illusion does not enable us to see the equal-sized circles for what they are, it is difficult to completely dispel preconceptions and prejudices that we breathe in daily, even if we learn that our "truths" and "common sense" are mere social constructs. My point is not resignation, however. Rather, it is that acknowledgement of this difficulty is the necessary first step we can take to deal with this shortcoming. When we harbor a judgmental knee-jerk reaction in our head, we can catch ourselves without shaming ourselves or denying it. We can make a habit of asking ourselves if we have solid evidence to support our intuitions and if we are not conveniently ignoring counterevidence. We can practice relativizing our "truths" by taking mental notes and putting asterisks to our gut feelings. Perhaps, fiction is a good place to start this practice because the characters in the pages won't be offended, even if we prematurely blurt out judgmental comments about them.

Going back to the idea that America is progressive when it comes to the matters of gender and sexuality, I would love for my readers to pause and probe this notion. In my view, the two major characteristics of gender-sexuality norms in American society are "hypermasculinity" and "erotophobia," which complement and reinforce each other as two sides of the same coin. To give quotidian examples to illustrate this, let us think of how North American English as well as the popular media in the U.S. tend to describe gender and sexuality. American society is generally tolerant of violence, an anti-social behavior robustly associated with maleness, and often glorifies violence by associating it with positive traits and images like bravery, justice, strength, and coolness. Conversely, there is a clear tendency to perceive sexuality, which is strongly associated with femaleness (think of what a "sexual photo," a "sexy outfit," or an "erotic body" looks like to most people), as something disturbing, embarrassing, sinful, immoral, abject, and disgusting. In movies, TV programs, and video games intended for tweens and adolescences, physical combat, shootings, explosions, and destruction are usually represented as something cool. Whereas parents are not usually alarmed by positive representations of violence, they are likely alarmed by depictions of eroticism and non-sexual nudity in the media; even a baby's naked bottom is a taboo in America. The most degrading and offensive insult for a man or a woman within the entire vocabulary of American English is one that refers to female genitalia, which makes a neat contrast to praising a man or woman for "having balls." In casual conversation, "to kill, beat, kick, destroy, or massacre" often means "to have great success," as in "Professor, I killed that interview!" (when I first heard this, I thought my student was saying s/he had performed poorly). A "gangster" is also synonymous with a "very cool person." Names for sports teams often evoke the image of combative figures, such as Fighters, Chargers,

Knights and Cavaliers, but there also exist transgressive or even criminal versions like Raiders, Pirates, Buccaneers, Marauders, and Vikings.

Most likely, hypermasculinity and erotophobia were embedded in the historical, religious, and political context wherein the "land of the free, home of the brave" was originally founded by Christian moral crusaders. It is telling that the United States is the only developed country that constitutionally guarantees the right of its citizens to bear arms. No matter how many innocent citizens, including small children, die in mass-shootings every year, a violent male person's right to bear arms is valued far more than a non-violent person's right to not get killed. This glorification of masculine transgressions needs to be contrasted with the fact that this year (2022), the Supreme Court of the United States overturned *Roe v. Wade*, the 49-year precedence of women's right to choose, which cannot be separated from the underlying stigmatization of female sexuality.

If American society would regard violence with as much abhorrence as it currently regards sexuality, and if it would celebrate human sexuality to the extent that it currently glorifies violence, the number of victims in mass-shootings and the number of sex workers and members of the LGBTQ community who are subjected to violence would diminish exponentially. Furthermore, the most despicable name one could call another would be a "killer" instead of the C-word, a woman's right to choose would never be taken away, victims of sexual violence would be able to openly denounce their perpetrators, and revenge porn would cease to exist. It is regrettable that feminism has not stigmatized violence enough, though it has often stigmatized sexuality.

For the past several decades, feminist scholars specializing in classical Japanese literature have published their discontentment about how literary characters behave (albeit according to the genre conventions) in courtly tales, particularly regarding matters of sex and polygyny. In contrast, the same scholars appear mostly or totally indifferent to the unambiguous depictions of brutal and gory violence depicted in military tales, such as the

Tales of the Heike (14th c.). If feminist scholars defend their position as a self-evidently moral one, why do they not denounce the ubiquity of this masculine vice that results in death in the story as well as in the real world if one acts on it? This, of course, is a rhetorical question. I am not actually encouraging my colleagues to expand their moral outrage to other literary tropes. Rather, I am attempting to highlight the double standard of my field's moral compass for judging violence and non-consensual sexual encounters, which aligns with the two sides of the same coin—hyper-masculinity and erotophobia—that characterize America's gender-sexuality norms.

5. Conclusion

Much like my friends and colleagues, I live a busy life that makes me feel like I am constantly struggling to simply tread water. Therefore, writing this essay provided me with a rare opportunity to look back on my entire adult life, including events and occurrences that I had not thought of for years. I graduated from university in Tokyo right after the bursting of the bubble economy; I was at a loss, not knowing what skills I had or how I could contribute to society. I am extremely lucky to have a career I love, the origin of which goes back to the late 1990s when I immigrated to this country, as I discussed above. I would not have been who I am today had I not undergone many challenges and awakenings. This, again, points back to the simple fact of life that categorizing everything into binaries of good or bad will miss the point of living a human life.

To conclude this essay, I would like to briefly discuss the meaning of literature as I see it, and this is the final partial answer to the question of why I do what I do. There is a general tendency for people to put more stock in quantifiable, numerical data for being "objective" and "credible" and value it as scientific evidence, whereas narratives tend to be dismissed and devalued for being "subjective" and "unreliable." Nevertheless, such simplistic binary is misleading, since it is still humans who quantify data and interpret it, and humans are known to manipulate data in order to achieve a specific result they are looking for (Ritchie 2020). Now, let us pretend that humans can perfectly quantify data and objectively interpret it at all times. This still does not mean that narratives play no part in knowledge creation or solving urgent global problems. For example, when a natural or man-made disaster occurs, it is necessary to quantify the damage, but to mobilize the people and influence the policymakers to prevent the recurrence of similar disasters, it is indispensable to hear the personal accounts of the survivors and witnesses. We humans are poor at processing or storing objective data in our minds. To understand complex phenomena, we often transform the data into a narrative so that we can grasp the meaning and significance of the matter, not only on the analytical level but also on the emotional level; both are necessary. If we look around, in all major domains of human life, be it history, philosophy, religion, politics, music, and even visual art, we rely on the power of narratives to break down and process abstract ideas.

We shape our worldviews by reading and listening to narratives. When we immerse ourselves in stories composed in a remote past and/ or a faraway land, the distance diminishes, while our outlook widens and brightens. By the same token, disinformation and prejudices are powerful narratives that can influence our opinions. In today's information overload, we are prone to saving time and mental energy by uncritically agreeing with what our tribes promote and rejecting whatever other tribes put forth. It goes without saying that the more we automate our thinking process, the more our ability to think critically will deteriorate, which will in turn exacerbate the existing political, socioeconomic, racial, and cultural divisions in our society. As such, narratives are inextricably connected to being human. It is my hope that, in some ways, what I do as a teacher and scholar of classical Japanese literature may benefit my fellow humans living in "the land of the free."

Neither Here nor There:
Libraries of Knowledge,
in English, in Japan

Dylan McGee (Nagoya University)

A few summers ago, I found myself in a tastefully appointed library in a one-bedroom, single-bath apartment *from* the Upper East Side of Manhattan. Notice how I said from the Upper East Side, not *on* it. I'll explain what that means in a moment.

The woman giving a tour of the place encouraged me to peruse the collection of books, all of which had been wrapped in cellophane and stacked eight shelves high, floor to ceiling. When I crouched down to inspect the old dictionaries and reference books on the bottom shelf, for signs of wear by the famous fingers that had flicked their pages, I was struck by how thickly the smell of toluene fumed through the cellophane. How quickly that smell spirited me to memories of subterranean crawls through the Firestone Library at Princeton University, the "submarine" of the C.V. Starr East Asia Library at Columbia University, the avalanche of books in my advisor's office at Kanazawa University, and all the way back to the pristine collection of modern Japanese literature in translation that had been assembled by Marleigh Grayer Ryan at my undergraduate alma mater, tucked away in the evergreens of upstate New York. Within the span of a few seconds, one whiff had taken me on a sentimental journey through my entire career of reading books about Japan.

Putting a knee to the parquet flooring, I righted myself to scan the higher shelves of the collection, from the works by Edward Seidensticker and Ivan Morris arranged at eye level, all the way up to the first editions of Mishima and Abe Kobo novels on the top shelf, abutting the crown molding. Spotting a first edition of E. Dale Saunders' translation of *Inter Ice Age 4*, just barely out of reach, I imagined what it must have been like for American readers in the 1960s and 1970s, back when people seemed to form impressions of Japan through fictional books, translated into English, with tastefully modern covers rendered in teal and turquoise.

My guide, taking note of my interest, asked me where I was from.

New York, originally.

She smiled and gestured towards a sloop-backed chair. Said come over here. Come over to this chair at the far end of the bookshelves, alongside this exotic-looking radiator.

Try sitting in it.

I smiled thanks but no thanks. I explained that I had just been swimming in the Sea of Japan. That my swim trunks might still be damp and briny. Which might ruin the upholstery.

Please, she said. *Keene-sensei would want you to.*

1. Neither Here nor There

At this point, I should probably come clean about the setting of this story. You'll remember that I opened by stating that this apartment was *from* the Upper East Side, not *on* it. In fact, this apartment I've been describing is originally *from* New York, specifically from the estate of Donald Keene, acclaimed scholar and translator of Japanese literature. Yet like Kamo no Chomei's hut, which during times of disaster could be mobilized for relocation in the foothills of Kyoto, Donald Keene's apartment has been transplanted to a small residential neighborhood in Kashiwazaki, Niigata Prefecture, where it has stood for the past ten years. The apartment is fascinating in so many ways, not least of all because of how it stands out from its surroundings. If you're not familiar with Kashiwazaki, you might picture it as a breezy coastal city, flanked by commercial fishing marinas on the Sea of Japan side and a welter of machine parts factories inland, with a constant caravan of class-7 conventional duty trucks passing in between. The main boulevard wends through a network of salt-rusted shopping arcades that date back to the heyday of Tanaka Kakuei-style clientelism. Karaoke cabarets. Mom-and-pop boutiques and "bar-ber" shops. A licensed Panasonic retailer, displaying a sun-blanched cardboard cutout of Matsushima Nanako, still in her teens, modelling a fax machine from 1992.

One would need to search closely for evidence of the events that sparked the strange movement of Donald Keene's apartment to this place. Yet the evidence is here, in cracked sidewalk tiles that have not been sealed and in a small Quonset hut, shaken off its foundation. In July 2007, a magnitude 6.6 earthquake seventeen kilometers off the coast of Kashiwazaki triggered landslides and the destruction of over three hundred buildings, mostly aging wooden structures with heavy ceramic tile roofs. Over 1,000 people were injured, and eleven lost their lives. Weeks later, a telephone rang at one of the reception desks in Kashiwazaki City Hall. I am assuming at the desk of culture and tourism. At a time when local officials were still preoccupied with cleanup and reconstruction efforts, it must have confused the person who answered the phone when they heard that Donald Keene, Professor of Japanese Literature at Columbia University in New York, was offering to come to Kashiwazaki to stage a long-lost puppet play about a fourteenth-century monk. A play whose last recorded performance had been over three hundred years earlier, in Jōkyō 2 (1685). A play whose only discernible connection to Kashiwazaki being that the mummified remains of the monk were interred at a temple in nearby Nagaoka. At this point in my envisioning of the phone call, I cue several seconds of dead air over the receiver. *Puppet play?* Even with the assurance that it would be of local interest, I wonder if the person taking the call had managed to piece together the logic of how an Edo-period puppet play had anything to do with anything.

Of course, it had everything to do with revival. The revival of this play, whose script had recently been discovered in the holdings of The British Museum, was meant to augur the revival of Kashiwazaki itself in the wake of the disaster. To offer hope. With the help of Niigata-born shamisen player Tsuruzawa Asazō V (also known as Echigo Kakutayū), the play was performed in Kashiwazaki in June 2009, just shy of the two-year anniversary of the disaster, to much acclaim in the local and national media. Two years later, following the 2011 Tohoku earthquake and tsunami, Donald Keene famously relinquished his American citizenship and became a Japanese citizen, aiming to live out the remainder of his life in solidarity with the Japanese people.

By this time, the project to relocate Donald Keene's apartment to Kashiwazaki was well underway. Starting in August 2011, over 2,500 items from Donald Keene's New York apartment—including books, paintings, vases, carpets, ottomans, heating fixtures, light switches, anything that wasn't bolted down, but even things that were, like the original brass doorknobs— were removed from their original placements, air shipped to Kashiwazaki, and rearranged piece by piece within a carefully curated recreation of the original apartment. The enormous expenses for this project were underwritten by the Bourbon corporation, whose previous work you may be familiar with if you've ever walked down the snack aisle of your local Japanese supermarket. Bourbon, which is based in Kashiwazaki, produces several popular brands of cookies. In fact, the company was founded in the wake of the 1923 Great Kanto Earthquake, with the mission of producing nutritious and high-quality biscuits that could tide the population over in times of disaster. With a corporate legacy that originated out of one of the most devastating earthquakes in modern Japanese history, it was perhaps only natural that the company took an interest in Donald Keene's cultural activism in the wake of two natural disasters.

Today, as a special accommodation to guests of the Donald Keene Center Kashiwazaki, Bourbon offers their full line of products in the museum gift shop, which can be accessed from the current incarnation of Donald Keene's parlor by way of a stairway. There, fans of Japanese literature can taste the richness of Bourbon's Alfort chocolate medallions, or their delectably flaky Le Monde crepe wafers, packaged in commemorative, Donald Keene Center editions sachets. And trust me when I say that after the first bite of a Le Monde, the pairing of America's best known Japanologist with Japan's most popular producer of European-style cookies suddenly feels far less ludicrous than it should.

Before you get the impression that I am merely reveling in the delightful weirdness of this curation, and the improbable convergence of academic, municipal, and commercial concerns that brought it into being, let me explain why this visit to Donald Keene's apartment in Niigata resonated so powerfully with me, and why I have chosen to make it the thematic focus of this essay. It didn't hit me until I had exited the Donald Keene Center at Kashiwazaki, and then within the space of a few steps, re-entered the actual city of Kashiwazaki, but somewhere in between, I was seized by this powerful sense of being neither here nor there. Of suddenly, physically being back in the forty-degree swelter of cicada-bleating Niigata, but not really being there. In some ways, it was like the disorienting experience of leaving a movie theater, when the soundtrack continues to rouse the senses, and the affective intensities that have sustained you through two hours of visual engagement and vicarious identification with the lead actor suddenly have nothing left to latch onto. And all you have left in their wake is the illusion, that bracing feeling that you too could become a decorated scholar of Japanese literature someday. Yet there was something more to it. Ludicrously, I had felt very much at home in Donald Keene's apartment, sitting in his upholstered chair and enjoying the gorgeous view of the sun setting over the Hudson River in overlapping currents of lavender and maroon—all of which had been convincingly rendered, more or less, on the digitally printed window shade. I knew that on the other side of that window shade, there was surely a less scenic view, perhaps of someone's Hijet flatbed K-truck parked alongside mounds of seaweed, sun-drying on top of old newspapers. In this part of Niigata, there is a type of maroon-colored seaweed called *ego* that can command premium prices on the open market, with lots of competition among amateur seaweed hunters combing the beaches for the biggest score. But I choose to block out that reality and indulge in the illusion of the Hudson River instead.

Which brings me to my last point about the apartment—which is the stinging realization I came to, that this wall of books, and the lofty accomplishments of scholarship they represented, seemed to have no relevance whatsoever to the city of Kashiwazaki, the place that gave them space to exist. I think my bewilderment at the time would have been best summarized by the headline of a feature about the Donald Keene Center that ran on a popular Japanese travel site, in which the writer bluntly asked *Why Kashiwazaki?* 何故、柏崎に？ All those books which Donald Keene had invested a career in writing, and me the better part of three decades reading and re-reading, they seemed to have about as much relevance to Kashiwazaki as wafer cookies to earthquakes. For example, I could walk over to the nearby Welcia Drug Store or the Veam Stadium Pachinko Parlor, and I could conduct a survey of the local residents, and I would probably not find a single person who has ever given a fleeting thought to Donald Keene's work as the translator of *The Battles of Coxinga.*

This led me to question, what is the point of English language scholarship about Japan? What relevance does it have to the everyday lives of people in Japan, especially in times of disaster? Had the apartment been relocated to any other part of Japan besides Niigata, I might not have been beset with these questions; but I think it was because I have long-standing ties to the area, with family living in the nearby town of Kawaguchi, and probably also because I have a tendency to internalize or perform Niigata values when I am visiting there, that I couldn't help but feel that people in Kashiwazaki viewed the museum as a peculiar use of space, if not, more judgmentally, as a vanity project that didn't quite belong in their town. Only after experiencing the radical juxtaposition of Donald Keene's gleaming blue museum with the raised beds of eggplants just steps away from the entrance—the "real world" of Kashiwazaki, if you will—did that incongruity became starkly apparent to me.

2. World within Walls

Since my visit, I have come to embrace Donald Keene's apartment, in all its fascinating displacements, as a metaphor for my own problematic position as a teacher and researcher in Japan. Well, maybe not even a metaphor. As I write this, I am taking visual stock of all the books in my office here at Nagoya University, stacked eight shelves high along two ten-meter long walls. About half of the books are in English. Some of these books, a few boxes worth, made the trip with me from New York when I took up my position here in April 2011. Some of the books are the exact same ones you would find in Donald Keene's apartment, some the exact same editions, and some are even arranged on the shelf in the exact same order. Occasionally, when I am hunting through their pages for bibliographic references, or for an excerpt I want to scan to PDF, I feel the ghost motions of the past, of previously handling these same books in different times and spaces, magically overlap with the haptic intensities of the present. That awareness of literally going through the same motions with the same books, and yet often finding something new and inspiring to share with my students, continually reaffirms for me the value of what so many scholars and translators of Japanese literature working in English have contributed to this field.

Which is not to say that I have an unproblematic relationship with these books. During my first years of "teaching about Japan" to international students at Nagoya University, I did not always comply with the mandate to use English as the only language of instruction. Not when I had highly motivated second-language learners who were keen to read Japanese texts in the original. Or a few intrepid native-speaking Japanese students from other departments, who wanted to try discussing (though not necessarily reading) Japanese literature in English. Why should I assign Donald Keene's translation of "Account of My Hut" without also giving students the option to read a Japanese annotated edition? Despite the widespread expectation that English-language instruction would internationalize our campus from within, I observed many curious ways in which it could render the opposite effect, and create separation between international students and everyone else. At times, I sensed that my own classroom might not be so different from Donald Keene's apartment—a small piece of American-style academia that had been relocated within a Japanese university. Just down the hall or even in the adjoining classroom, a colleague of mine might be teaching the exact same text, in Japanese, to a class of students who might never get to meet my students.

For the remainder of this essay, I would like to delve a bit more deeply into this theme of displacement I have been sketching out, through a flat ontological view of books as objects. Objects that can enter into surprisingly weird assemblages with other objects, people, and places. I would propose that well beyond what books contain, the physical placements and displacements of books can tell us a lot about the systems of knowledge that shape teaching and research about Japan—systems that I admit to being in some ways complicit. In doing so, I will also be drawing upon my experiences teaching and researching in Japanese literature, both during my tenure at Nagoya University and in the years prior, which I hope the reader will indulge me to describe with some humor and a taste for the absurd, since these are my prime mechanisms for making sense of my place in Japanese academia.

3. Library within a Library

One of my very first assignments, my very first day on the job at Nagoya University in April 2011, was to take stock of our collection of books about Japanese literature in English and make a list of recommended additions. To fill in the gaps, as it were. I brought a tiny moleskin notebook and a pen to the task of inspecting our collection, expecting that I would need to record very specific information. What I did not expect to find was a colossal rupture in our bibliographic system, in which "books for international students" were physically segregated from the rest of the open stacks. I opened my tiny notebook and drew a big exclamation point. Of course, I had been familiar with similar forms of segregation in other municipal and university libraries in Japan, where hilariously labelled "books for foreigners," which almost always meant books in English, were separated from books in Japanese—or sometimes more comically, "Nipponese." Perhaps such distinctions are made for practical and benign reasons, I don't know. Yet if only I could convey to librarians how embarrassing it is for someone who is very visibly a foreigner to schlep over to the "books for foreigners" section. It's like you're complicitly surrendering yourself to the fact that you will never be proficient enough in Japanese to actually read books in the language— or worse, that you are so convinced of the superiority of English-language books that you wouldn't deign to lay your eyes on anything written in another language. Either way, it's an awful mark of indignity to have hanging over your head. Come to think of it, this may explain why I felt so comfortable when I visited Donald Keene's library several years later. Sure, the books were wrapped in cellophane and cordoned off by stanchions, but at least I didn't have to contend with these internalized presumptions about foreigners in Japanese libraries. I could simply reach out for a book and open it up, without having some third party mediate or weigh in about the cultural politics of what I was doing.

Of course, I imagine that whoever proposed the idea of separating the books into a cozy niche on the second floor of the Central Library probably had a very different vision than the one I am describing. Utopian, even. Perhaps they envisioned a lively salon, where students from all over the world could converge on this idyllic spot overlooking a manicured garden of sago palms, pick up the latest issue of an English-language magazine like *Wired*, and enjoy a stimulating intellectual conversation. Evidence of just such an intent could be seen in the modular seating that had recently been purchased for this space, which allowed students to form a dozen upholstered wedges into any formation most conducive to collaboration or discussion. Sadly, the actual collection of books did not seem sufficient for sustaining this vision of intellectual foment. Translations of Murakami Haruki's first two novellas, a copy of Arthur Golden's *Memoirs of a Geisha*, and Morita Akio's 1988 autobiography *Made in Japan* rounded out a pretty underwhelming selection of books.

Somewhat discouraged, I decided to explore other areas of the library, to see what incoming students might be missing out on. When I reached the fourth floor of the open stacks and turned a corner into what I assumed would be a dark corridor of forgotten books, I stopped in my tracks and very nearly lost the notebook from my hand. Arranged before me was an almost perfect replica of the collection of Japanese literature that I had known as an undergraduate, which had been assembled by Marleigh Ryan in the main library of the State University of New York (SUNY). It was uncanny. Despite myself, I fingered the spine of a 1956 first edition of Edward Seidensticker's translation of *Snow Country*—a book that I had distinct memories of reading during the New York blizzard of 1996, seated in the library in front of a massive panorama window that overlooked blue pine trees. I opened to the first chapter to see if the decorative asterisks, arranged in brocade-like patterns by the book's overly ambitious typographer, still appeared to flutter down the pages like flakes of black snow. Those clusters of florets rematerialized in my memory as I searched for the inn in Echigo-Yuzawa where Kawabata Yasunari wrote his first drafts of *Snow Country*. How weird that just two years later after first reading this book in English, I would be visiting the setting of the novel with my wife, who lived just two station stops away from Echigo-Yuzawa. It was just one more reminder for me that the experiences reading and re-reading the books we love can sometimes form prophetic subplots within the stories of our own lives.

I remember how badly I wanted to read *Snow Country* in Japanese after reading the translation. How I took a train ride on the Hudson River Line to Grand Central Station. How I walked for blocks through the slush and snow to Kinokuniya Books in Rockefeller Center, where a single copy of the novel was available in the Shinchō bunko paperback edition for more than twice its original retail price. How I marveled at the novelty of its smallness, how an entire novel could be condensed into such a slim volume. And yet how its dreary cover design—no more than a blue background streaked with rain— and its lack of typographic creativity could leave me wanting for the aesthetic experience of reading the translation. How, on the train ride back, I squeegeed my fingertip across the condensation on the window, to see if an eyeball really could reflect so clearly in the glass, as Kawabata described it. How I smirked when what appeared in my little aperture was no reflective eyeball, but a tangle of phallic graffiti on a retaining wall outside of Tarrytown.

My Japanese language teacher, Marleigh Ryan, had kindly invited me to her office each week, so that we could read Kawabata together in Japanese—something that was not possible to do in the undergraduate courses she taught, where all the assigned readings were in English translation. She suggested we start with *The Dancing Girl of Izu* instead—much to my chagrin, after having just made a full-day trip to acquire a copy of *Snow Country*. During our meetings, she would often share anecdotes about her experiences studying Japanese literature at Columbia University under Donald Keene. Over time, I came to realize that many explications she offered about the text were based on notes she had kept as a graduate student in Keene sensei's seminars. I remember, for example, how she pulled out an impeccably executed set of notes, probably from the early 1960s, that had included a lengthy commentary about the expression *ama-ashi* 雨足, whose literal meaning, "feet of rain," was not making any sense to me. I was amazed to learn that it was an ancient expression found in Tang Dynasty poetry, and that it described a very specific form of precipitation for which English had no precise vocabulary to convey. But above all, I was amazed to learn that she had faithfully preserved her notebooks for nearly three decades and had kept them all neatly arranged within arm's reach of her workspace—as if the physical and temporal distances that separated her from Donald Keene's seminars were of no material concern. When Marleigh Ryan explained "feet of rain" to me, in a delightfully animated and evocative way, I felt like I was sitting in on Donald Keene's seminar back in the 1960s. Like I was partaking in a living tradition, of performative explications of literary texts that could only pass directly from teacher to student.

After spending nearly an hour with this hidden collection of books, reminiscing about my own personal history with them, I realized that I had still not attended to the task of creating a list of titles for acquisition. So I jotted down the first twenty or thirty titles that occurred to me. Slipped my notebook into my back pocket. In a weird way, I had kind of wished that the collection didn't need to be updated, that it could remain in its current form—a form that had magically transported me back to a different time and place. But I also knew that my sense of nostalgia would be of no service to our incoming students—nor to the books themselves. That if these books were to find new life in the hands of a new audience of readers, that they would need to be part of a continually updated and renovated collection, not a carefully preserved museum piece within a remote corner of our library.

4. Conclusion, or *How Japanese Literature Was Introduced to the World*

Lastly, I would like to conclude this series of reflections with one final note on the theme of displacement. In the Donald Keene Center Kashiwazaki, there is a small theater space where visitors can watch recordings of various lectures that Donald Keene has given over the years. Included in that video library is a recording of a talk he gave at Nagoya University on February 11, 2012, entitled "How was Japanese Literature Introduced to the World?". The talk is more or less a pastiche of dozens of other talks he had given in the past, a reworking of material from every memoir and newspaper article, every think piece, that he had published over his sixty-year career. Somehow, when mediated through the theater space at the museum, the lecture assumes a rather solemn tone, and it is difficult to feel anything but a sense of quiet reverence for Donald Keene as he recounts his early experiences with learning about the language and literature of Japan, beginning with his familiar anecdote about how his whole career in Japanese Studies began when he was eighteen, and encountered a copy of Arthur Waley's translation of *Tale of Genji* in a New York bookstore.

Yet having attended the very same lecture in person, as part of a capacity crowd at Toyoda Auditorium, I can attest to having sensed a much more lively and valedictory vibe in the building that day. Donald Keene was very much in the news those days, following his relinquishment of American citizenship and his move to Japan following the 2011 Tohoku earthquake and tsunami. In conversations with friends and colleagues, I sensed a genuine feeling of goodwill towards him for doing that, even among people who had never read his work before. Outside the main hall of the auditorium, I noticed a pair of tables displaying his many translations and monograph studies, along with a separate table with towering stacks of his most recent book, which was available for purchase. One of the students in my undergraduate literature class, who had scored a ticket to the event in the university-wide lottery, and who happened to be standing a few places ahead of me in line, turned and beamed, *I can't believe that we get to see the real Donald Keene!*

I smiled in response. During the lecture itself, I have to say that I was less impressed by the aura or presence of Donald Keene per se, than by the uncanny familiarity of his gestures and mannerisms. For hundreds of hours over the course of many years, I had read translations and literary histories written by Donald Keene, in a voice that I had created in my own mind. To be honest, I had never met him prior to his visit to Nagoya, and I had never heard him speak Japanese before. Therefore, I was surprised to discover in his heavily accented Japanese intimate echoes of ways that my relatives in New York used to speak. I felt very much at home listening to him. I also found in certain delicate turns of phrase, some hints of Marleigh Grayer Ryan's explications of literary texts, which affected me deeply. And so when I rose to my feet along with rest of the capacity crowd at Toyoda Auditorium to give Donald Keene a lengthy standing ovation, I think I was thanking him in my own way, for letting me know that it was okay to love studying about Japan even when you feel a bit out of place here, and that it's okay to feel sometimes that you are neither here nor there.

Epilogue

Sachi Schmidt-Hori

When I first thought of creating a bilingual collection of essays written by Japan Studies scholars based in Japan and in the United States, I asked my good friend Keiko Eguchi (who later contributed her own essay to this volume) which publisher I should pitch this idea to. She immediately told me to contact the editor-in-chief of Bungaku tsūshin, Mr. Keisuke Okada. Thank you, Keiko-san, for the introduction. It was a match made in heaven.

As I put together this volume, my other close friend, Setsu Shigematsu, provided me with candid and constructive feedback on my essay. Her tough love and encouragement made me a better critical thinker and writer. Thank you, Setsu.

I also want to express my deepest gratitude for all of my fellow co-authors, editor-in-chief of Bungaku tsūshin, Mr. Okada, and my editor Mr. Tetsushi Watanabe. Thank you, everyone, for your diligence, patience, and dedication.

Regrettably, I must share extremely sad news with my readers. Mark Bookman, who authored "My Life as a Disabled American in Japan: Intersectional Barriers and Inclusive Imaginaries," passed away on December 16, 2022. The last time I saw Mark was August 2022. That day, I arrived at Odaiba Marine Park station of the Yurikamome Line. One year had passed since the conclusion of the Tokyo 2020 Summer Olympics (which was delayed for one year due to the pandemic), the area looked eerily quiet. My photographer friend Peter Weld and I went to visit Mark's apartment in the futuristic Odaiba neighborhood to discuss a collaborative project for the "Springboard Japan" website. I remember clearly that it was a particularly hot and humid day and that Mark, Peter, Mark's caregiver (a Nepali gentleman whose name I cannot recall), and I constantly switched back-and-forth between English and Japanese. Even though the windows of Mark's apartment were shut and the air conditioner was on, the cicadas' cry reverberated across the entire place and the four of us kept wiping the sweat off our faces. I never dreamed that this was going to be the last time I would see Mark in person. Four months later, he departed this world at age 31. Japan Studies lost a talented young scholar-educator-activist who was truly beloved and respected by so many people.

参考文献／**References**

- 阿部泰郎監修、江口啓子・鹿谷祐子・玉田沙織編『室町時代の少女革命：『新蔵人』絵巻の世界』笠間書院、2014.
- 鹿谷祐子「『新蔵人』絵巻の「越境」性—AAS（アジア学会）での発表報告」『リポート笠間』58、2015.
- 堀あきこ・守如子編著『ＢＬの教科書』有斐閣、2020.
- 簗瀬一雄『校註阿佛尼全集増補版』風間書房、1981.
- 柳姃希・三本松政之「韓国における性的少数者の当事者組織形成過程に関する研究：当事者としての活動家に着目して」『立教大学コミュニティ福祉研究所紀要』3、2015.
- 脇田晴子『日本中世女性史の研究—性別役割分担と母性・家政・性愛』東京大学出版会、1992.
- Ahmed, Sara. *Living a Feminist Life*. Durham, NC: Duke University Press, 2017.
- Ashikari, Mikiko. "Cultivating Japanese Whiteness: The 'Whitening' Cosmetics Boom and the Japanese Identity." *Journal of Material Culture* 10, no. 1 (2005): 73–91.
- Bargen, Doris G. *A Woman's Weapon: Spirit Possession in the Tale of Genji*. Honolulu: University of Hawai'i Press, 1997.
- Bonnett, Alastair. "A White World?: Whiteness and the Meaning of Modernity in Latin America and Japan." In *Working through Whiteness: International Perspectives*, edited by Cynthia Levine-Rasky, 69–106. Albany: State University of New York Press, 2002.
- Bookman, Mark R. "Politics and Prosthetics: 150 Years of Disability in Japan." PhD diss., University of Pennsylvania, 2021.
- Childs, Margaret H. "Coercive Courtship Strategies and Gendered Goals in Classical Japanese Literature." *Japanese Language and Literature* 44, no. 2 (2010): 119–148.
- Coulthard, Glen Sean, and Gerald R. Alfred. *Red Skin, White Masks: Rejecting the Colonial Politics of Recognition*. Minneapolis: University of Minnesota Press, 2014.
- Crawcour, Sydney. "Review of *An Introduction to Japanese Kanbun*, by Akira Komai and Thomas H. Rohlich." *Monumenta Nipponica* 44, no. 2 (1989): 256–258.
- Crenshaw, Kimberlé. "Demarginalizing the Intersection of Race and Sex: A Black Feminist Critique of Antidiscrimination Doctrine, Feminist Theory and Antiracist Politics." *University of Chicago Legal Forum* 1989, no. 1(8) (1989): 139–67.
- Daniels, Peter, and William Bright. *The World's Writing Systems*. Oxford, The United Kingdom: Oxford University Press, 1996.
- Du Bois, W.E.B. *Darkwater: Voices from Within the Veil*. Verso, 2012 (1920).
- Fanon, Frantz. *The Wretched of the Earth*. New York, NY: Grove/Atlantic, 2007 (1963).
- Field, Norma. *The Splendor of Longing in the Tale of Genji*. Princeton, NJ: Princeton University Press, 1987.
- Frellesvig, Bjarke. *A History of the Japanese Language*. Cambridge, The United Kingdom: Cambridge University Press, 2010.
- Fujikawa, Takao. "Whiteness Studies in Japan: Visible and Invisible Types of Whiteness." In *Historicising Whiteness: Transnational Perspectives on the Construction of an Identity*, edited by Leigh Boucher, Jane Carey, and Katherine Ellinghaus, 26–34. Melbourne, Australia: RMIT Publishing, 2007.
- Fujitani, Takashi. "The Reischauer Memo: Mr. Moto, Hirohito, and Japanese American

Soldiers." *Critical Asian Studies* 33, no. 3 (2001): 379–402.

- Hall, Stuart, and Bram Gieben. "The West and the Rest: Discourse and Power." In *Race and Racialization, 2E: Essential Readings*, edited by Tania Das Gupta, 85–95. Toronto, Canada: Canadian Scholars, 1992.
- Handel, Zev. *Sinography: The Borrowing and Adaptation of the Chinese Script*. Leiden, The Netherlands: Brill, 2019.
- Hardacre, Helen. "Japanese Studies in the United States: Present Situation and Future Prospects." *Asia Journal* 1, no. 1 (1994): 17–36.
- Harootunian, Harry D., and Naoki Sakai. "Japan Studies and Cultural Studies." *positions: east asia cultures critique* 7, no. 2 (1999): 593–647.
- Harris, Cheryl. "Whiteness as Property." *Harvard Law Review* (1993): 1707–1791.
- Hirano, Katsuya. "Settler-colonialism, Ecology, and Expropriation of Ainu Mosir: A Transnational Perspective." In *Migrant Ecologies: Environmental Histories of the Pacific World*, edited by Edward Melillo and Ryan Jones, 135–153. Honolulu: University of Hawai'i Press, 2022.
- Horne, Gerald. *Race War: White Supremacy and the Japanese Attack on the British Empire*. New York, NY: NYU Press, 2004.
- Inoue Hisashi 井上ひさし. *Kirikirijin*. Tokyo: Shinchōsha, 1981.
- Jackson, Reginald R. *A Proximate Remove: Queering Intimacy and Loss in the Tale of Genji*. Oakland: University of California Press, 2021.
- Jung, Moon-Kie, and João Costa Vargas. *Antiblackness*. Durham, NC: Duke University Press, 2021.
- Konno Shinji 今野真二. *Furigana no rekishi*. Tokyo: Shūeisha, 2009.
- Koshiro, Yukiko. *Trans-Pacific Racisms and the U.S. Occupation of Japan*. New York, NY: Columbia University Press, 1999.
- Krebs, Gerhard. 2015. "Racism under Negotiation: The Japanese Race in the Nazi-German Perspective." In *Race and Racism in Modern East Asia*, edited by Rotem Kowne and Walter Demel, 217–241. Leiden, The Netherlands: Brill, 2015.
- Lee Yangji 李良枝. *Yuhi*. Tokyo: Kōdansha Bungei Bunko, 1988.
- Lie, John. *Multiethnic Japan*. Cambridge, MA: Harvard University Press, 2009.
- Lipsitz, George. "The Possessive Investment in Whiteness: Racialized Social Democracy and the 'White' Problem in American Studies." *American Quarterly* 47, no. 3 (1995): 369–387.
- Matsumura, Wendy. "Resignation from UCSD Critical Gender Studies Program Executive Committee," 2022. https://kashmir-scholars.org/2022/02/10/why-solidarity-and-how/.
- McCormick, Melissa. "Mountains, Magic, and Mothers: Envisioning the Female Ascetic in a Medieval *Chigo* Tale." In *Crossing the Sea: Essays on East Asian Art in Honor of Professor Yoshiaki Shimizu*, edited by Gregory P. A. Levine, Andrew M. Watsky, and Gennifer Weisenfeld, 107–133. Princeton, NJ: Princeton University Press, 2012.
- Nihon gakusei shien kikō 日本学生支援機構 (JASSO). "Reiwa 2-nendo daigaku, tanki daigaku oyobi kōtō senmon gakkō ni okeru shōgai no aru gakusei no shūgaku shien ni kansuru jittai chōsa kekka no gaiyō nado ni tsuite" (2021).
- Osada, Masako. *Sanctions and Honorary Whites: Diplomatic Policies and Economic Realities in Relations between Japan and South Africa*. Westport, CT: Greenwood Publishing Group, 2002.
- Owen, Stephen, Ding Xiang Warner, and Paul Kroll. *The Poetry of Du Fu*. Boston, MA: De Gruyter Mouton, 2015.

- Levi McLaughlin, Kimberlee Sanders, Jolyon Thomas, and Michelle Wang. "Petition to AAS to Support Black Scholars of Asia." https://jolyon.thomasresearch.org/news/2020/6/15/ petition-to-aas-to-support-black-scholars-of-asia.
- Rimer, J. Thomas, Mitsuya Mori, and Cody M. Poulton. *The Columbia Anthology of Modern Japanese Drama*. New York, NY: Columbia University Press, 2014.
- Ritchie, Stuart J. *Science Fictions: How Fraud, Bias, Negligence, and Hype Undermine the Search for Truth*. New York, NY: Metropolitan Books, 2020.
- Rodriguez, Dylan. *White Reconstruction: Domestic Warfare and the Logics of Genocide*. New York, NY: Fordham University Press, 2021.
- Russell, John. "Replicating the White Self and Other: Skin Color, Racelessness, Gynoids, and the Construction of Whiteness in Japan." *Japanese Studies* 37, no. 1 (2017): 23–48.
- Saitō, Mareshi, Ross King, and Christina Laffin, eds. *Kanbunmyaku: The Literary Sinitic Context and the Birth of Modern Japanese Language and Literature*. Leiden, The Netherlands: Brill, 2021.
- Sakiyama Tami 崎山多美. "Mienai machi kara shonkanee ga." *Subaru* 28, no. 5 (2006).
- Sarra, Edith. *Unreal Houses: Character Gender and Genealogy in the Tale of Genji*. Cambridge, MA: Harvard University Asia Center, 2020.
- Schmidt-Hori, Sachi. "The New Lady-in-Waiting Is a *Chigo*: Sexual Fluidity and Dual Transvestism in a Medieval Buddhist Acolyte." *Japanese Language and Literature* 43, no. 2 (2009): 383–423.
- Shigematsu, Setsu. "The Sky is Falling: On Asian American Imperial Entitlement to Life." In *Society and Space*, 2021. https://www.societyandspace.org/articles/the-sky-is-falling.
- Shindō Sakiko 進藤咲子. "Furigana no kinō to hensen." In *Kōza Nihongogaku 6: Gendai hyōki to no shiteki taishō*, edited by Morioka Kenji. Tokyo: Meiji Shoin, 1982.
- Suzuki Torao 鈴木虎雄. *To Shōryō shishū*. Tokyo: Kokumin Bunko Kankōkai, 1928.
- Tanaka, Stefan. *Japan's Orient: Rendering Pasts into History*. Berkeley: University of California Press, 1995.
- Vargas, João Costa. *The Denial of Antiblackness: Multiracial Redemption and Black Suffering*. Minneapolis: University of Minnesota Press, 2018.
- Vargas, João Costa. "Blue Pill, Red Pill: The Incommensurable Worlds of Racism and Antiblackness." *Kalfou* 8, no. 1/2 (2021): 183–205.
- Wynter, Sylvia. "Unsettling the Coloniality of Being/Power/Truth/Freedom: Towards the Human, After Man, Its Overrepresentation—An Argument." *CR: The New Centennial Review* 3, no. 3 (2003): 257–337.
- Yokoyama Yūta 横山悠太. *Wagahai wa neko ni naru*. Tokyo: Kōdansha, 2014.
- Yoshikawa Kōjirō 吉川幸次郎. *Toho nooto*. Osaka: Sōgensha, 1952.

プロフィール／Profiles ［執筆順］

シュミット堀佐知　SCHMIDT-HORI, Sachi
…奥付参照

佐々木孝浩　SASAKI, Takahiro
慶應義塾大学附属研究所斯道文庫教授
著書に『日本古典書誌学論』（笠間書院、2016）、『芳賀矢一　「国文学」の誕生』（岩波書店、2021）などがある。

日比嘉高　HIBI, Yoshitaka
名古屋大学大学院人文学研究科教授
著書に『プライヴァシーの誕生　モデル小説のトラブル史』（新曜社、2020）、『文学の歴史をどう書き直すのか　二〇世紀日本の小説・空間・メディア』（笠間書院、2016）、『ジャパニーズ・アメリカ　移民文学、出版文化、収容所』（新曜社、2014）などがある。

江口啓子　EGUCHI, Keiko
豊田工業高等専門学校准教授
著書に『室町時代の女装少年×姫：『ちごいま』物語絵巻の世界』（共著、笠間書院、2019）、『異性装　歴史の中の性の越境者たち』（共著、集英社インターナショナル、2023）、論文に「男装と変成男子：『新蔵人』絵巻に見る女人成仏の思想」（『中世文学』65 号、2020）などがある。

マーク・ブックマン　Mark Bookman
東京大学国際高等研究所東京カレッジポストドクトラル・フェロー
著書に"Can the Tokyo 2020 Paralympic Games Spur Change?" (*The Japan Times*, September 6, 2021), "The Coronavirus Crisis: Disability Politics and Activism in Contemporary Japan," *Japan Focus: The Asia-Pacific Journal*, 18 no. 3 (2020): p. 1–13. などがある。

セツ・シゲマツ　Setsu Shigematsu

カリフォルニア大学リバーサイド校准教授

著書に *Scream from the Shadows: The Women's Liberation Movement in Japan* (University of Minnesota Press, 2012) などがある。

監督兼プロデュース作品に *Visions of Abolition* (2012), *Abolish ICE and All Border-Prisons* (2023) がある。

末松美咲　SUEMATSU, Misaki

名古屋学院大学商学部専任講師

著書に『室町時代の女装少年×姫：『ちごいま』物語絵巻の世界』(共著、笠間書院、2019)、論文に「『児今参り』物語の再創造と室町期女房の文芸活動」(『説話文学研究』54号、2019)、「性空型『硯わり』と近世前期における物語の制作」(『伝承文学研究』70号、2021) などがある。

クリストファー・ローウィ　Christopher Lowy

カーネギーメロン大学現代語学部助教授

論文に「『婉曲の踏み車』と変わらないイデオロギー－エイズ、サル痘、〈悪所〉のハッテン場を中心に」(『ユリイカ』2022年8月号)、「新型コロナ騒動から日本エイズ文学を考える」(『現代思想』2020年5月号) などがある。現在はひつじ書房のウェブマガジン「未草」にて今野真二氏と「日本語表記のアーキテクチャ／ The Architecture of Written Japanese」を協同連載中。

ディラン・ミギー　Dylan McGee

名古屋大学大学院人文学研究科准教授

著書に *Interdisciplinary Edo*（共著、Routledge, 2023）, *A Kamigata Anthology, Literature from Japan's Metropolitan Centers*（共著、University of Hawai'i Press, 2020）, *A Tokyo Anthology: Literature from Japan's Modern Capital, 1850-1920*（共著, University of Hawai'i Press, 2017）などがある。

■訳者

シュミット堀佐知・渡辺哲史・Brian Bergstrom・Yuanhao Chen Emma Cool・James Dorsey・Rhiannon Liou・Jason Saber

編者

シュミット堀佐知　SCHMIDT-HORI, Sachi

ダートマス大学（米国）アジア社会文化言語学部准教授
著作に*Tales of Idolized Boys: Male-Male Love in Medieval Buddhist Narratives*（University of Hawai'i Press, 2021）、"Yoshitsune and the Gendered Transformations of Japan's Self-Image," *The Journal of Japanese Studies* 48, no. 1（2022）、"The Erotic Family: Structures and Narratives of Milk Kinship in Premodern Japanese Tales," *The Journal of Asian Studies* 80, no. 3（2021）などがある。

執筆者

シュミット堀佐知　SCHMIDT-HORI, Sachi
佐々木孝浩　SASAKI, Takahiro
日比嘉高　HIBI, Yoshitaka
江口啓子　EGUCHI, Keiko
マーク・ブックマン　BOOKMAN, Mark
セツ・シゲマツ　SHIGEMATSU, Setsu
末松美咲　SUEMATSU, Misaki
クリストファー・ローウィ　LOWY, Christopher
ディラン・ミギー　MCGEE, Dylan

なんで日本研究するの？／Why Study Japan?

2023（令和5）年 10 月 20 日　第 1 版第 1 刷発行

ISBN978-4-86766-019-5　C0036　©著作権は各執筆者にあります

発行所　株式会社 文学通信
〒 114-0001　東京都北区東十条 1-18-1 東十条ビル 1-101
電話 03-5939-9027　Fax 03-5939-9094
メール info@bungaku-report.com ウェブ http://bungaku-report.com

発行人　岡田圭介
印刷・製本　モリモト印刷

ご意見・ご感想はこちら
からも送れます。上記
のQRコードを読み取っ
てください。

※乱丁・落丁本はお取り替えいたしますので、ご一報ください。書影は自由にお使いください。